THE MARVELLOUS IN FIELDING'S NOVELS

Mitchell Kalpakgian

University Press of America

Copyright © 1981 by
University Press of America, Inc.[TM]
P.O. Box 19101, Washington, DC 20036

All rights reserved
Printed in the United States of America

ISBN: 0-8191-1506-1 Perfect
0-8191-1505-3 Case
Library of Congress Number: 80-1411

DEDICATION

To Joyce, Gregory, Aram, and Mark, the marvellous in my own history, and to Khatchig (Archie) Kalpakgian and Meline Manouelian Kalpakgian, through whom the first and greatest gift of Fortune arrived.

TABLE OF CONTENTS

Chapter		Page
I.	ART AS THE ABILITY TO CONCEAL ART: VARIETY AS A SOURCE OF WONDER IN JOSEPH ANDREWS	1
	A. The Classical Basis of Fielding's Art	2
	B. The Epic Variety of Joseph Andrews	20
II.	NATURE AND FORTUNE AS INTELLIGIBLE MYSTERIES: BEAUTY AND LUCK AS SPECIES OF WONDER IN TOM JONES	55
III.	THE HEROIC AND THE MARVELLOUS: VIRTUE OR MAGNANIMITY AS A SOURCE OF WONDER IN AMELIA	105
IV.	THE MIRACLES OF DIVINE PROVIDENCE: GOD AS THE SOURCE OF WONDER	147
	A. Introduction	147
	B. Science	161
	C. Religion	167
	D. History	182
V.	CONCLUSION: FIELDING'S MARVELLOUS AND THE EIGHTEENTH CENTURY SUBLIME	199
VI.	BIBLIOGRAPHY	221

ABOUT THE AUTHOR

Mitchell Kalpakgian was born in Milford, Massachusetts, and graduated from Milford High School. He received his B.A. in English from Bowdoin College in 1963, his M.A. from the University of Kansas, and his Ph.D. from the University of Iowa. Since 1967 he has taught at Simpson College in Indianola, Iowa, where he is currently an Associate Professor of English. He is a regular contributor to the <u>Armenian Weekly</u> and a book reviewer for <u>Ararat</u>.

CHAPTER I

ART AS THE ABILITY TO CONCEAL ART: VARIETY AS A SOURCE OF WONDER IN JOSEPH ANDREWS

Is it for the Christian to consider any work "his own," when even Christ has said that "I do nothing of myself"? or for the Hindu, when Krishna has said that "the Comprehensor cannot form the concept 'I am the doer'"? or the Buddhist, for whom it has been said that "To wish that it may be made known that 'I was the author' is the thought of a man not yet adult"?
>   --Ananda Coomaraswamy, *Christian and Oriental Philosophy of Art*

But in Epic poetry, owing to the narrative form, many events simultaneously transacted can be presented; and these, if relevant to the subject, add mass and dignity to the poem. The Epic has here an advantage, and one that conduces to grandeur of effect, to diverting the mind of the hearer, and relieving the story with varying episodes. For sameness of incident soon produces satiety, and makes tragedies fail on the stage.
>   --Aristotle, *The Poetics*

A. The Classical Basis of Fielding's Art

In <u>Christian and Oriental Philosophy of Art</u>, Ananda Coomaraswamy speaks of the traditional artist as an anonymous man, a humble artisan or maker who sought the perfection of his product rather than personal fame. He strove to create useful works that served the essential needs of man, not seeking popularity by indulging man's eccentric tastes and immoderate appetites for novelties and sensations. According to Coomaraswamy, the humility or anonymity of the medieval-Christian or oriental artist derives from the idea that "<u>I</u> am the doer" or "<u>I</u> was the author" is childishness:

> In traditional arts it is never Who said? but only What was said? that concerns us: for "all that is true, by whomsoever it has been said, has its origin in the Spirit."[1]

In other words, truth is universal, commonplace. It is like the wisdom in the Book of Proverbs crying aloud on the housetops. "A private property in ideas is inconceivable," to quote Coomaraswamy; "there cannot be an authorship of ideas, but only an entertainment."[2] Originality, then, in this classical-Christian-oriental philosophy of art (the <u>philosophia perennis</u>) means to discover an old truth in a new way rather than to make a bold startling pronouncement. Strictly speaking, the artist does not create. He discovers or finds in the classical sense of <u>inventio</u>; he arranges old materials to form a new creation. As Sir Joshua Reynolds explains this process of invention in Discourse 2 of <u>Discourses on Art</u>:

> Invention, strictly speaking, is little more than a new combination of those images which have been previously gathered and deposited in the memory: nothing can come of nothing: he who has laid up no materials, can produce no combinations.[3]

Invention recognizes its debt to Nature and the ancients for its materials or stock of ideas. For example, Imlac in Rasselas mentions how he read all the poets of his nation and acquired a knowledge of nature and stored his mind with "all that is awfully vast or elegantly little" (chapter x) as a prelude to his performances as a poet. Nothing can come of nothing. Hence Imlac asserts, "To a poet nothing can be useless." As Reynolds says in Discourse 6, "The greatest natural genius cannot subsist on its own stock" (p. 77). Artistic genius, originality in the sense of inventio, requires all available knowledge before it begins to operate: it needs the matter given by Nature and the stock of ideas provided by the ancients. Once this originality begins to work, it still depends on its source. It attempts to find form in matter, the universal in the particular--essences which are also already there. That is, the artist does not heighten or transform the real through his creative imagination, the "lamp" that M. H. Abrams refers to in The Mirror and the Lamp which provides meaning or "light" to a dark universe devoid of it. Rather he reads the intelligibility of the universe which the world reflects like a "mirror." The artist sees the form that inheres hidden in matter, in the same way that Shakespeare's Prospero sees the form of Ariel camouflaged in the matter of a tree. He does not impose form on matter or create ex nihilo. As C. S. Lewis says in The Discarded Image:

> Spin something out of one's own head when the world teems with so many noble deeds, wholesome examples, pitiful tragedies, strange adventures, and merry jests which have never yet been set forth quite so well as they deserve? . . . Why make things for oneself like the lonely Robinson Crusoe, when there is riches all about you to be had for the asking? The modern artist often does not think the riches is there. He is the alchemist who must turn base metal into gold.[4]

That is, the perennial philosophy teaches that the
world as given or created reflects the divine art
of the Creator, that it radiates, to use Dante's
phrase, "significant form." It is an intelligible
mystery. The humility of the artist arises because he senses his great debt to a copious universe, to a generous Nature. The humility of the
artist follows from a metaphysic. If the truth is
universal and cries aloud to everyone, if the
world's open secret is intelligible and only needs
to be read by a seer, if the subject matter or raw
material or art is copious and inexhaustible--
then, to quote Jacques Maritain, "Being superabounds."[5] Thus the humility of the traditional
artist relates to his idea of originality, which
in turn is based on a metaphysics. As Father John
D. Boyd writes in The Function of Mimesis and Its
Decline:

> "Aristotle," says Else, "is a Greek for
> whom creation means discovery (heuresis),
> the uncovering of a true relation which
> already exists somehow in the scheme of
> things." Yet this is not the same thing
> at all as scientific or philosophic research, but the mysterious insight into
> things which we associate with the truly
> gifted poet.[6]

This whole notion of heuresis lies at the heart of
Fielding's art: the "discovery" of Joseph Andrews' true identity as an open secret; "the true
relation which already exists somehow in the
scheme of things" when Tom Jones discovers that
Bridget Allworthy was his true mother and that he
is really related to Allworthy, his legitimate
uncle.

As an inheritor of the classical-Christian
tradition, Fielding follows the perennial philosophy. He reveals the humility of the traditional
artist by disavowing any claims of originality.
He conceals his own art by acknowledging his immense debt to the ancients. For example, in the
opening book of Tom Jones, Fielding compares his

novel to a feast at a "public ordinary" rather than an exquisite "eleemosynary treat"[7]; "all persons are welcome" to this banquet, not just the select few who attend the private entertainment of a gentleman. That is, Fielding offers a plain, general bill of fare at his "ordinary," not anything rare or exotic--no novel foreign foods but old English roast beef. He admits that as a host he lacks all originality since his plain fare consists only of a well-known food: "The provision, then, which we have here made is no other than Human Nature." Just as the art of the cook depends, not on the rarity of the animal or bird, but on the cook's talent to bring out the essence or aroma of naturally delicious flavors that inhere in good food, so too the art of the novelist involves the ability to educe: to bring out the universal truths that dwell in particular examples, to lead out the form from matter, to abstract the one from the many. As Fielding says in this same chapter: "In like manner, the excellence of the mental entertainment consists less in the subject than in the author's skill in well dressing it up." The subject matter, then, of Fielding's novels is as old as Human Nature and as common as roast beef--"What oft was thought." Indeed Fielding's metaphor of art as "cookery" and the artist as a cook skilled in "dressing it up" derives from the oft-quoted couplet of Pope which Fielding cites and expands in the first chapter of Tom Jones:

> True wit is nature to advantage drest;
> What oft was thought, but n'er so well exprest.
>   (p. 2, Bk. I, ch. i)

Like Pope, who endorses Aristotle's mimetic view of art in An Essay on Criticism ("First follow Nature, and your judgment frame/ By her just standard, which is still the same," ll. 68-69), Fielding of course also subscribes to Aristotle's "Art imitates Nature" and the classical view of originality that goes with this theory. As Father Boyd points out in The Function of Mimesis and Its

Decline:

> This mimetic principle asserts the "given" quality which the Greeks saw in all reality, hence its imitability; it maintains the stubborn autonomy of form in nature transformed into theme that is independent of private whim, structure that is fruitful in being self-sufficient, and pleasurable contemplation that needs no justification beyond itself.[8]

That is, "true wit" and <u>mimesis</u> go together. The artist exercises wit when he sees or discovers this 'given' form in nature; when he seizes on an eternal truth ("What oft was thought") in a startling, fresh way ("n'er so well exprest"); when he finds a new metaphor or "dress" or "seasoning" for a commonplace.

In expressing his own endorsement of the mimetic view of art, Fielding always stresses the gratuitous quality of the Nature which his art imitates and the classical idea of wit which imitation requires. He humbly acknowledges his debt to Nature, his Alma Mater, in much the same way that the good cook appreciates the "prodigious variety" of Nature's plenty. The infinite variety of Human Nature, the matter of the novelist, is as inexhaustible as the copiousness of Mother Nature's animal and vegetable kingdom, the matter of the cook: ". . . in Human Nature, though here collected under one general name, is such prodigious variety, that a cook will have sooner gone through all the several species of animal and vegetable food in the world, than an author will be able to exhaust so extensive a subject" (<u>Tom Jones</u>, p. 2, Bk. I, ch. i). Likewise, in his <u>Journal of a Voyage to Lisbon</u>, Fielding marvels at Nature's abundance in her creation of fish: "Of all the animal foods with which man is furnished, there are none so plentiful as fish."[9] In short, Nature's wealth, the already available subject matter or raw material of art or cooking, awes Fielding because of its boundless immensity. He expresses a profound sense of wonder at Nature's fecundity, a sense of astonishment comparable to Milton's ". . . Nature boon/ Poured forth profuse . . ." in <u>Paradise Lost</u> (IV, ll. 242-243). To acknowledge <u>this</u> givenness of Nature like Aristotle or to sense the creativity of God in the universe like a Milton or Fielding awakens a sense of gratitude and inspires an author to admire and praise the glory of God, Being, or Nature rather than to seek personal fame.

Fielding constantly shows gratitude to the source of his art, Nature. For example, in the "Author's Preface" to <u>Joseph Andrews</u>, Fielding confesses: ". . . everything is copied from the book of nature, and scarce a character or action produced which I have not taken from my own observations and experience."[10] In short, Nature provides all. She offers a comic writer ample materials for his art. As Fielding again notes in the "Author's Preface," "life <u>everywhere</u> furnishes an accurate observer with the <u>ridiculous</u>" (p. xxxiii; italics added). In <u>Joseph Andrews</u> Fielding excoriates the writers of romances who do not imitate Nature: "who, without any assistance from nature or history, record persons who never were, or will be, and facts which never did, nor possibly can, happen: whose heroes are of their own creation, and their brains the chaos whence all the materials are selected" (p. 217, Bk. III, ch. i). In other words, they have tried to be creative or original by consulting imagination and fancy instead of exercising invention or wit. They have resorted to novelty, sensationalism, oddities-- everything Fielding means by the term "the Monstrous" in the "Author's Preface." When Fielding condemns the writers of romance for "forming originals from the confused heap of matter in their own brains," it resembles Swift's criticism of the moderns in <u>The Battle of the Books</u>: the moderns spin cobwebs from their own minds while the ancients produce honey by gathering nectar from the flowers. The ancients respect the abundance of Nature, whereas the moderns complain of its dearth. As the bee tells the spider, "yet, if the materials be nothing but Dirt, spun out of your own Entrails (the Guts of Modern Brains), the Edifice will conclude at last in a Cobweb." The bee, a true Aristotelian, recognizes that art thrives on Nature: "For the rest, whatever we have got, has been by infinite Labor, and search, and ranging thro' every Corner of Nature."[11] Fielding, like Swift, acknowledges the subordination of art to Nature and the superiority of the ancients to the moderns. He recognizes his debt not only to Mother Nature but also to the wisdom of the ancients--the materials upon which his own power of invention works.

Just as Fielding acknowledges the inexhaustible, "prodigious variety" of Human Nature and the diversity of Nature's animal and plant life in the first chapter of Tom Jones and the profusion of Nature in his description of Allworthy's estate, likewise he views the ancients as an abundant storehouse of wisdom. In Tom Jones (p. 537, Bk. XII, ch. i), "Showing what is to be deemed plagiarism in a modern author, and what is to be considered as lawful prize," Fielding addresses himself to the problem of originality, which Swift also treats in The Battle of the Books. In the battle of ancients versus moderns, the moderns charge the ancients with plagiarism, a gross lack of all originality as well as an act of theft. Thus the spider accuses the bee: "Your Livelihood is an universal Plunder upon Nature; a Freebooter over Fields and Gardens; and for the sake of Stealing will rob a Nettle as readily as a Violet."[12] Fielding, however, arguing like Swift's bee, distinguishes between quoting ancient authors and plagiarizing modern writers. He explains that to translate from the ancients, even "without quoting the original, or without taking the least notice of the book from whence they were borrowed," is neither plagiarism nor unoriginality. "The ancients may be considered a rich common, where every person who hath the smallest tenement in Parnassus hath a free right to fatten his muse." Fielding's humorous analogy compares the ancients to wealthy squires whose property the poor moderns may plunder. Like the givenness of Nature created for man's use, the ancients are "there" for the benefit of all. Like Nature's copious variety, the ancients too offer a fertile common. "In like manner are the ancients, such as Homer, Virgil, Horace, Cicero, and the rest, to be esteemed among us writers as so many wealthy squires, from whom we, the poor of Parnassus, claim an immemorial custom of taking whatever we can come at" (p. 537, p. 538; Bk. XII, ch. i). To translate Latin and Greek passages into English without citing chapter and verse or quoting the original, then, is only to draw from the world's accumulated wisdom. It is to practice the art of Swift's bee who selects from only the best flowers, proceeding "by an universal Range, with long Search, much Study, true Judgment, and Distinction of Things, brings home Honey and Wax."[13] Thus, acknowledging his debt to Nature and to the ancients, Fielding lays no claim to originality in the "modern" sense of the spider. Recognizing that the opulent wisdom of the ancients in its fullness compares with Nature's prodigious variety in its copiousness, Fielding admits that he owes all to Nature and the ancients.

Unlike so many authors of the eighteenth century--Colley Cibber, Pope's dunces, Swift's moderns or spiders, Fielding's Trapwit in Pasquin-- Fielding hardly attempts to cultivate his own worldly reputation or to pursue personal fame. Rather he belongs to a classical tradition that views the poet as the custodian of fame, a singer who praises others and gives fame to heroes and great men--not as a seeker of glory for himself. O. B. Hardison's The Enduring Monument covers in great depth this topic of the poet as the giver of fame, honor, and glory. In his book Professor Hardison writes, "The idea that poets are the special custodians of fame is repeated by Horace, Cicero, and a host of other classical writers."[14] This notion contrasts markedly with the Renaissance cult of glory described by Jacob Burckhardt in The Civilization of the Renaissance in Italy-- what Burckhardt calls "the great desire to achieve something great and memorable" that prompted Dante not only to write great poetry but also to want "to be esteemed the first in his own walks."[15] In this cult of glory an artist seeks immortality and everlasting fame by creating a masterpiece or by performing a famous or infamous deed that will endure forever. Self-glory is essential, not accidental; primary, not secondary.

Fielding writes from the classical tradition of the poet as the custodian of fame, not as an heir of the Renaissance who pursues the cult of self-glory. Two statements in <u>Joseph Andrews</u> especially relate him to the view of the poet as the singer of others' praise. Noting that human examples are more efficacious than abstract precepts and that a good man is a better teacher than a good book, Fielding continues:

> In this light I have always regarded those biographers who have recorded the actions of great and worthy persons of both sexes. Not to mention those ancient writers which of late days are little read (Plutarch and Nepos) . . .; our own language affords many of excellent use and instruction, finely calculated to sow the seeds of virtue in youth, and very easy to be comprehended by persons of moderate capacity (the history of John the Great, the history of Earl of Warwick, the lives of Argalus and Parthenia, the history of the Champions of Christendom). (Pp. 3-4, Bk. I, ch. i)

In the mode of the great biographies that he cherishes, Fielding's own novels also praise the "actions of great and worthy persons of both sexes," heroes like Tom Jones, Allworthy, Wilson, and heroines like Amelia. His novels belong to the most ancient of all genres, the literature of Praise and Blame, to cite O. B. Hardison's terms. That is, the praise afforded a heroine like Amelia evokes admiration and creates attraction, the desire to be near and to emulate the good and the beautiful. On the other hand, the blame given a villain like Jonathan Wild arouses loathing, the desire to shun the monstrous or ugly, the characteristics of evil. As Fielding writes in the opening chapter of Jonathan Wild, the lives of famous men offer "lively examples of whatever is amiable or detestable, worthy of admiration or abhorrence" and illustrate "the true beauty of virtue and deformity of vice."[16] This idea of virtue as a species of the beautiful and vice as a species of the ugly recurs in Fielding's work. In "An Essay on the Knowledge of the Characters of Men," Fielding writes, "It is truly said of Virtue, that, could men behold her naked, they would be all in love with her."[17] In one of the articles for The Champion, Fielding describes vice as "a tawdry, painted harlot, within, all foul and impure, enticing only at a distance . . ." (Tues., Jan. 24, 1739-40).[18] Thus Fielding, who praises the beauty of virtue through noble paragons of goodness and blames the ugliness of vice through loathsome examples of evil and ridiculous paradigms of folly, belongs to the tradition of the poet as the giver of fame. In Joseph Andrews (p. 215, Bk. III, ch. i), "Matter prefatory in praise of biography," Fielding again endorses the ancient view of the poet as the guardian of fame: ". . . it is most certain, that truth is to be found only in the works of those who celebrate the lives of great men, and are commonly called biographers . . ." (italics mine). Like the biographer or epic poet who writes for the noble purpose of praising a great hero and exhorting his fellow man to love virtue and hate vice--rather than perpetuating his own name--Fielding's own biographical novels or "histories" imitate this classical pattern, a point more fully discussed later in the chapter. It suffices here to say that all of Fielding's novels deal with the life or biography of the main character. Also the histories within the History (the history of Leonora or Wilson in Joseph Andrews; the history of Mrs. Fitzpatrick, the Man of the Hill, or Nightingale in Tom Jones; the history of Mrs. Bennet or Mr. Trent in Amelia) all qualify as biographical lives. Furthermore, Fielding's best known poems belong to the literature of Praise: "Of True Greatness" honors George Dodington as a model of true magnanimity, and "Of Good-Nature" celebrates the charity of the Duke of Richmond.

Throughout his work Fielding attacks the vainglory of mediocre authors: authors who write only to establish a reputation as learned men or to win fame through publication; writers who ignore all canons of good taste or the first principles of art, such as instruction and delight; scribblers who titillate the mob's prurient interest in the grotesque, improbable, or unnatural--the typical fault of bad travel books. For example, in "Of True Greatness" Fielding laments how the pretenders to greatness have corrupted the poet's sacred calling--"The poet's noble name and laureate wreath":

> Leave, scribblers, leave the tuneful
>   road to fame,
> Nor by assuming damn a poet's name.[19]

In his criticism of the mad pursuit of fame, Fielding describes common fame in <u>The Covent-Garden Journal</u> (No. 12) as "a loud, rattling, impudent, overbearing lie."[20] In <u>The Champion</u> (Tues., Nov. 27, 1739) he calls fame "but the breath of man." It is a dainty or sweet which fattens a poet, the insubstantial food of both a soldier and an author. Translating Horace in this essay, Fielding compares the obsession with fame to the monomania of avarice:

>   For selfish men,
> The gift of fame like that of money
>   dream;
> And think they lose, whene'er they give
>   esteem.[21]

Thus the greedy pursuer of self-glory who niggardly withholds praise perverts the whole classical notion of the poet as the giver of fame.

Along with hoarding glory and denying praise, the mad pursuit of fame leads to pride and envy. "Writing seems to be understood as an arrogating to yourself a superiority . . . of the understanding," Fielding asserts in The Champion (Sat., Mar. 1, 1739-40). To acquire a reputation involves "the art of puffing," falsely ascribing a well-known name like Shakespeare or Jonson to a recent work.[22] The art of puffing of course is a form of envy. In the words of Pope, quoted by Fielding for another essay in The Champion (Tues., Nov. 27, 1739):

> Envy will merit, as its shade pursue,
> But, like a shadow, proves the substance true.[23]

An author can also win glory through infamy or notoriety. As Jacob Burckhardt noted, "How many who could distinguish themselves by nothing praiseworthy, strove to do so by infamous deeds!"[24] Like the man who burned the temple of Ephesus or the English villain who comforted himself on the way to the gallows (The Champion, Sat., May 3, 1740), "that his name would get into history, and he should live on record"[25]--a form of notoriety that resembles the "greatness" of a Jonathan Wild-- there are authors like Colley Cibber or Pope's dunces who have won fame because of their "excellence in badness" or "consummate imperfection."[26] In this article in The Champion, Fielding cites the characters who appear in Pope's Peri Bathous, the frequenters of Hurlothrumbo, where pleasure arises from "the exquisite badness of the performance," and Cibber's Apology, "the saddest stuff that was ever writ," as examples of fools who have acquired reputations through notoriety. They resemble the vain adepts in fox-hunting or cock-fighting who take special pride in "qualities which are themselves very mean and trivial" (The Champion, Tues., Apr. 15, 1740).[27]

Fielding criticizes vain authors not only for their self-centered love of fame but also for their violation of the canons of good taste, for their ignorance of the noble end of art, namely, both instruction and delight--not mere entertainment or titillation. Mediocre writers fail to teach the beauty of virtue and the ugliness of vice, the true moral purpose of art for Fielding. In his "Preface" to the <u>Familiar Letters</u>, his sister's epistolary novel about the adventures of David Simple, Fielding refers to a virtuoso as a corrupter of good taste, a kind pseudo-artist ignorant of the real purpose of art:

> These are a kind of burlesque natural philosopher, whose endeavours are not to discover the beauties, but the oddities and frolicks of nature. They are indeed a sort of natural jugglers, whose business it is to elevate and surprize, not to satisfy, inform, and entertain.[28]

That is, the virtuoso, to use Samuel Johnson's distinction, merely "diverts" rather than "pleases." In his dictionary, as Jean H. Hagstrum notes in <u>Samuel Johnson's Literary Criticism</u>, "to <u>divert</u> implies something more lively, and to <u>please</u>, something more important." Johnson defines <u>diversion</u> as "sport; something that unbends the mind by turning it off from care." On the other hand, he associates <u>pleasure</u> with a rational, intellectual type of satisfaction: he defines it as "delight; gratification of the mind or senses."[29] In Letter XL of <u>Familiar Letters</u>, assumed to be written by Fielding, Valentine complains to David Simple about the inane entertainments of the town, which amount to no more than "diversions" in Johnson's sense. The "Fustian of Lee and Rowe with French and Italian buffoonery" have monopolized the stage.[30] In Letter XLIII from Miss Lucy Rural to Miss Prudentia Flutters, the country girl ridicules the idle amusements of the city which she learns about from Prudentia: "Indeed, dear Prue, so far from having my opinion raised of the town pleasures . . . I am the more convinced of the impertinence and stupidity of a town life." She also is disenchanted with operas and "the Beaus" that Prue mentioned in her letter:

"Sure the Opera must be a very wretched entertainment, or you would never suffer such animals (the beaus) to divert your attention from it." Finally, Miss Lucy prefers the innocent country pleasures, the hearty celebration of Christmas and its true English hospitality, which she humorously calls a "trumpet," in mock imitation of Prue's favorite pastime in town, the "drum."[31] Thus Fielding laments the decline of the noble vocation of poet or artist from the lofty station of custodian of fame and teacher of the beauty of virtue to the low role of a clever juggler or insipid entertainer.

Fielding especially attacks the irrational, subhuman amusements of his day in Pasquin. Mrs. Mayoress and her daughter wish to enter the beau monde and thus partake of the pleasures of the town: ridottos, rope dancing and tumbling, and cards. In the play within the play, all these "polite" entertainments belong to the forces of Queen Ignorance:

> Queen Ignorance is landed in your realm,
> With a vast power from Italy and France
> Of singers, fiddlers, tumblers, and rope-
>   dancers.

Trapwit's play assumes that the end of art is only to entertain or divert, not to teach and instruct. As Fustian says, plays need to be protracted by the "art of spinning," by introducing unnecessary actions and characters in order to consume time: "But the business of the play, as I take it, is to divert, and therefore every character that diverts is necessary to the business of the play." In order to protract the play with extraneous diversions that will amuse the audience, Fustian has written an extraordinary third act:

> it is, sir, so crammed with drums and
> trumpets, thunder and lightning, battles
> and ghosts, that I believe the audience
> will want no entertainment after it: it
> is as full of show as Merlin's cave it-

self, and for wit--no rope-dancing or
tumbling can come near it.

The corruption of good taste (the dethronement of
Queen Common Sense) has degenerated so far that
the great plays of Shakespeare, Jonson, and Vanbrugh need to be abridged to allow time for the
antics of jugglers. Fustian remarks:

> but I have often wondered how it was possible for any creature of human understanding, after having been diverted for
> three hours with the productions of a
> great genius, to sit for three more, and
> see a set of people running about the
> stage after one another, without speaking
> one syllable.[32]

Thus Fustian only seeks popularity or fame, the
approval of the ignorant mobs. He will resort to
any kind of tactic or trick to achieve it: the
violation of probability, the use of spectacular
deus ex machina, the frivolities of foreign entertainment. He wants to outrival all the other popular performers of the day. This play neither
praises nor blames or teaches and delights. He
seeks originality, not in the exercise of classical inventio, but in the use of innovation--by
writing, so to speak, "what n'er was thought" and
staging "what n'er was done"; in short, by resorting to the Monstrous.

Along with his criticism of the mad pursuit
of fame and the superficial art of his age, Fielding also rejected the idea of novelty found in
travel books of the eighteenth century, that is,
the appeal to oddities and eccentricities as a
form of originality. In his "Preface" to the
Journal of a Voyage to Lisbon, Fielding cites the
appeal to man's idle curiosity as the reason for
the popularity of travel books. "This indeed, it
is in the power of every traveller to gratify; but
it is the leading principle in weak minds only."
The mediocre voyage writer publishes because of
his vainglory; he craves instant fame, some out-

ward mark of his superiority, the visible proof of distinction that constitutes what Burckhardt calls "the modern form of glory."[33] To quote again from the "Preface":

> The vanity of knowing more than other men is, perhaps, besides hunger, the only inducement to writing, or at least to publishing, at all. Why then should not the voyage writer be inflamed with the glory of having seen what no man ever did or ever will see but himself?

Fielding goes on to express his dislike for Pliny's assertion of facts and events that defy God's commandments, Nature's laws, the recorded history of mankind, and common sense places his work in the category of the Monstrous. Pliny resembles the travel writer who fills his pages "with monsters which nobody hath ever seen, and with adventures which never have, nor could possibly, happened to them. . . ."[34] Fielding here reflects the same distaste for the Monstrous--the unnatural, improbable, or curious--that he reflects in the "Author's Preface" to Joseph Andrews, where he distinguishes his comic epic in prose from burlesque and Caricatura: burlesque exhibits "what is monstrous and unnatural" and Caricatura exhibits "monsters, not men." A similar critical pronouncement appears in the discussion of "the Marvellous" in Tom Jones (p. 332, Bk. VIII, ch. i). Fielding contends that it is a duty of the writer to keep "within the bounds of possibility" and hence exclude all spectacular deus ex machina. He cites the precept of Horace, "to introduce supernatural agents as seldom as possible," and the rule of Aristotle that probable impossibilities should be preferred to improbable possibilities. To evoke the marvellous or astonishing, one of the chief ends of literature, the poet "must confine himself to what really happened" and thus avoid causing surprise by an appeal to the Monstrous or incredible. That is, the author of the Marvellous who confines himself to Nature (the given or old) discovers, through the power of *inventio*, the astonishing or new dimension of the commonplace; the eternal youthfulness of old Mother Nature (Thoreau); "the dearest freshness deep down things" (Hopkins). In this sense Joseph Andrews' discovery of his true father, Tom Jones' discovery of his real mother, and Amelia's learning about her mother's original will consist of revelations that simply unveil the surprising, unique freshness of an old truth, a commonplace, that was always "there" as an open secret waiting to be found.

Another example of Fielding's criticism of travel books as full of "monsters" occurs in *Jonathan Wild*. In this novel the idea of travel does not resemble the process of *heuresis* or discovery that the journey in *Joseph Andrews* and *Tom Jones* imitates, whereby Joseph's pursuit of Fanny and Tom's quest for Sophia compare with a man's search for wisdom, traditionally personified as a "she" and called *sophia* in Greek. In *Jonathan Wild* (p. 106, Bk. II, ch. xii), "The strange and yet natural escape of our hero" describes the incredible, miraculous rescue of Jonathan Wild through a supernatural deity. Just after Mrs. Heartfree's improbable deliverance from rape by a gallant French captain who, like a *deus ex machina*, appears from nowhere to save her from Wild's clutches, Wild himself is immediately rescued in the same extraordinary, unbelievable way. Mother Nature performs the office of a god machine:

> She, therefore, no sooner spied him in the water than she softly whispered in his ear to attempt the recovery of his boat, which he immediately obeyed, and, being a good swimmer, and it being a perfect calm, with great facility accomplished it.

Wild manages to survive on six biscuits and with a leaky boat that has just received a broadside!

Fielding's satire of travel literature with its cult of the Monstrous and its notion of pseudo-wonder--that is, creating astonishment by the use of the "incredible" that distorts Nature rather than the Marvellous which inheres in Nature--resembles Swift's parody of travel books in <u>Gulliver's Travels</u>. The irony of Gulliver's self-portrait as the author of a travel book which purports to avoid "every Fault with which common writers of Travels are often too justly charged" (p. 239, Part IV, ch. 12) is that Gulliver commits all the typical faults. Gulliver, for example, indulges his love of fame and his fondness for the Monstrous or grotesque by his fascination with the Struldbrugs and Houyhnhnms. Gulliver asserted he was studious of the truth and did not "affect" any ornaments of vain learning, yet his chapter on the Struldbrugs flaunts his pedantry. He included it, he maintains, because it was a rare, curious item, a novelty, "a little out of the common way; at least I do not remember to have met the like in any Book of Travels that hath come to my hands" (p. 172, Part III, ch. xi). In such a statement Gulliver reveals the trivial mind and vainglorious nature that seek novelties to publicize his reputation in the world.

Thus Fielding, like Swift, criticizes the vainglory of authors, the worldly idea of fame, and the new eighteenth-century conception of originality. These eighteenth-century phenomena contradict the perennial view of art held by Fielding. The vainglory of authors who gloat to see their name in print defies the traditional notion about the anonymity of the artist who regards himself primarily as the instrument rather than the doer of the work. The worldly idea of fame, "the modern form of glory" spoken of by Burckhardt, clashes with the traditional notion of the poet as the custodian who sings or praises, that is, <u>gives</u> fame and honor to others instead of winning and securing it exclusively for himself. The new eighteenth-century conception of originality (implied by Samuel Johnson's definition of <u>novel</u> as "unusual" in his <u>Dictionary</u>) seen in travel books that deal in the Monstrous opposes the Aristotelian concept of "general nature" ("What oft was thought") shared by the classical minds of the age --Swift, Pope, Fielding, Johnson, Reynolds, Austen. When originality in the sense of the Monstrous becomes the end of art, the general becomes sacrificed to the particular; the streaks of the tulip are numbered at the expense of large appearances; art does not imitate Nature; and amusement without instruction becomes the end of art. Instead of gratefully acknowledging the givenness of Nature's universal forms or wondering at the inexhaustible, fecund variety of Nature's materials as a rich commons for the writer to cultivate, the bad voyage writer tends to view Nature as barren, limited, or exhausted ground that will not bear fruit; he views Nature as Swift's spider does in The Battle of the Books. Rather than discover the marvellous or surprising that inheres in Nature by relating "what really happened" and by utilizing the power of inventio, the traveller seeks novelties and pursues wonder by visiting strange lands and gaping at curiosities in the manner of a Gulliver who can be impressed only by size or oddity. While Fielding admits his special debt to his Alma Mater, Nature, and to the wisdom of the ancients as an act of humility and gratitude, Gulliver or the scribblers of the age constantly make invidious comparisons between their own publications and the works of others in an exhibition of boastfulness.

B. The Epic Variety of Joseph Andrews

Fielding not only attacks these anti-classical tendencies of his age by exposing the mediocre works and authors of the eighteenth century but also practices in his own art the same principles he uses to judge others. First of all, he avoids the vainglory of authors by refusing to boast about the merits of his novels in the style of a Defoe, Richardson, or Cibber. Second, he does not cater to Lady Fame by abandoning the canons of good taste or compromising the principles of good art in order to divert the masses with stupid entertainments, as the playwright does in Pasquin.

He always strives to mix profit and delight, to "instruct by pleasing." Hence he writes biographies, lives, or "histories" (the literature of Praise) or satires like Jonathan Wild or Tom Thumb (the literature of Blame) in order to teach the beauty of goodness and the ugliness of evil. Third, although some of his major works like Joseph Andrews and Tom Jones involve the idea of travel and the notion of variety, Fielding avoids the excesses of bad travel literature, the improbable adventures that fill these books. Each one of these three aspects of Fielding's art will be studied in turn, and the discussion will focus on Joseph Andrews.

To use but two examples, Fielding's novels avoid the pretentiousness of Defoe's Robinson Crusoe and Richardson's Pamela. Defoe's "Preface" to Robinson Crusoe is no more than an advertisement that ascribes to the novel merits which it lacks. It deserves to be quoted at length for its boastfulness:

> If ever the story of any private man's adventures in the world were worth making public, and were acceptable when published, the editor of this account thinks this will be so.
> The wonders of this man's life exceed all that (he thinks) is to be found extant; the life of one man being scarce capable of a greater variety.
> The story is told with modesty, with seriousness, and with a religious application of events to the uses to which wise men always apply them (viz.) to the instruction of others by this example, and to justify and honour the wisdom of Providence in all the variety of our circumstances, let them happen how they will.[35] (italics mine)

Robinson Crusoe pretends to be a serious, moral history, a probable story, "a just history of fact"; whereas it is only an incredible romance that provides amusement without instruction, a mediocre travel book that deals in the Monstrous: the unbelievable rescues that deliver Crusoe from death, the use of Providence as a piece of god machinery, the oddity of a noble, happy savage like Friday, and the sensationalism of the episode with the cannibals. Defoe's custom of promising one thing in the title page and offering another thing in the story is the kind of practice that perturbed Fielding. As he says in <u>Joseph Andrews</u> (p. 91, Bk. II, ch. i):

> And in these inscriptions I have been as faithful as possible, not imitating the celebrated Montaigne, who promises you one thing and gives you another; nor some title-page authors, who promise a great deal, and produce nothing at all.

According to Fielding, Richardson also commits this same kind of fault, a form of hypocrisy. He promises a paragon of virtue in Pamela, but he delivers an accomplished coquette. He promises "a great deal" but produces "nothing at all" as Fielding's <u>Shamela</u> illustrates. For Fielding virtue, especially a woman's character, is always associated with modesty or purity of heart, as seen in the portraits of his ideal women, Fanny, Sophia, and Amelia. Thus Fielding addresses his readers in <u>Amelia</u>: ". . . the best of all things, which is innocence, is always within thy own power."[36] In the same novel Dr. Harrison commends Amelia's womanhood for its "openness of heart." As he says, "I may call her an Israelite indeed, in whom there is no guile" (p. 146, Bk. IX, ch. viii). When Fielding compares virtue to a beautiful woman in "An Essay on the Knowledge of the Characters of Men," he writes: "Nothing can, in fact, be more foreign to the nature of virtue than ostentation."[37] Because Richardson identifies virtue with a vain woman who always flaunts her innocence and who, in "self-approving joy," proudly repeats the compliments paid to her ("so that they could hardly talk of anything else; one launching out upon my complexion, another upon my eyes, my hand, and, in short . . . upon my whole person and behaviour"),[38] Fielding questions Richardson's whole concept of virtue. For Fielding virtue does good by stealth, not with a trumpet; it seeks the good of the other person, not the prize of "Virtue Rewarded."

Like Richardson's *Pamela*, which promises a model of virtue but delivers a worldly woman, Colley Cibber's autobiography promises an unpretentious, modest autobiography which will prevent an actor's life from "being so oddly besmear'd (or at best but flatly white-wash'd)."[39] However, it offers an apology for the folly and vanity of the author. For example, Cibber admits, "He who assumes praise to himself, the world will think overpays himself. . . . Praise, tho' it may be our due, is not like a bank-bill, to be paid upon demand; to be valuable, it must be voluntary" (p. 23). He goes on to compare the merit of a writer to the beauty of a woman: These virtues "are never mended by their talking of them: how amiable is she that seems not to know she is handsome!" (p. 33). However, Cibber contradicts these principles because throughout the autobiography he cannot forget his fame as an actor and poet laureate. Even the criticism he receives he interprets as indirect praise: "If I were quite good for nothing, the peddlers in wit would not be concerned to take me to pieces . . . ." (p. 26). Cibber calls his folly wisdom: "If I can please myself with my follies as the best part of my fortune, have I not a plentiful provision for life?" (p. 15). Like Richardson's Pamela, who equates virtue with reward, Colley Cibber associates folly with happiness; both commit non-sequiturs. Richardson and Cibber presume to elevate the mediocre into the heroic, to ennoble the trivial. They violate the essence of biography because they do not choose worthy subjects, "the lives of great men" as Fielding puts it in *Joseph Andrews* (p. 215, Bk. III, ch. i); "the best and most perfect individuals of that species," to use a phrase from *Tom Jones* (p. 411, Bk. VIII, ch. xv). In short, Pamela and Cibber do not belong to the literature of

Praise but to the literature of Blame. They are examples to shun rather than to imitate. They arouse loathing or laughter instead of desire or admiration. They belong to the "true Ridiculous," a species of the ugly, as Fielding defines the term in the "Author's Preface" to Joseph Andrews. Affectation in the form of Cibber's vanity or in the form of a Shamela's hypocrisy prompts laughter or ridicule, a desire to shun such folly. To pretend one thing and be another or, in the case of authors, to promise one thing and give another denotes artfulness--concealment in the form of deceit, not in the sense of modesty. "Art as the ability to conceal art" refers to the humility of the artist, not his hypocrisy. It is one thing to cloak the mediocre in the disguise of excellence, as Defoe, Richardson, and Cibber do. It is another thing to camouflage excellence in the garb of the commonplace, to hide an epic in the comedy of Joseph Andrews or of Tom Jones as Fielding does.

 As a corrective to Richardson's Pamela and Cibber's Apology, objects of satire in Joseph Andrews, Fielding's novel, a biography that belongs to the literature of Praise, will follow the classical tradition and record "the actions of great and worthy persons" (p. 27, Bk. I, ch. i). As a therapeutic to those title-page authors like Montaigne who promise one thing in the preface and offer another thing in the story, Joseph Andrews is faithful to Fielding's original promise in the preface to the novel, the vow to write a comic epic in prose. In his preface and in the first chapter of the novel, then, Fielding offers the two essential ideas which will inform his novel, the notion of the epic and the concept of biography; he implicitly shows how his art differs from the work of the authors he criticizes.

 One aspect of the epic which Fielding incorporates into the novel is the sense of variety, the diversity within unity symbolized, for example, by the shield of Achilles in Homer's Iliad where good and evil exist side by side--where a wedding and a lawsuit occur at the same moment;

where one city lives in peace while its neighboring city is beleaguered by war. Each of the various designs on the shield illustrates, with a different example, this universal truth about the mixed quality of life, the simultaneity of life and death, peace and war, good and evil. In his preface Fielding refers to this quality of the epic: "its action being more extended and comprehensive; containing a much larger circle of incidents, and introducing a greater variety of characters." In his dialogue with Wilson, Parson Adams lauds Homer's sense of variety: "If we consider their variety, we may cry out with Aristotle in his twenty-fourth chapter, that no part of this divine poem is destitute of manners" (p. 230, Bk. III, ch. ii). However, Fielding's idea of variety differs from the kind of diversity Defoe strives after in Robinson Crusoe when Defoe refers to the story of his hero as "the life of one man being scarce capable of a greater variety." Whereas Fielding, like Homer, dedicates himself to the idea of the one and the many ("I describe not men but manners; not an individual but a species"), Defoe separates universals from particulars, stressing the singular, peculiar novelty of his hero's experiences in the style of romance ("the wonders of this man's life exceed all that . . . is to be found extant")--not the Everyman, Tom Jones quality of his characters' histories.

Fielding portrays characters who are both individuals and types. Characters from all the novels as diverse as Parson Adams, Tom Jones, Booth, and Heartfree belong to a species of men who epitomize Good-Nature and Imprudence. Characters as distinct as Lady Booby, Jonathan Wild, Blifil, and Colonel James all reflect Ill-Nature and False Prudence. Various magnanimous characters like Wilson, Allworthy, Amelia, and Dr. Harrison typify Good-Nature and True Prudence, the cardinal virtue of right reason. "The proper study of mankind is Man" as a generic type summarizes Fielding's classical view of character which relates the individual to the species.

The idea of Ill-Nature and False Prudence recurs throughout Joseph Andrews and illustrates Fielding's sense of the one and the many, the idea of epic variety. Several different characters exemplify prudence in its perverted sense. The passengers on the stagecoach who stop to ponder the fate of Joseph Andrews--beaten, robbed, and naked in a ditch--reveal their lack of good-nature. The coachman is in too much of a hurry to stop for a poor wretch; the lady is too modest to tolerate naked men; the old gentleman fears for his own safety; and the lawyer worries about the liability of the passengers, the technicalities of the law. In short, they all practice prudence in the corrupt sense of self-interest: charity begins at home. They all assume that prudence means fear, caution, and distrust. They regard it as a negative quality: not trusting a stranger, not wasting their money, time, or clothes, not taking a chance with the law. For them prudence denotes saving for one's self rather than helping or providing for others. It becomes a form of wariness or circumspection concerned solely with one's own safety; a form of profit-loss calculation interested only in one's pleasure, advancement, or security rather than the justice due to another person. Josef Pieper's The Four Cardinal Virtues clearly explains the distinction between the cardinal virtue and false prudence:

> For we think of prudence as far more akin to the idea of mere utility, the bonum utile, than to the ideal of nobility, the bonum honestum. In colloquial use, prudence always carries the connotation of timorous, small-minded self-preservation, of a rather selfish concern about oneself. Neither of these traits is compatible with nobility; both are unworthy of the noble man.[40]

Lady Booby's advances and Mrs. Slipslop's overtures to Joseph show the same kind of false prudence. In her calculating, coquettish way, Lady Booby tries to seduce Joseph while safeguarding her reputation: she cautiously conducts her flirtation with Joseph in the privacy of her bedchamber rather than in public and carefully plays at love when she is supposedly mourning the death of her husband. She acts with stealth. When Joseph's male virtue rejects her favors, Lady Booby banishes him to avoid all threats to her reputation: "Have I not exposed myself to the refusal of my footman?" (p. 32, Bk. I, ch. viii). Mrs. Slipslop practices the exact type of worldly prudence. Her watchful reckoning appears in her deliberations: "The truth is, she was arrived at an age when she thought she might indulge herself in any liberties with a man, without the danger of bringing a third person into the world to betray them" (p. 21, Bk. I, ch. vi). Like Lady Booby, Slipslop wants both to have her pleasure and also to enjoy her reputation--without any risk of betrayal. Another example of Slipslop's self-interest is her decision to continue to serve Lady Booby, in spite of their disagreement concerning Joseph's character: "The prudent waiting-gentlewoman had duly weighed the whole matter, and found, on mature deliberation, that a place in possession was better than one in expectation" (pp. 35-36, Bk. I, ch. ix). In other words, to quote the well-known political maxim, "Interest will not lie."[41] Lady Booby bribes Mrs. Slipslop, who listened through the keyhole when her lady tempted Joseph, to keep the secret. Their compromise serves the self-interest of both.

The history of Leonora, a seeming digression, enlarges Fielding's portrayal of worldly prudence, ill-nature, and the idea of "interest will not lie." Like the lawyer on the stagecoach who figured that the passengers had more to lose than gain if they left Joseph by the roadside--"if he should die they might be called to some account for his murder" (p. 46, Bk. I, ch. xii); like Mrs. Slipslop who reckoned that she had more to lose than gain by leaving Lady Booby's service, Leonora, after she does all the arithmetic, breaks her engagement with Horatio to marry Bellarmine. Thus she adds and subtracts:

> Can he give me an equipage, or any of those things which Bellarmine will make me mistress of? How vast is the difference between being the wife of a poor counselor, and the wife of one of Bellarmine's fortune! If I marry Horatio, I shall triumph over no more than one rival; but by marrying Bellarmine, I shall be the envy of all my acquaintance. What happiness! (p. 118, Bk. II, ch. iv)

Leonora's politic aunt of course applauds her niece's decision and assures her that "The world is always on the side of prudence and would surely condemn you if you sacrificed your interest to any motive whatever" (p. 119, Bk. II, ch. iv). They both regard prudence as an economic quality devoted to self-profit, not as a cardinal virtue concerned with justice.

The history of Leonard and Paul also expands the discussion of prudence and enriches Fielding's concept of the one and the many, the sense of epic variety. In this story Paul, the confidant of both Leonard and Leonard's wife, tries to arbitrate their family quarrels. Rather than risk the friendship of either husband or wife, he reassures both in private that they are right. Instead of distinguishing right from wrong--the essential task of the cardinal virtue of prudence or right reasons--Paul worries about maintaining his image as the good friend of both husband and wife rather than doing justice to either party, in the same way the lady on the stagecoach concerns herself more with her reputation for modesty than in practicing charity toward a naked man. In his own way Paul is as overly watchful about his fame for friendship as Joseph is about his reputation for chastity. He is like the physicians in the novel who ignorantly diagnose Joseph's illness; they artfully describe Joseph's condition as fatal. In that way if the patient dies, they escape all blame; if the patient recovers, they win glory for their miraculous cure. Paul, likewise, wanting to eliminate all risk and to avoid a commitment, does nothing--neglecting to practice the charity of a friend and the justice of an arbiter. Like Lady Booby who wants to preserve her reputation for modesty without being chaste, like the physician who expects the prestige of an authority without knowing how to cure a patient, Paul also wants the distinction of friendship without showing the sincerity of a friend. They all resemble those mediocre authors like Cibber or Defoe who pretend to greatness without possessing the true merit which they ascribe to themselves. They all fail to meet Fielding's criteria for true greatness, the test for moral excellence or genuine merit that he presents in The Champion (Tues., Mar. 4, 1739-40):

> There is a consciousness in true merit, which renders a man careless of the reception it meets with. He disdains to fly to little arts to inform the world of what it wants only judgment to discover of itself. He is rather studious to deserve than acquire praise. Whereas, the man of contrary character is always forward to acquaint others with his deserts. He is not desirous of virtue itself, but only the reputation of it, therefore is more solicitous to carry virtue in his countenance than in his heart.[42]

The false prudence of ill-natured characters and the artfulness of specious authors, then, only seek the reputation of virtue or greatness. Lady Booby, Mrs. Slipslop, Leonora, and Paul and Richardson and Cibber, according to Fielding, "fly to little arts" to safeguard or publicize their names. To state that true merit is "not at all busied in courting the acclamations of the crowd" and that it only strives "to deserve than acquire praise" as Fielding does in this article of The Champion is to say again that art is the ability to conceal art.

The caution of the falsely prudent characters

from <u>Joseph Andrews</u> mentioned above receives more elaboration when Fielding calls attention to the deed of the constable. This watchman wanted to eliminate every possible risk as he watched his prisoner. Although he guards his captive with weapons, the constable fears that his prisoner might overtake him by surprise. To prevent this danger, he locks the captive in the room and stations himself as a guard outside the door--forgetting that the room contains a window. Thus Fielding concludes from the example of the cautious constable about the nature of false prudence in general:

> But human life . . . very much resembles a game at chess; for as in the latter, while a gamester is too attentive to secure himself very strongly on one side the board, he is apt to leave an unguarded opening on the other; so doth it happen in life. (p. 69, Bk. I, ch. xvi)

For all of the above-mentioned "prudent" characters, in spite of all their calculation and wariness, leave an "unguarded opening" that foils their careful plans. Despite Lady Booby's elaborate preparations to seduce Joseph and safeguard her reputation, Joseph's male chastity refuses to be tempted and Mrs. Slipslop manages to spy out her lady's secret by listening through the keyhole, the unguarded opening. Just as Mrs. Slipslop is about to seize Joseph in an amorous embrace, Lady Booby's bell--a possibility or opening Slipslop ignored--frustrates her scheme. Leonora, who received two marriage offers, ends her life as an old maid, an "unfortunate jilt," because her father did not grant Bellarmine the exorbitant dowry he demanded; this accident she never anticipated. Paul, once the dear friend of both Leonard and his wife, is suddenly banished from their household as a traitor to both, "the occasion of almost every dispute which had fallen out between them" (p. 388, Bk. IV, ch. x): they discover that Paul gave his opinion on both sides--a coincidence that Paul's discretion failed to foresee. The constable's prisoner escapes through the window, another unguarded opening.

This whole discussion of Joseph Andrews illustrates several points. First, Fielding borrows from the ancients; he imitates Homer. Thus he does not view himself as a creator or originator. Second, he exercises invention, arranging and combining the given, the commonplace, the old (Cervantes' Don Quixote, Homer's Iliad, classical biography) to discover a new composition, the comic epic in prose. Third, in the tradition of the poet as the custodian of fame Fielding praises the truly great or admirable, the magnanimity of those characters like Wilson who embody Good-Nature and True Prudence. He blames evil and loathes its ugliness, as personified in those characters like Lady Booby who typify Ill-Nature and False Prudence. He ridicules folly, satirizing all the falsely prudent characters cited earlier. That is, he does not praise the ugly, the foolish, or the mediocre, as Richardson, Cibber, and Defoe tend to do. Fourth, unlike the title-page author who offers less than what he promised, Fielding offers more than he promised in the preface. Joseph Andrews begins as a satire against Richardson and Cibber but becomes more than a parody of Pamela and the Apology, as the previous discussion of the one and the many illustrates. Indeed Fielding's modest explanation of the comic epic in prose in the preface hardly does justice to all the real merits of the novel, a point which the following remarks will elucidate.

When Parson Adams in his dialogue with Wilson praises the greatness of Homer, he remarks, "I am at a loss whether I should rather admire the exactness of his judgment in the nice distinction or the immensity of his imagination in their variety" (p. 230, Bk. III, ch. ii). That is, he wonders at Homer's genius in seeing both the one and the many, the species and the individual--his ability to discern essential similarities and qualitative differences among men. Adams goes on to explain:

> . . . how accurately is the sedate, in-
> jured resentment of Achilles, distin-
> guished from the hot, insulting passion
> of Agamemnon! How widely doth the brutal
> courage of Ajax differ from the amiable
> bravery of Diomedes; and the wisdom of
> Nestor, which is the result of long ex-
> perience, from the cunning of Ulysses,
> the effect of art and subtlety only!
> (p. 230, Bk. III, ch. ii)

Adams' comment on Homer's genius also applies to Fielding's art. He too exercises, to use the well-known eighteenth-century terms, wit (the ability to see resemblances) and judgment (the power to make distinctions)--two concepts which Fielding explains in Book IX of <u>Tom Jones</u>. Here he defines the powers of the mind in terms of "ge-nius," which includes "invention" (wit), "a quick and sagacious penetration into the true essence of all the objects of our contemplation," and "judg-ment," capable of "distinguishing their essential differences" (p. 415, Bk. IX, ch. i). Just as the wrath of Achilles and Agamemnon are alike and dif-ferent, so too the prudence of Lady Booby and the constable are essentially similar although dis-tinct. Lady Booby intends harm toward others: she banishes Joseph, she tries to prevent the mar-riage of Joseph and Fanny, she threatens to evict Parson Adams and his family. On the other hand, the constable bears no malice toward anyone; he merely fears for his own life. Likewise, there are general similarities and fine distinctions be-tween the prudence of Leonora and Paul. They both exemplify the injustice caused by worldly pru-dence: Leonora is unfair to Horatio and Paul is dishonest to both Leonard and his spouse. How-ever, their motives, their degree of guilt, and their punishments all vary. Leonora seeks her own self-interest by deserting Horatio and preferring the wealthier Bellarmine, whereas Paul's concern for his reputation does not amount to such gross selfishness; he is more innocent than Leonora. Also Leonora's preference for Bellarmine results in a duel that almost proves fatal to him, whereas

Paul's vacillation results in no such catastrophe, only a family quarrel; again Leonora is more guilty. Hence she receives the greater punishment, the loss of two potential husbands, whereas Paul loses two friends. Thus Fielding, the Bow Street magistrate, reveals his "judgment" in a manner that resembles Allworthy's nice distinction between Tom Jones' and Jennie's crime of fornication. Adams' remarks on Homer, then, implicitly comment on Fielding's art.

Just as Adams notes the difference between the ripened wisdom of Nestor and the cunning of Ulysses, Fielding too distinguishes between the true wisdom and genuine prudence of Mr. Wilson and the worldly wisdom and the artfulness of a Lady Booby. Like Nestor's wisdom which Adams alludes to, Wilson's prudence results from "long reflection and experience," his past mistakes as a fop and rakehell in London. His prudence belongs to the classical-Christian tradition of the cardinal virtues, prudence as right reason or moral conscience rather than "reckoning" as Hobbes defines it or as self-interest. Wilson's prudence includes charity or good-nature as he welcomes Adams' party into his home, pours out his hospitality, and provides his guests with necessaries as they continue their journey. Unlike the passengers on the stagecoach who wanted to ignore Joseph, Wilson's prudence transcends petty caution and contains an element of daring--a sense of "divine foolishness," to use Paul Tillich's terms, as opposed to "safe reasonableness."[43] Wilson takes a chance by inviting total strangers into his home in the middle of the night. Thus by adventuring to take a risk instead of fearing danger, by practicing charity instead of self-interest, and by using foresight to provide for others instead of calculating one's own reward, Wilson embodies the cardinal virtue of prudence. Thus the contrast between the true wisdom of Wilson and the worldly wisdom of Lady Booby is as marked as the difference between the knowledge of Nestor and the cunning of Ulysses. It appears, then, that Fielding indirectly, modestly, comments on his own novel through Adams' observations on the Iliad.

In his faithfulness to the idea of the epic with its copious, harmonious variety, Fielding delivers in the story of Joseph Andrews what he promised in the preface, a comic epic in prose. The novel, with its histories within a History and with its various individuals who comprise a species, follows the principle of the one and the many that Homer's shield of Achilles portrays. As the Iliad illustrates the truth that each man receives a mixed lot from Zeus, a life comprised of ingredients from both the jars of good luck and bad luck, so Fielding's comic epic depicts the universal that "life everywhere furnishes an accurate observer with the ridiculous" and the commonplace that "no man is wise at all hours" (Nemo mortalium omnibus horis sapit). The vanity of a Joseph Andrews proud of his chastity, the folly of Parson Adams vain about his sermons, the foppery of Wilson's early life, the hypocrisy of Lady Booby--all depict the universality of Fielding's truth. Unlike a Defoe who promises a history but offers a romance or a Gulliver who claims to avoid the faults of a travel book but commits all of them or a Richardson who intends to paint a paragon of virtue but actually creates an acquisitive, ambitious upstart, Fielding not only gives what he intended but also offers more than he promised.

Fielding understates rather than boasts. The "Author's Preface" to Joseph Andrews and the prefatory chapters to each book hardly do justice to the merits of the novel. They only state the principles of Fielding's philosophy of art ("Art imitates Nature") and acknowledge his debt to the ancients (Homer, Cervantes)--thus concealing his own original use of these old materials, his, to quote again from Discourse 2 of Sir Joshua Reynolds, "new combination of those images which have been previously gathered and deposited in the memory" (p. 16)--a true mark of originality or genius in the classical sense of invention. Adams' humorous lecture to Wilson on the greatness of Homer seems no more than another vain exhibition of the parson's bookish learning. However, Adams' comments on Homer's wit and judgment, his love of the individual and his fondness for variety, provide a clue to the art of Joseph Andrews, as explained earlier. Fielding camouflages the seriousness of his point by including it in the remarks of a fool --a wise fool. In other words, Fielding half-reveals and half-conceals when he discusses his own work. He states that the art of Joseph Andrews involves a mystery or secret. The reader will not be able to "see two chapters before him" or predict the ending. It is not a simple book, "easily to be seen through." The art of the novel slowly will disclose itself; the secret will become open only by "small degrees" as in the process of heuresis (p. 40, Bk. I, ch. xi), although Fielding himself will never offer any explicit clarification--as Richardson does, for example, in his itemized catalogue of the moral lessons of Pamela, the "few brief observations" (p. 530) with which he concludes the novel.

Fielding hints rather than tells. He provides no clear explanation for the histories within the History, the biography of Leonora, the history of Wilson, or the story of Leonard and Paul. He only confesses, "There are certain mysteries or secrets in all trades, from the highest to the lowest" (p. 90, Bk. II, ch. i), and the art of dividing a novel into books and chapters constitutes one of those mysteries. Although it might seem to serve no useful purpose besides providing a means "to swell our works to a much larger bulk than they could otherwise be extended to," these divisions lead to practical ends. They function as resting stops or inns to refresh the weary reader; they preserve the beauty of a book by preventing the practice of turning down the leaves of a book to mark the page; an author's dividing his book compares with a butcher's jointing his meat, "for such assistance is of great help to both the readers and the carver" (p. 93, Bk. II, ch. i). That is, what appears useless (the art of dividing) is essential, a form of relief. What appears light or comic (Fielding's prefatory chapters) is serious. What appears foolish (Parson Adams) is wise. This is the same metaphysical principle referred to by Jacques Maritain: ". . . the best way of hiding anything is to make it common, to place it among the most ordinary objects."[44] Thus what seems a lack of art or mere digression, the histories within the History, proves to be true art. What seemed like an episodic story, the worst of all possible plots according to Aristotle ("Of all plots and actions the episodic are the worst"), turns out to have unity of action, a requirement for all great works of literature according to Aristotle--"an action that is complete, and whole, and of a certain magnitude," to quote again from the Poetics.[45] Wilson's history seems to strike Joseph as a long, tedious tale that has no interest or relevance for him, whereas it contains the mystery of his birth, the mention of a lost son and a strawberry birthmark. Like Joseph, who falls asleep, ignores Wilson's story, and fails to discover the secret of his true identity during his sojourn at Wilson's home, the reader who grows inattentive or dismisses the histories of the minor characters will miss the mystery or art of Fielding's novel. Thus Fielding cautions his reader not to fall asleep or ignore seemingly insignificant details or digressions: "I would not advise him to travel through these pages too fast; for, if he doth, he may probably miss some curious productions of nature" (p. 91, Bk. II, ch. i). He makes a similar point in Tom Jones in his distinction between two kinds of travellers, the "ingenious traveller" and the "money-meditating tradesman." The former "always proportions his stay at any place to the beauties, elegancies, and curiosities which it affords." The tradesman, on the other hand, always plods along at the same pace, unaware of the beauties of landscape or architecture: "On they jog, with equal pace, through the verdant meadows or over the barren heath, their horses measuring four miles and a half per hour with the utmost exactness" (p. 531, Bk. XI, ch. ix). The imperceptive, dull, inattentive reader or traveller, then, will overlook the beauties that are concealed in art or Nature as open secrets which require an observant eye to "discover" them in the sense of <u>heuresis</u>. Because of this notion of the open secret, the reader should not dismiss Fielding's light chapters, such as the chapter that justifies the art of dividing as a pause analogous to resting at an inn. For here Fielding camouflages the serious (just as Nature does nothing in vain, so the novelist includes everything for a purpose) with the comic (a reason for divisions in books is to provide bookmarks). Fielding half-reveals and half-conceals in the way he mixes the serious and the comic. The words of Sir Joshua Reynolds from Discourse 4 are most apropos:

> An inferior artist is unwilling that any part of his industry should be lost upon the spectator. He takes as much pains to discover, as the greater does to conceal, the marks of his subordinate assiduity. (p. 42)

Fielding not only understates rather than boasts or hints rather than tells but also implies rather than inculcates his moral instruction. The moral lesson taught by the folly of the falsely prudent characters needs no comment. False prudence invites bad luck, which enters through the "unguarded opening" in the game of chess they play with life. Fielding's noble characters, like Wilson, teach in an implicit way, by providing an example, by living a good life; they do not instruct in the overtly didactic manner of a Parson Adams, Thwackum, or Square, who only recite empty formulas or hollow abstractions and rely on moral systems. As Fielding writes in <u>Joseph Andrews</u> (p. 3, Bk. I, ch. i), "It is a trite but true observation that examples work more forcibly on the mind than precepts"; a good man is of greater use than a good book. The way that Wilson instructs Adams, by example, surpasses the method Adams employs to teach Joseph--through precept. For Adams does not practice what he preaches, as when he counsels Joseph to moderate his grief at the loss of Fanny and then grieves immoderately himself when he hears that his youngest son has drowned. On the other hand, Wilson's actions do not contradict his words. During his short stay at Wilson's home, Adams appreciates Wilson's art of living. As an artist at living, Wilson combines profit and delight. He enjoys cultivating his garden which also provides food for his family. He raises a family and educates his children while he also delights in their company. Adams admires the way Wilson and his family live, the practical wisdom of husband and wife which combines prudence and charity and leads to good works such as well-bred children and hospitality to strangers. Wilson's inspiring example moves Adams to conclude, "This was the manner in which the people had lived in the golden age" (p. 269, Bk. III, ch. iv). The beauty of Wilson's life attracts Adams; his good example excites imitation. Adams' natural attraction to Wilson's virtuous life illustrates Fielding's statement that a good example "inspires our imitation in an irresistible manner" (p. 3, Bk. I, ch. i). That is, virtue is a species of the beautiful and awakens desire like a comely woman. As Fielding remarks in "An Essay on the Knowledge of the Character of Men," "It is truly said of Virtue, that, could men behold her naked, they would all be in love with her."[46] In the same way a beautiful woman naturally awakens desire without flaunting her attractions and virtue naturally inspires emulation without boasting of its merit, so too Wilson easily instructs Adams without resorting to overt didacticism--the kind of obvious pedantry Adams shows when he refers people to his sermons.

Likewise, an author need not, in the solemn tone of a Defoe or Richardson, publicize or elucidate the moral quality of his work. The former announces in his preface to Robinson Crusoe that the story proceeds "with a religious application of events . . . to justify and honour the wisdom of Providence in all the variety of our circumstances, let them happen how they will"--a gross overstatement. Richardson concludes Pamela with a kind of sermon, a tedious list of moral platitudes, such as "let children see what a blessing awaits their duty to their parents, though ever so low in the world"--a form of grave moralizing that Fielding avoided. As mentioned earlier, Fielding mixes the serious with the comic; he instructs by pleasing and never separates delight from profit-- in the same way that Wilson combines work and play and unites his vocation and avocation. Fielding's comment on English pantomime or the art of contrast in Tom Jones summarizes this view:

> This entertainment consisted of two parts, which the inventor distinguished by the names of the serious and the comic. The serious exhibited a certain number of heathen gods and heroes, who were certainly the worst and dullest company into which an audience was ever introduced; and (which was a secret known to few) were actually intended to be, in order to contrast the comic part of the entertainment, and to display the tricks of the harlequin to the better advantage. (p. 162, Bk. V, ch. i)

The histories of Leonora, Wilson, and Leonard and Paul follow the principle of this "secret known to few," the ability to conceal art through the idea of contrast; they both instruct and delight by weaving the serious and the comic. As resting stops or inns along the way, they refresh or please the reader. They also delight by virtue of their contrast with the rest of the story. For Fielding the idea of beauty or the experience of pleasure requires contrast and variety: "A volume without any such places of rest resembles the opening of wilds or seas, which tries the eye and fatigues the spirit when entered upon" (Joseph Andrews, p. 91, Bk. II, ch. i). However, by including histories that comment on some aspect of prudence, an essential theme of the novel, Fielding teaches as well as pleases. In other words, the union of work and play, profit and delight, the serious and the comic all exemplify the art of contrast--the art of concealing.

Indeed Fielding generally mocks all forms of solemn gravity: Joseph Andrews' seriousness about his male virtue, Parson Adams' sermons, the austere Square, "sober, discreet, pious" Blifil, Mrs. Graveairs, the humorless wise man. For example, in A Journey from This World to the Next, one of Julian's adventures treats of his life as a monk. Following the life of a morose recluse, Julian the monk despises all forms of play:

> As I was of a sour morose temper, and hated nothing more than the symptoms of happiness appearing in any countenance, I represented all kind of diversion and amusement as the most horrid sins. I inveighed against cheerfulness as levity, and encouraged nothing but gravity . . . .[47]

In another adventure Julian plays the part of a wise man. Born to be a sage, even as a child Julian spurned play; at two years old he breaks his rattle, a happy omen for a babe destined for wisdom. Later in his school days the boy refuses to join the games of his friends. As a man Julian rejects the pleasures of marriage as inconsistent with the title of a wise man: "I could by no means prevail with myself to sacrifice that character of profound wisdom, which I had with such uniform conduct obtained, and with such caution hitherto preserved."[48] Finally he prefers to marry a rich widow, a match he regards as consistent with his idea of wisdom even though it contains no element of love. He buys the reputation of wisdom by sacrificing all pleasure. After a long, miserable marriage he knows only one consolation, the congratulation of his friends on the "prudence" of his marriage. Fielding never associates wisdom with cheerlessness any more than he speaks of instruction without delight or virtue without beauty.

Fielding's statements on true wisdom in Tom Jones refute the views of Julian the monk and Julian the wise man. For Fielding a truly wise man despises neither riches, pleasures, or worldly blessings; he "may enjoy a handsome wife or hearty friend, and still remain as wise as any sour Popish recluse, who buries all his social faculties and starves his belly while he well lashes his back" (p. 226, Bk. VI, ch. iii). In "The Characters of Men," Fielding also ridicules the affectation of wisdom in the form of gravity. He remarks that "an austere countenance is no token of purity of heart," and he agrees with Shaftesbury that "gravity is of the essence of imposture."[49] Rather than equate wisdom with gravity, Fielding connects it with folly--the idea of the wise fool seen in Parson Adams and Tom Jones who are wise in their practice of good-nature (i.e., charity, cheerfulness, sociability) but foolish in their neglect of prudence. Instead of relegating wisdom to the solitary life of a Man of the Hill or a Julian the monk, Fielding relates it to the sociable world of Allworthy, Wilson, and Amelia. In short, wisdom is related to good-nature, not to sullenness. "The wise man gratifies every appetite and every passion while the fool sacrifices all the rest to pall and satiate one" (<u>Tom Jones</u>, p. 226, Bk. VI, ch. iii) is a statement that refers to the wise man's ability to enjoy--not to despise--the variety of life's pleasures. Thus the blend of wisdom and cheerfulness that Fielding's wise fools and prudent wise men embody is no more contradictory than the union of work and play in Wilson's art of living, the mixture of profit and delight in Fielding's digressions, the marriage of comedy and epic in <u>Joseph Andrews</u>, or the combination of the marvellous and the natural in Fielding's work. All involve the art of contrast, the art of concealing precious metals, so to speak, in common minerals.

    This last notion, the interfusion of the marvellous and the natural, informs Fielding's conception of travel literature. Unlike the typical voyage writer whom he satirizes in his preface to <u>A Journal of a Voyage to Lisbon</u>, Fielding does not cultivate the Monstrous that has no basis in reality. Rather he seeks the Marvellous which inheres in Nature. The travel in Joseph Andrews is not a journey to a remote spot like Gulliver's trips to Laputa, Balnibarbi, Luggnagg, Glubbduddrib, and Japan or like Crusoe's voyage to a deserted island. Like the journey in Tom Jones, the travel in Joseph Andrews covers old, familiar English roads, the well-known route to London. The "adventures" in the novel, a basic element of all travel literature, do not deal in absurdities or improbabilities, such as Crusoe's eerie battle with the cannibals in a faraway place, Jonathan Wild's incredible escape in the middle of the ocean, or Gulliver's grotesque experience with the Struldbrugs in a strange land. The adventures in Joseph Andrews deal with commonplace occurrences at well-known sites: the robbery of a stagecoach on a thoroughfare; the arrival of unexpected guests at a public inn; the meeting of old acquaintances on the road to London; the hunting of squires in the countryside. For example, the adventures at Mrs. Towwouse's inn or the inn at Upton in Tom Jones are both marvellous and probable happenings. When Adams and Joseph or Tom and Sophia meet, wonder or surprise occurs. However, their meeting at a "common-place," an inn on the old road to London, confirms Fielding's theory about the Marvellous or surprising dwelling amidst the natural or probable. Even the most marvellous event in Joseph Andrews, Wilson's discovery of his lost son, allows for an explanation through natural causes. Wilson finds a lost son whom he has not seen for twenty-one years--a marvellous occurrence; yet he identifies Joseph through a strawberry birthmark, a natural sign. Wilson providentially arrives at Booby Parish at the exact moment when Joseph's identity is in question--a marvellous coincidence; yet Wilson had promised to visit Adams when they parted, a natural gesture of friendship. Adams accidentally alights upon the home of Joseph Andrews' real father, another instance of marvellous good fortune; yet for a lost, weary traveller to go to the nearest home and hope for hospitality is a most natural reaction. By uniting the Marvellous and the natural, then, Fielding's idea of travel in Joseph Andrews avoids the Monstrous, the improbabilities of other travel books and romances.

As romantic travel literature, both <u>Robinson Crusoe</u> and <u>Gulliver's Travels</u> violate the criteria of Samuel Johnson's "preface" to Lobo's <u>Voyage to Abysinnia</u>. They both favor the cult of primitivism and promote the idea of the happy, noble savage that Johnson's classical view challenged. As Johnson said, Lobo's <u>Voyage</u> offered no picture of "Hottentots without religious polity or articulate language; no Chinese perfectly polite, and completely skilled in all sciences." In their primitivism <u>Robinson Crusoe</u> and <u>Gulliver's Travels</u> do not subscribe to Johnson's classical view that human nature is everywhere the same; rather they endorse the fallacy that, in Johnson's words, "life in one part of the globe is so very different from life in another."^{50} For example, during his stay on the island, Crusoe concludes that his uncivilized existence offers a happier state than his civilized life in English society:

> From this moment I began to conclude in my mind that it was possible for me to be more happy in this forsaken, solitary condition than it was probable I should ever have been in any other particular state in the world; and with this thought I was going to give thanks to God for bringing me to this place. (p. 114, "I Travel Across the Island")

Crusoe portrays Friday as a noble savage with a natural religion, a form of deism: "his simple, unfeigned honesty appeared to me more and more every day." Together they live the good life, uncorrupted by society: ". . . the three years which we lived there together (were) perfectly and completely happy, if any such thing as complete happiness can be formed in a sublunary state" ("We Make Another Canoe"). Gulliver too believes in the superiority of the primitive life, the simple way of the Houyhnhnms who do not erect human institutions like government, business, and education and who have no use for civilized customs like the use of clothes, money, and an alphabet. The horses have truly "returned to nature." After his sojourn with the Houyhnhnms Gulliver embraces the happy life of these noble horses and spurns society:

> My Design was, if possible, to discover some small Island uninhabited, yet sufficient by my Labour to furnish me with Necessaries of Life, which I would have thought a greater Happiness than to be first Minister in the politest Court in Europe; so horrible was the Idea I conceived of returning to live in the Society and under the Government of Yahoos. (p. 232, Part IV, ch. xi)

Thus by perpetuating the myth of the noble savage and denying that human nature remains everywhere the same, the mediocre travel book tends toward romance rather than history. It does not present individuals who are members of a species; instead it offers curiosities or rare specimens like the honest cannibal or rational horses, more examples of the Monstrous.

On the other hand, Fielding's idea of the journey in Joseph Andrews meets Johnson's criteria and shows, to quote again from the preface to Lobo's Voyage, "that wherever human nature is to be found, there is a mixture of vice and virtue, a contest of passion and reason." For example, Fielding does not sentimentalize the country life of Wilson or idealize Tom Jones' experience in Somersetshire or celebrate the man of the hill's solitary existence. Fielding's portraits of country life show no trace of primitivism, for he does not identify evil with civilization and good with the cult of "return to nature." Even in Wilson's simple life, which Adams compares to the golden age, tragedy occurs when a cruel squire maliciously kills an innocent spaniel, the favorite pet of Wilson's daughter. "She expressed great agony at his loss; and the other children began to cry for their sister's misfortune; nor could Fanny herself refrain" (p. 268, Bk. III, ch. iv). Likewise, Allworthy's estate is not as idyllic as its beautiful landscape suggests: Allworthy's discovery of a bastard at his doorstep alone proves that fact. The man of the hill retreated from civilization in order to avoid all the ills of society, all the "dishonesty, cruelty, ingratitude, and treachery" of man. However, even though he now lives secluded from men and the corruptions of London, he is nearly robbed and killed by thieves. In rejecting the idea of utopia associated with primitivism and by persisting in the traditional view that human nature remains everywhere essentially the same, Fielding defends the classical view or originality or invention--finding the marvellous in the natural, the new (the "wonder-full") in the old (Alma Mater). Thus Fielding writes about merry old England, not about foreign or imaginary lands. The adventures, such as Wilson's discovery of his lost son, consist of astonishing but probable occurrences, not incredible fictions. His novels deal with an old subject (Human Nature) or commonplaces rather than cults or relative truths. Fielding's idea of travel rejects the view of the grand tour that the "parson-hunting" squire represents in Joseph Andrews:

> He made in three years the tour of Europe, as they term it, and returned home well furnished with French clothes, phrases, and servants, with a hearty contempt for his own country; especially which had any savour of the plain spirit and honesty of our ancestors.
> (p. 288, Bk. III, ch. vii)

Enthralled with French novelties, the squire despises everything English--as Gulliver does after he returns home from the island of the horses. Spurning the old and the familiar, his ancestors and his country, the squire cultivates his taste for the Monstrous: "but what distinguished him chiefly was a strange delight which he took in everything which is ridiculous, odious, and absurd in his own species" (p. 288, Bk. III, ch. vii). Instead of using travel to learn about the variety and unity of human nature, to know men and manners --the real purpose of travel--the squire only observes eccentricities.

Indeed the true use of travel teaches man to see both the similarities and differences among men, to discern the idea of the one and the many, to exercise wit and judgment. For Fielding an essential element in the education of man, along with "genius," "learning," and "a good heart" is the knowledge of experience--what he terms "conversation" or what he means when he cites "Mores hominum multorum vidit," the epigraph to Tom Jones:

> Again, there is another sort of knowledge, beyond the power of learning to bestow, and this is to be had by conversation. So necessary is this to the understanding of the characters of men, that none are more ignorant of them than those learned pedants whose lives have been entirely consumed in colleges and among books; for however exquisitely human nature may have been described by writers, the true practical system can be learnt only in the world. (Tom Jones, p. 416, Bk. IX, ch. i)

It is this knowledge of men and manners that allows a host at an inn to correct Adams' theory on physiognomy and that permits Joseph to challenge the parson's views on public education. The host questions Adams' ability to read character by a close examination of a man's countenance; he appeals to experience: "if you had travelled as far as I have, and conversed with the many nations where I have traded, you would not give any credit to a man's countenance" (p. 210, Bk. II, ch. xvii). On the basis of his own observations Joseph also doubts one of Adams' pet notions: he refutes Adams' grand theory that public schools are dens of iniquity by appealing to concrete examples from life. He replies to Adams, ". . . you know my late master, Sir Thomas Booby, was bred at a public school, and he was the finest gentleman in all the neighborhood" (p. 271, Bk. III, ch. v). Conversely, Joseph cites examples of gentlemen who received a private education at home, "who were educated within five miles of their own houses, and are as wicked as if they had known the world from their infancy" (p. 272, Bk. III, ch. v)--another proof that human nature remains constant everywhere, regardless of geography, climate, or country. Tom Jones' episode with the Gypsies also proves how experience or travel corrects theories and generalizations. Prior to this incident, Jones accepted the common prejudice against the Gypsies. He admits to the king of the Gypsies, "I must confess, sir, I have not heard so favorable an account of them as they seem to deserve" (p. 586, Bk. XIII, ch. xii). He learns, however, that the Gypsies are not, as opinion would have it, a thieving, immoral, uncivilized race of barbarian people but a human society with its own stable institutions and civilized customs. Tom appreciates the hospitality and courtesy of these people, their gaiety and friendliness, and their form of government. In short, he senses their essential humanity; he no longer views them as a singular race of men. Like a good traveller, Tom, exercising wit and judgment, recognizes both the common humanity and discrete individuality of the Gypsies. They are unique in their absolute form of government and their use of shame as a form of punishment. As a distinct people ". . . they differ from all other people and to which perhaps this their happiness is entirely owing, namely, that they have no false honours among them, and that they look on shame as the most grievous punishment in the world" (p. 588, Bk. XII, ch. xii). Fielding's idea of conversation with the world, then, criticizes the character who, like the man of the hill, fears travel or experience and the character who, like Parson Adams, desires to travel only in books.

Both types fail to sense the immense variety

of life, the diversity of men and manners, the exceptions to the rule which experience alone can teach. They see only the one at the expense of the many. The man of the hill regards all men as depraved; Parson Adams sees all men as good-natured. False prudence distrusts everyone; imprudence believes everyone. On the other hand, the traveller who pursues the Monstrous sees only the many at the expense of the one, describing differences without noting similarities. Gulliver, for example, keeps repeating, "the different Nations of the World had different Customs." In contrast to these two extreme views, Fielding's own profound sense of the one and the many receives one of its foremost expressions in "Characters of Men":

> Those who predicate of man in general, that he is an animal of this or that disposition, seem to me not sufficiently to have studied human nature; for that immense variety of characters, so apparent in men even of the same climate, religion, and education, which gives the poet a sufficient licence, as I apprehend, for saying that,
> "Man differs more from man, than man from beast,"
> could hardly exist, unless the distinction had some original foundation in nature itself.[51]

Because Nature provides this prodigious, amazing variety, it offers an inexhaustible source of wonder, of the Marvellous. For Fielding, as for Mark Twain, truth is indeed stranger than fiction.

To summarize: Fielding reveals the humility of the traditional artist in many ways. First, he remembers his debt to Nature who provides all and to the ancients who offer a wealth of wisdom. He acknowledges his sources and teachers; he does not hail his own creativity or originality. Second, he belongs to the classical tradition of the poet as the giver of fame, not to the Renaissance cult of self-glory. Fielding sees the sacred calling of the poet or artist as related to justice, the rendering to others--the great, the heroic, the admirable--their due in the form of fame, honor, and glory. The poet as judge or critic is obliged to praise the good and the beautiful, not the mediocre or the foolish as Pamela and Cibber's Apology do. Third, Fielding understates rather than boasts, he offers more than he promised: Joseph Andrews gives more than an imitation of Don Quixote, an epic modeled upon Homer, a classical form of biography, a parody of Pamela, or a treatise on prudence; it overflows or transcends these categories and definitions. As a work of art in imitation of Nature, it is as inexhaustible in its own way as Nature's prodigious variety. Fourth, Fielding hints rather than tells; he educes rather than dictates. Like a Socratic teacher who gradually leads his pupil to the truth, Fielding slowly unveils the purpose of his plot. Just as Socrates' pupil must discover the truth for himself, so Fielding's reader must see the form in matter, the art concealed by art. He must abstract the idea of the one from the many in the same way that Joseph needs to find his missing Fanny and Wilson is obliged to recognize his lost son. Fifth, Fielding implies rather than inculcates his moral instruction; he camouflages the serious in the comic, the profitable in the delightful, wisdom in folly, and the marvellous in the ordinary. In short, Fielding's view of art as the ability to conceal art, to half-reveal and half-conceal the open secret, is founded on a metaphysical principle so aptly expressed in the quotation from Bacon cited by Norman O. Brown and Marshall McLuhan:

> It is a game of hide and seek: "The glory of God is to conceal a thing, but the glory of the king is to find it out; as if, according to the innocent play of children, the Divine Majesty took delight to hide his works, to the end to have them found out; and as if kings could not obtain a greater honour than to be God's playfellows in that game."[52]

Or, in the words of Jacques Maritain:

> Metaphysics, the supreme human science, possesses a characteristic in common with the Gospels. What is most precious and most divine is hidden under what seems most commonplace.[53]

NOTES TO CHAPTER I

[1] Ananda Coomaraswamy, Christian and Oriental Philosophy of Art (New York: Dover, 1956), p. 40.

[2] Coomaraswamy, p. 69.

[3] Sir Joshua Reynolds, Discourses on Art (Indianapolis: Bobbs-Merrill, 1965), pp. 15-16. All further references to this work come from this edition. The page reference will hereafter be given in parentheses in the text.

[4] C. S. Lewis, The Discarded Image (Cambridge: Cambridge Univ. Press, 1967), p. 211.

[5] Jacques Maritain, Creative Intuition in Art and Poetry (Cleveland and New York: Meridian, 1966), p. 92.

[6] John D. Boyd, S. J., The Function of Mimesis and Its Decline (Cambridge, Mass.: Harvard Univ. Press, 1968), p. 24.

[7] Henry Fielding, Tom Jones (New York: Modern Library, 1950), p. 1. All further quotations from Tom Jones are taken from this edition. References to the page number, book, and chapter of the novel will hereafter be provided in parentheses in the text.

[8] Boyd, p. 304.

[9] Henry Fielding, Miscellaneous Writings in The Works of Henry Fielding, ed. William Ernest Henley (New York: Croscup and Sterling, 1902), XVI, 264--hereafter cited as Works throughout the remainder of the book.

[10] Henry Fielding, Joseph Andrews (New York: Modern Library, 1950), xxxix. All further quotations come from this edition; references to the page number, book, and chapter are provided in parentheses in the text.

[11] Jonathan Swift, *Gulliver's Travels and Other Writings* (New York: Modern Library, 1958), p. 378. All further references to either *The Battle of the Books* or *Gulliver's Travels* come from this edition. Page number, section, and chapter will hereafter be provided in parentheses within the text.

[12] Ibid., p. 376.

[13] Ibid., p. 377.

[14] O. B. Hardison, *The Enduring Monument* (Chapel Hill: Univ. of North Carolina Press, 1962), p. 27.

[15] Jacob Burckhardt, *The Civilization of the Renaissance in Italy* (New York: Modern Library, 1954), p. 109; p. 115; p. 115; p. 108.

[16] Henry Fielding, *Jonathan Wild* (New York: Signet, 1962), p. 7. Further references to the novel come from this edition; page numbers, book, and chapter are cited in parentheses in the text.

[17] *Works*, XIV, 300.

[18] *Works*, XV, 167.

[19] *Works*, XII, 255.

[20] *Works*, XIV, 120.

[21] *Works*, XV, 78; 80.

[22] *Works*, XV, 223; 224.

[23] *Works*, XV, 86.

[24] Burckhardt, p. 115.

[25] *Works*, XV, 297.

[26] *Works*, XV, 280.

[27] *Works*, XV, 280; 279.

[28] *Works*, XVI, 29.

[29] Jean H. Hagstrum, *Samuel Johnson's Literary Criticism* (Chicago: Univ. of Chicago Press, 1967), p. 79.

[30] *Works*, XVI, 30.

[31] *Works*, XVI, 43-46.

[32] *Works*, XI, 209; 211; 217; 222.

[33] Burckhardt, p. 108.

[34] *Works*, XVI, 180; 183, 182, 183.

[35] Daniel Defoe, *Robinson Crusoe* (New York: Signet, 1961), p. 7. Further references are incorporated in the text; the title of the chapter is cited and the page number of this edition is given.

[36] Henry Fielding, *Amelia* (New York: E. P. Dutton, 1962), p. 69. Further references are incorporated in the text; page number, book, and chapter are cited in parentheses.

[37] *Works*, XIV, 300.

[38] Samuel Richardson, *Pamela* (New York: Norton, 1958), pp. 302-303. All further references are based on this edition; page numbers are cited in parentheses in the text.

[39] Colley Cibber, *An Apology for his Life* (London: J. M. Dent; New York: E. P. Dutton), p. 6. All further references come from this edition; page numbers are cited in parentheses in the text.

[40] Josef Pieper, *The Four Cardinal Virtues* (Notre Dame: Univ. of Notre Dame Press, 1966), p. 4.

⁴¹J. A. W. Gunn's essay, "Interest Will Not Lie: 17th-Century Political Maxim," Journal of the History of Ideas XXXIX (Oct.-Dec., 1968), 551-564, provides an excellent discussion that explains how prudence degenerates from its status as a cardinal virtue to a form of statistical calculation or political arithmetic based on the maxim that self-interest or worldly prudence is a constant factor in predicting the behavior of other men or nations.

⁴²Works, XV, 228.

⁴³Paul Tillich, The Eternal Now (New York: Scribner, 1963), p. 161.

⁴⁴Jacques Maritain, A Preface to Metaphysics (New York: Mentor-Omega, 1962), p. 87.

⁴⁵Walter J. Bate, ed., Criticism: The Major Texts (New York: Harcourt, Brace, & World, 1952), p. 25; p. 24.

⁴⁶Works, XIV, 300.

⁴⁷Henry Fielding, Miscellanies in The Works of Henry Fielding (Philadelphia: John D. Morris, 1902), VI, 80.

⁴⁸Ibid., p. 91.

⁴⁹Works, XIV, 284; 285.

⁵⁰Mona Wilson, ed., Johnson: Prose and Poetry (Cambridge: Harvard Univ. Press, 1963), p. 15 ff.

⁵¹Works, XIV, 281.

⁵²Norman O. Brown, Love's Body (New York: Vintage, 1966), pp. 245-246.

⁵³Jacques Maritain, A Preface to Metaphysics, p. 88.

CHAPTER II

NATURE AND FORTUNE AS INTELLIGIBLE MYSTERIES:
BEAUTY AND LUCK AS SPECIES OF WONDER IN
TOM JONES

> Great and wondrously sublime is simplicity when it thus reconciles in itself these apparently opposite virtues. It is the highest expression of the beautiful. For the beautiful is harmony, the splendor arising out of unity and diversity; and the greater the diversity, the more profound is the unity, the more extraordinary is the beauty.
> --Garrigou-Lagrange, Providence

> The ποιητής was for the Greeks the type of the Creator, who was poet and composer (i.e., musician) at the same time . . . .
> --Leo Spitzer, Classical and Christian Ideas of World Harmony

Fielding's description of Allworthy's estate in Tom Jones (pp. 8-11, Bk. I, ch. iv) emphasizes the irregular, unsystematic, unmethodical, asymmetrical character of Nature. Neither the lay of the land nor the course of the water follows the order of mathematics or geometry. The terrain offers more than sheer meadows, pure woods, or all mountains; instead of the "clear and distinct ideas" of a Descartes, it comprises "all the diversity that hills, lawns, wood, and water" can create. The trees that adorn the estate do not belong to one species but represent many varieties: oaks, beeches, elms, firs. Even the most level part of the land, the lawn, goes "sloping downhill" to avoid monotony. The water, likewise, flows in unexpected ways. The cascade does not progress in "a regular flight of steps" but tumbles "in a natural fall over the broken and mossy stones." The water "winds" and "meanders" through the woods and follows no straight line. The right hand scene and the left hand view do not symmetrically parallel each other: on the right of the grove towers an old abbey; on the left of the grove appears a park. Finally, "a ridge of wild mountains" provides another example of Nature's bold, irregular art. Thus the uneven lay of the land, the wandering course of the water, the diversity of the trees, and the jaggedness of the mountains all reveal Nature as "unmethodized."

Fielding never depicts Nature as a great chain of being, a geometrical design, or as a machine or clock. Nature is not the closed system that Pope's Essay on Man delineates, the purely rational, systematic, linked universe of Leibnitzian optimism where Nature's plan assumes the unmysterious, self-evident clarity of geometry--"the best of all possible worlds." Fielding's portrait of Nature opposes the chain of being in several ways. First, in contrast to the linked or closed quality of the chain of being, Fielding stresses the openness, the "prospects," the vistas of Nature. Second, in contrast to the chain of being's pure, clear ideas--"All Nature," "All chance," "All discord," "All partial evil" (Essay on Man, I, 11. 289-292)--Fielding sees Nature as chiaroscuro, both light and dark, as half-revealed and half-concealed. Third, in contrast to the simple, monistic view of Nature that the chain of being concept offers ("One truth is clear, whatever is, is right"), Fielding observes the multiplicity of Nature, her "prodigious variety."

The location of Allworthy's house illustrates the first idea, the open, unconfined quality of nature. The building is situated on a hill that provides "a most charming prospect of the valley beneath." The front of the house permits a full, open view of the lake that fills the center of the plain. To the right of the valley "opened" another vista that revealed the villages in the distance. To the left of the valley "the view of a very fine park" affords another wide margin. The last detail in the description, the ridge of mountains, "the tops of which were above the clouds," provides another panorama, the boundlessness of the heavens as opposed to the closed universe of the chain of being. Secondly, Fielding's view of Nature conflicts with the chain of being because he sees her as a mysterious woman rather than as a clear system, as a modest beauty rather than as an intricate clock. Just as the circuitous course of the water as it meanders on its way to the ocean often remains hidden to the human eye, so too these full, wide prospects do not always provide a comprehensive view. Although the lake appears visible from every room in the front of the house, this clear view ends--"the prospect was closed"-- after the lake joins the river and heads for the sea. The right hand scene of the valley, which provides a glimpse into distant villages, suddenly becomes "terminated by one of the towers of an old abbey." In the way that Nature opens and closes these scenes, then, she reveals and conceals, mixing light and dark, proving both her intelligibility and her mystery. Fielding challenges the chain of being in yet another way: he opposes the variety, fickleness, and mystery of Nature as beautiful, creative woman to the simplicity, regularity, and predictability of Nature as watch or machine. The sudden rises and falls in the land, the unexpected turns and twistings of the river, the curves of the wild mountains, the park's "very unequal ground" all illustrate Nature's fickle, feminine quality, her ability to surprise and cause wonder, to evoke a sense of the Marvellous. Thus Fielding, in his description of Allworthy's estate as well as in a number of other passages, portrays Nature as open rather than closed, as infinite rather than bounded, as musically harmonious rather than geometrically symmetrical, or, in the context of this chapter, as an "intelligible mystery" rather than a "clear and distinct idea." That is, Nature, full of the Marvellous or what Aristotle in the *Poetics* called "the wonderful," transcends man's ideas, concepts, and systems which try to circumscribe or delimit her. As a dynamic *Natura naturans* ("Nature naturing"), to use a phrase from medieval philosophy, rather than as a static chain of being, she shows a copious, infinite variety that refuses to be reduced to narrow rules or mathematical logic.

This notion of Nature's copious variety, however, is not to be confused with the fullness or plenitude that forms a basic element in the chain of being. When Pope writes in the *Essay on Man*,

> Of systems possible, if 'tis confessed
> That Wisdom Infinite must form the best,
> Where all must full or not coherent be,
> (I, ll. 43-45)

he views Nature as a plenum, "the assumption," to quote A. O. Lovejoy, "that 'nature makes no leaps.'"[1] The principle of plenitude does not mean Nature's love of beautiful variety or musical harmony but a deterministic idea, the notion of "necessary 'fullness'" or "eternal logical necessity"[2] that A. O. Lovejoy refers to. In Pope's phrase, "Where all *must* full or not coherent be." This principle of plenitude, then, explains the fullness of the universe, not as the effect of divine providence or God's love as in *Paradise Lost*, but as a consequence of cosmic determinism. As A. O. Lovejoy explains:

> . . . all things follow *ex necessitate divinae naturae*, and . . . the existent universe is just such a system as Spinoza had represented--logically inevitable in its last detail, so that no alternative could ever have been so much as conceived by an infinite intellect.[3]

Thus fullness or the plenum in the chain of being tends to mean explicitness, enumeration, gradation, the elimination of all voids; in Locke's words:

> In all the visible corporeal world we see no chasms or gaps. All quite down from us the descent is by easy steps, and a continued series that in each remove differ very little one from the other.4

Of course Fielding's description of Nature at Somersetshire, with its open vistas or gaps (the cascade suddenly drops by "tumbling in a natural fall" rather than by logically progressing in "a regular flight of steps") challenges the tenet that "nature makes no leaps" and that her pattern is "logically inevitable in its last detail." As mentioned earlier, the water that originates in a hidden spring and is destined for the ocean pursues a random, devious, unpredictable course. In short, Fielding sees Nature's handiwork as the masterpiece of an artist, as the beauty of a woman in her infinite variety, as the harmony of a musical composition--not as a regular clock or a linked chain. Fielding, for example, comments upon Nature's "admirable taste," her beautiful colors and artistic touches, in her creation of the variegated countryside of Somersetshire. That is, he admires Nature's qualities, the "old" oaks, the "mossy" stones, the "pebbly" channel, the "wild" mountains--not the size or quantity of the estate. He admires the organism of Nature's body, not the mechanism of Nature as res extensa.

In another chapter of Tom Jones, Fielding again praises the wonder of Nature's art:

> At Eshur, at Stowe, at Wilton, at Eastbury, and at Prior's Park, days are too short for the ravished imagination; while we admire the wondrous power of art in improving nature. In some of these, art chiefly engages our admiration; in others, nature and art contend for our applause; but, in the last, the

former seems to triumph. Here Nature appears in her richest attire, and Art, dressed with the modestest simplicity, attends her benignant mistress. Here Nature indeed pours forth the choicest treasures which she hath lavished on this world; and here human nature presents you with an object which can be exceeded only in the other. (p. 531, Bk. XI, ch. ix)

Here Fielding portrays Nature as imaginative artist, as a beautiful woman, and as a provident mother. As an artist her wisdom outrivals man's knowledge; she is the queen and man is the servant. As a beautiful woman she displays resplendent colors and appears "in her richest attire." As a generous mother she "pours forth" her gifts on mankind. Her copiousness oversteps narrow, fixed boundaries. When Fielding goes on to praise the "taste" and "imagination" of Nature, "which luxuriously riots in these elegant scenes," he places Nature's profusion and beauty in the realm of the Marvellous, as inexhaustible wonders that surpass man's power of description or definition. "Days are too short for the ravished imagination" to admire fully Nature's masterpieces. That is, Nature often appears so wise, so beautiful, or so generous that she defies man's systems or methods of classification. The irregular, unpredictable way Nature reveals her beauty is an aspect of the Marvellous. As Fielding explains in the same chapter, to appreciate Nature's art "the ingenious traveller" as opposed to the "money-meditating tradesman" proportions or varies his pace according to a natural rhythm. He lingers over the lovely prospects, "the woods, the rivers, the lawns of Devon and of Dorset," but he hurries past the heath of Bagshot. On the other hand, the tradesman's jog trot methodically proceeds "with <u>equal</u> pace, through the verdant meadows or over the barren heath, their horses <u>measuring</u> four miles and a half per hour with <u>the utmost exactness</u>" (p. 531, Bk. XI, ch. ix; italics added). The good traveller, like the good novelist, must imitate the rhythm or music of Nature, not the clockwork of man. He must "sometimes . . . stand still, and sometimes . . . fly" (Tom Jones, p. 41, Bk. II, ch. i) and be in tune with the world.

Along with his description of Somersetshire and the picture of Eshur, Devon, and Dorset, Fielding's portrait of Sophia also clarifies his view of Nature. For Fielding Sophia is Nature personified; she is "a copy from nature" as he describes her in the opening chapters of Book IV. Sophia is "adorned with all the charms in which nature can array her; bedecked with beauty, youth, sprightliness, innocency, modesty, and tenderness." Her mental powers are "derived from nature," and her courtesy and refinement are "natural gentility" (p. 108 ff., Bk. IV, ch. ii). Like the "amazing variety of meadows and woods" that adorned Allworthy's estate and like the Nature that "pours forth the choicest treasures which she hath lavished on this world" in her creation of Eshur, Stowe, and Elton, Sophia's physical appearance reflects the bounty of Nature. Her features exemplify Nature's plenty: "luxuriant" hair, "full" eyebrows, "all the charms" of Nature's gifts. Like the undulating land, the "unequal ground," and the winding river--all sharp, surprising turns--Sophia reveals marked, unique, individual features that make her a nonpareil, an original beauty who outrivals the Venus de Medicis, the ladies of Hampton Court, and the darlings of the Kit-Cat club. Sophia's special beauty distinguishes her from all these other paragons: "for she did not exactly resemble any of them" (p. 110, Bk. IV, ch. ii). Fielding accents the distinct curves and lines of her particular attributes: her "curled" hair, her "regular" nose, her "oval" cheeks, her "long" neck "finely turned." Sophia is another example of Nature's asymmetrical art, the musical harmony of her compositions. Fielding goes on to note that Sophia's chin was neither "large or small, though perhaps it was rather of the former kind." That is, her beauty is not a matter of quantity, large or small, but a quality that defies exact measurement. Nor does the color of Sophia's cheeks follow a geometric pattern, an exact balance of red and white; instead it reflects pied beauty: "Her complexion had rather more of the lily than of the rose." The radiance of Sophia's white neck also defies exact measurement or easy description: "Here was whiteness which no lilies, ivory, nor alabaster could match." Causing wonder, her beauty becomes a source of the Marvellous and transcends man's "clear and distinct ideas"; Sophia's splendor, for all its brightness, is not a simple idea to grasp:

> Nitor spledens Pario´marmore purius.
> A gloss shining beyond the purest brightness of Parian marble. (pp. 110-111, Bk. IV, ch. ii)

In short, Nature's abundance and variety shape both the land around Somersetshire and the body of Sophia. Both Allworthy's estate and Sophia's splendor reveal the beauty of proportion, not of symmetry. The various, individual parts form a harmonious whole, not a simple, mathematical unity. As sources of the "wonder-full," both the landscape and Sophia represent marvels of beauty, miracles that cannot be fully comprehended by man's conceptual systems. As Dennis Quinn's article on the wane of wonder and the love of clarity in the seventeenth and eighteenth centuries points out: "It is not, to be sure, simply the love of clarity which is the enemy of wonder . . . but rather the demand for a reductive, final, and exhaustive knowledge which characterizes all forms of rationalism."[5] By admitting that "our highest abilities are very inadequate to the task" of describing Sophia's sublime beauty, by remarking that "days are too short" to admire fully Nature's wonders, and by acknowledging Nature's "amazing variety" and "admirable taste" at Somersetshire-- Fielding views the Marvellous as synonymous with inexhaustible and irreducible, beyond method or system.

Like Nature who is both delightful and useful, Sophia is both beautiful and good. Allworthy's estate functions as more than a romantic setting; it is the site of Allworthy's home. The sheep graze there. The water serves an essential purpose by causing things to grow. As Fielding commented in another incident in the novel, the scene where Tom fights Thwackum and Sophia faints at the sight of blood:

> we mentioned a murmuring brook which brook did not come there, as such gentle streams flow through vulgar romances, with no other purpose than to murmur. No! Fortune had decreed to ennoble this little brook with a higher honour than any of those which wash the plains of Arcadia ever deserved. (p. 210, Bk. V, ch. xii)

With Sophia in his arms Tom rushes toward the rivulet, sprinkles water on her face, and revives his beloved. Nature's murmuring brook is thus both functional as well as decorative. Likewise, Sophia in the course of the novel gives several examples of her virtue which complement her beauty: her devotion to her father, her goodness to the Seagrim family, her forgiveness of Tom. Sophia herself does not separate the enjoyable from the useful. In defending her scrupulous obedience to her father's wishes, she explains: "for besides that I am barely discharging my duty, I am likewise pleasing myself. I can truly say I have no delight equal to that of contributing to my father's happiness" (p. 141, Bk. IV, ch. x). In other words, harmony prevails between two elements that seem contrary: the useful and the pleasing, the good and the beautiful. Sophia's name, the Greek <u>sophia</u>, reinforces this concept of harmony: it signifies both the immaterial truth of wisdom and the physical beauty of a woman.

The many become one not only in the countryside of Somersetshire through the harmonious variety of "hills, lawns, wood, and water" and in the physical appearance of Sophia by the agreeable consonance of hair, eyes, nose, cheeks, and neck--

that is, in the congruity of the physical dimensions—but also in the union of the external and the internal, of the visible and the hidden, of form and matter. Just as the more physical land or "body" of Allworthy's estate is matter (<u>Mater</u>) or feminine, so the less visible water, the <u>hidden</u> spring and meandering river, resembles form, the masculine principle. Likewise, Fielding observes the harmony or analogy between Sophia's body and soul, between her outside and inside:

> Such was the outside of Sophia; nor was this beautiful frame disgraced by an inhabitant unworthy of it. Her mind was every way equal to her person; nay, the latter borrowed some charms from the former. (p. 111, Bk. IV, ch. ii)

That is, her soul or mind "in-forms" or animates her physical attractiveness, giving her an essence that is congruous with her appearance: "for when she smiled, the sweetness of her temper diffused that glory over her countenance which no regularity of features can give." Indeed this agreement between the outward and the inward man, this shining out of the form, underlies Fielding's whole theory of character—the notion of character in the classical sense of outward "mark," stamp, or impression; the idea of a man's nature as visible through his actions and words. As Fielding states in "An Essay on the Knowledge of the Characters of Men":

> . . . I conceive the passions of men do commonly imprint sufficient marks on the countenance; and it is owing chiefly to want of skill in the observer that physiognomy is of little use and credit in the world.[6]

Thus as the many outward parts become one, as the outward and the inward, matter and form, agree, and as opposites like the pleasing and the useful, beauty and virtue, complement one another, Fielding shows the amplitude or fullness inherent in the universal principles of Nature's harmony--the boundlessness that characterizes the Marvellous.

In addition to these forms of harmony, Fielding provides another example, the consonance between art and Nature, that is, between man's handiwork and Nature's masterpieces. Allworthy's estate, for example, owes its beauty to the art of man as well as Nature. Allworthy's house is a marvel of architecture; in imitation of Nature's laws of harmony, it mixes elements from both "the Gothic style" and "the beauties of the best Grecian architecture." One of the vistas from the valley shows a glimpse of civilization, "several villages," and another example of man's art, an old ruined abbey. The park shows evidence of man's influence and Nature's genius, though "owing less to art than to Nature." Similarly, the beauty of Eshur, Stowe, Wilton (in the quotation cited earlier) reflects the handiwork of man and Nature. Sometimes man's art improves Nature; sometimes they both show their genius as "nature and art contend for our applause." At other times Nature "seems to triumph." These different mixtures that combine both man's skill and Nature's art in varying degrees resemble the changing proportions of land and water in the scenes at Somersetshire. There the spring gushing from a rock, the lake at the center of a plain, and the river winding through the woods are all combinations which mix the two elements of earth and water in different ratios, not in exact halves.

Sophia as a masterpiece also reflects the influence of human art in addition to Nature's gifts: "It may, however, be proper to say, that whatever mental accomplishments she had derived from nature, they were somewhat improved and cultivated by art" (p. 111, Bk. IV, ch. ii). Sophia's manners and courtesy result from art's ability to enhance Nature. When man's art or science fails to improve, refine, or temper Nature, then a kind of uncultivated wilderness follows, like the uninhabitable island in The Tempest that Prospero's art or magic transforms into a civilization. Similarly, Tom's innate good-nature, without the art of prudence, leads to intemperance, the "wantonness, wildness, and want of caution" that harass him throughout the novel. Tom must bring into accord his actions and his intentions by learning an art that he does not natively possess: "It is not enough that your designs, nay, that your actions, are intrinsically good; you must take care they shall appear so. If your inside be never so beautiful, you must preserve a fair outside also" (p. 97, Bk. III, ch. vii). Fielding again stresses this harmony or cooperation between art and Nature in his discussion of the qualified writer or historian (pp. 413-418, Bk. IX, ch. i). A good writer needs both native ability and acquired talents. In addition to Nature's gifts of "genius" or natural reason and a "good heart," an author needs to supplement these endowments with "a good share of learning" and "a competent knowledge of history and of the belles-lettres." Then he must add to his natural talents and his acquired learning the knowledge of experience or "conversation," the knowledge of men and manners. Thus the interaction between man's art and Nature's gifts in the creation of beautiful landscape and educated men involves the same concept of harmony, an order based upon the model of music rather than the ideal of mathematics.

Thus Fielding's concept of order and Nature was atypical of his age. As Leo Spitzer observes in <u>Classical and Christian Ideas of World Harmony</u>, the eighteenth century witnessed a process of "de-musicalization," a loss of a sense of world harmony based upon "the musical unity of the world," the death of the harmony of the spheres notion: "our 'God-and-music-forsakenness' . . . dates from the eighteenth century; it is in fact a remnant of the eighteenth-century anti-Christian movement. . . ."[7] In an era that prized the univocal mind in love with clarity and unity at the sacrifice of mystery and diversity, as seen in Square's citations about the "eternal fitness of things," Fielding cherished the analogical mind that discerned similarities and differences--the powers of invention and judgment that he discusses in the introductory chapter of Book IX. Allworthy as judge needs to compare and contrast the crimes of fornication committed by Jenny and Tom. The reader as critic needs to see that the beauty of Somersetshire and the beauty of Sophia are both alike and different. Justice and beauty are not clear, univocal ideas: Allworthy always mixes mercy with justice, and beauty is always pied beauty for Fielding. As W. F. Lynch describes the analogical mind in Christ and Apollo:

> I should say we must achieve some kind of interpenetration of unity and multiplicity, sameness and difference, a kind of interpenetration in terms of which the two contraries become one and the same thing--but "become" this only because existentially they have always been it.[8]

In an era that often viewed Nature as barren or exhausted, as seen in the Ancients versus Moderns quarrel, Fielding marvelled at Nature's fecundity, the fullness of her "prodigious variety." John B. Bury's The Idea of Progress relates this whole question of the battle of the books to the larger issue about Nature's powers:

> The question, Can the men of today contend on equal terms with the illustrious ancients, or are they intellectually inferior? implied the larger issue, Has nature exhausted her powers; is she no longer capable of producing men equal in brains and vigour to those whom she once produced; is humanity played out, or are her forces permanent and inexhaustible?[9]

Almost in answer to this very kind of question, the opening chapter of Tom Jones can be read as Fielding's reply. Here Fielding assures his reader that the topos of Human Nature is not a hackneyed, depleted subject: "nor can the learned reader be ignorant, that in Human Nature, though here collected under one general name, is such prodigious variety, that a cook will have sooner gone through all the several species of animal and vegetable food in the world, than an author will be able to exhaust so extensive a subject." Finally, as Dennis Quinn's "Donne and the Wane of Wonder" so aptly illustrates, the epoch that saw the eclipse of the traditional idea of wonder ("wonder as the beginning of philosophy") also saw the rise of pseudo wonder, the false sublime, as well as the return of the stoic <u>nil admirari</u> ("marvel at nothing"): Professor Quinn cites Gulliver as the champion of "vulgar astonishment" and Descartes as the advocate of the <u>nil admirari</u> position.[10] Fielding, in his rejection of the mathematical ideal of absolute clarity and in his aversion to the false wonder of what he called the Monstrous, reaffirmed the classical-Christian idea of wonder when he asserted the existence of the Marvellous or the wonderful as inherent in Nature--a topic that he discusses at length in the first chapter of Book VIII of <u>Tom Jones</u>. This traditional conception of wonder, "sudden light filled with darkness" as Professor Quinn calls it, of course relates to the notion of Nature as an intelligible mystery that is part-revealed and part-concealed. For to wonder is to know only in part. To quote St. Albert the Great's summary of the classical-Christian synthesis of the idea:

> Now the man who is puzzled and wonders apparently does not know. Hence wonder is the movement of the man who does not know on his way to finding out, to get at the bottom of that at which he wonders and to determine its cause. . . . Thus Aristotle shows in that branch of logic which is called poetic that the poet fashions his story for the purpose of exciting wonder, and that the further effect of wonder is to excite inquiry. Such is the origin of philosophy, as Plato shows with respect to the stories of Phaeton and Deucalion. The single

> purpose of these stories is to excite one
> to wonder at the causes of the two del-
> uges of fire and of water . . . , so that
> through wonder the cause would be looked
> for, and the truth discovered.[11]

Fielding, deriving his notion of wonder primarily from Aristotle and Horace whom he alludes to in the introductory chapter to Book VIII as well as from Longinus whom he cites as one of the "noble critics" (p. 490, Bk. XI, ch. i) in a class with Aristotle and Horace, defended the concept of the Marvellous in an age that distrusted miracle and mystery. Fielding saw as aspects of the wonderful not only the inexhaustible fullness of Nature's bounty and the incomparable beauty of a Sophia but also Fortune's miracles of good luck and the true greatness of a hero or magnanimous man. The luck of Tom Jones, whom Sophia calls "the most fortunate man in the world" (p. 875, Bk. XVIII, ch. xii), and the goodness of Allworthy, "a man, who is not only the darling of all good men who know him, but a blessing to society, the glory of his country, and an honour to human nature" (p. 199, Bk. V, ch. ix), are also matters for true astonishment.

Fielding's view of Nature as musically harmonious and as full of the wonderful, then, relates to the larger questions of eighteenth century thought. Given Fielding's conception of Nature as both open and closed or as semi-clear and semi-dark, as varied yet unified, as orderly yet surprising, as obedient to higher laws yet defiant of narrow rules, as pied rather than monochromatic-- in short, as an intelligible mystery rather than as a closed system--how does the plot of <u>Tom Jones</u> imitate Nature's complex order? Since Nature, in Fielding's thought, avoids the formalism of a symmetrical garden and the aimlessness of a murmuring brook that merely flows "with no other purpose than to murmur," how does <u>Tom Jones</u> avoid these two extremes: the strict rules of neo-classical art and the formlessness of the "monstrous" romances that Fielding condemned?

The plot in Tom Jones does not follow any strict decorum, such as the ideal of unity of time or place or the practice of poetic justice--the precise rules of neo-classical art. Indeed in "Of The Serious in Writing, and for what purpose it is introduced" (p. 159, Bk. V, ch. i), Fielding, like Johnson in the Preface to Shakespeare, challenges the whole rationale for the unities of time and place: "Who ever demanded the reasons of that nice unity of time or place which is now established to be so essential to dramatic poetry?" The rules that prescribe absolute adherence to these neo-classical unitiés, the decorum that forbids "low" humor on the stage--Fielding considers these laws as nothing more than the arbitrary "dictates of the critic," as "dogmatical rules . . . without the least foundation." The neo-classical critics do not judge art by a close examination of the actual practices of great writers, in the way that Aristotle based the Poetics on Homer's epics and the masterpieces of Greek drama. Instead, as Fielding remarks in Tom Jones, "the critics have been emboldened to assume a dictatorial power, and have so far succeeded that they are now become the masters, and have the assurance to give laws to those authors from whose predecessors they originally received them" (p. 160, Bk. V, ch. i). These narrow critics do not, strictly speaking, criticize in the true sense of the word: "This word critic is of Greek derivation, and signifies judgment" (p. 487, Bk. XI, ch. i). They condemn on the basis of an ipse dixit, they resort to the malice of slander, or they condemn the whole work because of a small fault, "a single expression," "one scene" (p. 491, Bk. XI, ch. i). Unlike the true critic or judge who, like Allworthy, tries to see in men both the good and the bad in their right proportion and who mixes justice and mercy after weighing all the particulars--the whole situation--the bad critic "tends to pass a severe sentence upon the whole merely on account of some vicious part" (p. 490, Bk. XI, ch. i).

Thus Fielding rejects neo-classical criteria

for essentially the same reasons as Johnson. First, art, though it obeys certain first principles, such as unity of action or the notion of <u>mimesis</u> in its broad sense, transcends narrow rules. In Johnson's words, "but there is always an appeal open from criticism to nature."[12] In Fielding's words, many of the neo-classical tenets "have not the least foundation in truth or nature . . ." (p. 160, Bk. V, ch. i). Second, the rules hinder and interfere with a true imitation of Nature, which is not one thing, a clear idea, either pure tragedy or simple comedy, but a motley affair, always mixed and various--as Shakespeare's tragi-comedies and Fielding's comical epics illustrate. Johnson said that Shakespeare's plays defied rigid classification as either comedy or tragedy; they revealed "the real state of sublunary nature, which partakes of good and evil, joy and sorrow, mingled with endless variety or proportion and innumerable modes of combination."[13] Likewise, Fielding opposed the strict rules and pure genres of formalist critics with Nature's love of variety and contrast. In the same chapter, after he rejects the criteria of formalism, Fielding cites Nature's art of contrast as a model of beauty: "This vein is no other than that of contrast, which runs throughout all the works of the creation, and may probably have a large share in constituting in us the idea of all beauty, as well natural as artificial" (p. 161, Bk. V, ch. i). Third, the <u>form</u> in literature is not to be prescribed by the categorical assumptions of a critic who dictates, <u>a priori</u>, the unity of time or place, the purity of a genre, or the decorum of poetic justice. Rather <u>form</u> is to be discovered or unveiled in a heuristic manner; it becomes known or revealed in the process of going from the many to the one, from the particular to the general; that is, <u>a posteriori</u>. <u>Form</u>, in the Aristotelian sense, is not a tangible, measurable thing, an external shape, a clear idea of mathematics that can be proved or shown in a cursory way. Rather <u>form</u> is a semi-hidden universal or open secret that goes deeper than surface appearance or physical description. The fact that philosophers deny immaterial things like love and virtue does not, according to Fielding, destroy their reality: "for who ever heard of a gold-finder that had the impudence or folly to assert, from the ill success of his search, that there was no such thing as gold in the world?" (pp. 214-215, Bk. VI, ch. i). Mrs. Western's inability to read the open secret of Sophia's love for Tom--"scarce visible to the naked eye" (p. 163, Bk. V, ch. ii)--does not eliminate that hidden truth. <u>Form</u>, then, is an immaterial reality, like the soul or love, which can shine out in matter; it veils or camouflages itself in the physical or material in a half-revealing, half-concealing way, providing signs, hints, and clues--in a way that Sophia modestly betokens her love for Tom:

> Notwithstanding the nicest guard which Sophia endeavoured to set on her behaviour, she could not avoid letting some appearances now and then slip forth: for love may be likened to a disease in this, that when it is denied a vent in one part, it will certainly break out in another. What her lips, therefore, concealed, her eyes, her blushes, and many little involuntary actions, betrayed. (p. 166, Bk. V, ch. ii)

Thus <u>form</u> is not self-evident like an axiom in geometry or like Square's rule of right; it is not, by its shape, appearance, or body, patently visible to the naked eye. In short, it cannot be fully known or completely seen and hence evokes wonder[14]--the sense of the Marvellous that accompanies the revelation of the truth in Fielding's novels as seen, for example, in Allworthy's state of mind at the end of <u>Tom Jones</u>: "'Madame,' says Allworthy, 'I am under such an astonishment at what I have heard, that I am really unable to satisfy you; but come with me into my room. Indeed, Mrs. Miller, I have made surprising discoveries, and you shall soon know them.'" (p. 854, Bk. XVIII, ch. viii). Since <u>form</u> hides itself in matter and opens its secret by signs in slow, gradual

ways to those true critics or seers who love
truth, its revelation resembles the mystery of
woman, a Sophia. Sophia (sophia) must be sought
with loving desire, not with the rapacity of a
Lord Fellamar or the coldness of a Blifil. Sophia
yields herself only to a lover with pure, sincere
intentions--not to a Lord Fellamar who only wants
her body or to a Blifil who only eyes her fortune.
Hence Johnson in Rasselas and Fielding in Tom
Jones and Joseph Andrews employ the metaphor of
life as a journey in quest of truth (form) which
needs to be sought and discovered in the painstaking, ardent way that Tom pursues Sophia, Joseph
seeks Fanny, and Rasselas searches for the choice
of life. Form, in Fielding's classical view of
art, refers to an immaterial reality, an intelligible mystery, a deep interior principle that can
be known in part but not exhausted or measured in
any mathematical way. Form goes beyond the superficies of style that neo-classicists prized; it
is, in W. J. Bate's phrase, "the internal intention," not "the external accompaniments," of a
work of art.[15] This is precisely Fielding's point
when he attacks those critics who confuse form
with formalism by mistaking "mere form [appearance] for substance": "They acted as a judge
would, who should adhere to the lifeless letter of
law and reject the spirit" (Tom Jones, p. 160, Bk.
V, ch. i).

In the light of Fielding's broad conception
of Nature and his Aristotelian idea of form, Tom
Jones offers a history that will proceed in irregular, unmethodical ways. Fielding asserts that he
will write like the selective historian who dwells
on significant, extraordinary events, the Marvellous, and not merely record a bare, chronological
narrative. He will focus on worthy events like
"the revolutions of countries" rather than "to
preserve the regularity of his series . . . fill
up as much paper with the detail of months and
years in which nothing remarkable happened . . ."
(p. 40, Bk. II, ch. i). Stressing quality rather
than quantity, Fielding will escape the inane formalities of a newspaper, "which consists of just

the same number of words, whether there be any news in it or not," and he will avoid the mechanical motions of a stagecoach, "which performs constantly the same course, empty as well as full" (p. 40, Bk. II, ch. i). Thus there will be chasms, not always links, in Fielding's narration as he imitates Nature's ordered but unsystematic course, not "Nature methodized." He will sometimes stand still and sometimes fly, imitating the rhythms or music of Nature; he will not become the slave or "amanuensis" of time who follows the regularity of the clock or the progression of the calendar. In short, Fielding, modelling his history upon "what really happened" or might have happened (p. 335, Bk. VIII, ch. i), which always includes the wonderful or surprising, bases his plot upon Nature's varied harmony with its bold, unforeseen strokes, its sudden, unpredictable movements--not upon the graduated scale of a clock or chain of being that permits no gaps or chasms, that eliminates wonder and surprise.

Tom Jones' extraordinary history, full of the surprises and wonders of the Marvellous--the ups and downs of Fortune who "seldom doth things by halves" (p. 204, Bk. V, ch. x)--does not form a closed system, any simple, predictable pattern of events. By ascribing to Fortune such a prominent role in the life of Tom Jones, as well as in the histories of the other characters, Fielding sees in history not only the visible actions of men but also the unseen elements of luck. As Fielding explains in <u>The Champion</u> (Dec. 6, 1739), Fortune plays an important role in the lives of men and nations. Like Plato who paid "a religious respect to chance and fortune," like the Romans who erected a temple to the goddess Fortuna and regarded it as blasphemy not to share the glory of victory with her, like the Anglo-Saxons who "use to decide all controversies by lot," Fielding reveres the divinity of Fortune: ". . . I imagine wisdom to be of very little consequence in the affairs of this world: human life appears to me to resemble the game of hazard, much more than that of chess." He cites the life of Oliver Cromwell as an illustration of Fortune's uncanny role in the life of a man: "Whoever considers the former part of the life of Oliver Cromwell, may perceive a much greater probability of his ending his days in a gaol, than in a palace at the head of the nation."[16] The same kind of prediction was made of Tom Jones, "born to be hanged." Instead of denying Fortune's role and attributing success or failure solely to human foresight and planning like Machiavelli in his famous advice to rape Fortune, instead of crossing out the word "unfortunate" from the dictionary and placing all responsibility upon man in the style of a Richelieu[17]-- Fielding sees the mysterious interaction of two elements rather than one factor as the dominant force in the history or life of a man: man's actions, the visible, intelligible element, and Fortune, the invisible, mysterious element; the known and the unknown; the explainable and the wonderful. Just as Sophia's body and soul, her beauty and goodness, are interfused, just as the land and the water are intermixed throughout Allworthy's estate, so too man's actions and Fortune's whims interpenetrate in human events and do not detach themselves as clear, distinct, separable ideas in accordance with Descartes' ideal. The history of Tom Jones is not a predictable system that can be foreseen by a simple formula such as "born to be hanged" or a clear idea like "interest will not lie." Tom Jones' good fortune, the perennial luck of the fool, is not completely intelligible to pure reason. History does not prove any naive moral theory such as "virtue rewarded" or follow the neo-classical decorum of poetic justice. As R. S. Crane said in his famous essay on the plot of *Tom Jones*, "We are not disposed to feel, when we are done laughing at Tom, that all is right with the world or that we can count on Fortune always intervening, in the same gratifying way, on behalf of the good."[18] In Fielding's own words:

> There are a set of religious, or rather moral writers, who teach that virtue is the certain road to happiness, and vice to misery, in this world. A very whole-

some and comfortable doctrine, and to which we have but one objection, namely, that it is not true. (p. 690, Bk. XV, ch. i)

In the opening scene of the novel, Fielding shows the role that both the actions of men and the caprices of Fortune play in Tom's history. He refutes the simplistic theories of "born to be hanged," "interest will not lie," and "virtue rewarded," which attempt to reduce life's boundless variety and open prospects to a clear idea and a narrow view. The "odd accident" or whim of Fortune that surprises Allworthy on his return home is the strange infant he finds in his bed, a mystery that causes wonder: "He stood some time lost in astonishment at this sight" (p. 6, Bk. I, ch. iii). By bringing Tom into Allworthy's home, then, Fortune has played its secret part in this stage of Tom's history. Allworthy's decision to adopt the child and raise it as his own son is the human action, the known part, of Tom's early life. The Marvellous asserts itself at Tom's birth and in Allworthy's normal, everyday life; the miraculous inheres in the natural, upsetting the laws of statistical probability. For Tom is not only lucky to escape the common fate of bastards--abandonment before the church warden's door--but also fortunate to avoid death. According to Deborah Wilkins, there is always the chance that abandoned waifs will die before they are found: "and, if it was well wrapt up, and put in a warm basket, it is but two to one but it lives till it is found in the morning" (pp. 7-8, Bk. I, ch. iii)--her own prediction that Tom is born to die--"and it is, perhaps, better for such creatures to die in a state of innocence, than to grow up and imitate their mothers." However, just as Tom's fortunate lot is not the common fate of bastards and disproves Mrs. Wilkins' prophecy that he was born to die or be a menace to society, so too Allworthy's magnanimity refutes Mrs. Wilkins' unstated formula that "interest will not lie." He disregards her warnings that "the world is censorious," that "it hath been many an honest man's hap to pass for the father of children he never begot," that Allworthy is not obliged to succor a foundling which the parish can support. Welcoming Tom into his home as an adopted son, Allworthy exposes himself to the calumny of the world. His example, thus, negates the "virtue rewarded" or "virtue is the certain road to happiness" formula.

Tom's romance with Sophia also happens as a result of the combination of Fortune and man, accident and choice. After Sophia hears of Tom's affair with Molly, Western's daughter tries to curb her own inclinations. She resolves to avoid Tom's company altogether and thus decides to visit one of her aunts. "But Fortune, who had other designs in her head, put an immediate stop to any such proceeding . . ." (p. 149, Bk. IV, ch. xii). A mishap, the accident that occurs when she is hunting with her father, forces Sophia to alter her plans. Losing control of her horse, in danger of falling and suffering a fatal wound, she is suddenly rescued by Tom whose gallant protection of Sophia causes him to break an arm. Like Tom's rescue of Sophia's bird, "a trifling incident" with "some future consequences" (p. 112, Bk. IV, ch. iii), this episode of Tom's rescue of Sophia qualifies as one of those "many little circumstances . . . from which events of the utmost importance arise" (pp. 172-173, Bk. V, ch. iv). For during the interlude of Tom's recuperation at Squire Western's home, "the full secret" of Tom and Sophia's love becomes revelation to both of them. Because of Fortune's intervention in causing the accident that befell Sophia and because of Tom's heroic decision to rescue Sophia from the horse, both Fortune and man cooperated to determine the future history of Tom and Sophia's romance. Fortune presented the situation, and Tom willingly acted to help the distressed woman--in the same way that chance greeted Allworthy's homecoming with an unusual circumstance but allowed him to exercise his free choice in adopting Tom. Fortune proposes; man disposes.

During the interlude of Tom's recovery at

Squire Western's estate, Fortune's whims and man's actions interact in other ways. Only Mrs. Honour plays the part of fickle Fortune. This time man proposes and Fortune disposes: Tom declares his love for Sophia to Mrs. Honour, and Mrs. Honour, as changeable as Fortune, breaks her vow of secrecy to Tom and passes on his compliments to Sophia. Once Mrs. Honour saw Tom put his hands into Sophia's muff and kiss it. Another time Tom, hearing Sophia play the harpsichord, mentioned to Mrs. Honour how much he envied the happiness of Sophia's future husband. On another occasion Tom confessed to Mrs. Honour that he revered Sophia as a goddess. Not intending these remarks as subtle ingratiation, "flattery at second hand," Tom does not design that his compliments should be transmitted from Mrs. Honour to Sophia. As Mrs. Honour explains, "for he gave me a crown never to mention it, and made me swear upon a book, but I believe, indeed, it was not the Bible" (p. 157, Bk. IV, ch. xiv). It is Tom's luck, however, that Mrs. Honour breaks her promise and relays Tom's praises to her lady, an accident that has "such an effect on Sophia" that Fielding decides to refrain from description. Mrs. Honour's fondness for whispering secrets also prompts her to carry news about Sophia to Tom. Tom learns that although Sophia has bought a lovely new muff, she refuses to part with the old one--the one that Tom kissed and fondled. According to Mrs. Honour, ". . . she hath worn it upon her almost ever since, and I warrants hath given it many a kiss when nobody hath seen her" (p. 172, Bk. V, ch. iv). This minor incident with the muff affects Tom in the same profound way it touches Sophia,. causing "so violent an effect" on Tom that he dismisses all thoughts of Molly and succumbs to Sophia. It is Tom and Sophia's luck, then, that the accident with the horse occurred and that Mrs. Honour broke her promise. Fortune intervened and showed her power in the lives of men. However, without human cooperation and willingness, Fortune's efforts alone would not have materialized. If Tom did not seize the opportunity to rescue Sophia, if he never uttered words of praise about her, if Sophia had not preferred her old muff, Fortune would have acted in vain and Mrs. Honour could have disclosed no secrets.

    This scene illustrates not only the intricate coalescence between chance and choice but also the subtle mixture of good and evil. The interlude of Tom's convalescence is a bittersweet, neither all evil or all good as Thwackum and Square respectively interpret it. According to Thwackum, Tom's broken arm signifies God's divine punishment: "that he ought to look on his broken arm as a judgment from Heaven on his sins." In Square's view the so-called evil of the broken arm is for the universal good, "for the good of the whole": "He said, 'It was a mere abuse of words to call those things evils in which there was no moral unfitness.'" (p. 164, Bk. V, ch. ii). Neither one sees the <u>form</u> of love that is camouflaged in these incidents. Thwackum notices only the visible punishment of Tom's broken arm. Square, on the other hand, ignores what he sees: the pain is not real, "below the consideration of a wise man," "the most contemptible thing in the world." The clear ideas of Thwackum and Square which see everything as either black or white reduce life's complex variety to a closed system--Thwackum's virtue rewarded-vice punished formula and Square's rule of right. The <u>form</u> or significance of the experience, however, is not a clear idea or simple moral lesson but an intelligible mystery or open secret: the riddle of choice and accident; the paradox of good brought out of evil; the wonder of a great event, the revelation of love, caused by a little thing, a "trifling" incident like the muff episode. This is essentially the <u>form</u> or deeper meaning in the opening scene of the novel. Tom's illegitimate birth is an evil; Allworthy's adoption of Tom illustrates how good can intertwine itself with evil, how the wheat and the chaff often grow side by side. In both instances, the extraordinary occasion of Tom's birth and the astonishing events that lead to the revelation of love, the Marvellous weaves itself into common, everyday events or minor incidents.

Like the union or harmony of opposites mentioned earlier--land and water, beauty and goodness, body and soul, art and Nature--Fortune and man or Providence and free will form another one of these subtle knots. However, Fielding not only shows those moments when chance and choice cooperate--Allworthy adopting Tom and Tom saving Sophia --but also those occasions when Fortune refuses to lend assistance to man or man fails to respond to Fortune. For example, when Capt. Blifil suddenly dies of an apoplexy, "just at the very instant when his heart was exulting in meditations on the happiness which would accrue to him by Mr. Allworthy's death" (p. 69, Bk. II, ch. viii), Fortune frowns. On the other hand, when Tom arrives at the inn at Upton and Fortune smiles by directing Sophia to the same place, Tom does not reciprocate. Entangling himself with Mrs. Waters at the inn, Tom misses Sophia; he frustrates Fortune's intentions and causes his own bad luck. Like the other forms of natural order in the novel, luck is a matter of harmony, of being in tune with the world--often a result of the consonance of prudence and charity, of reason and will, in human nature. For Fielding sees a harmony or analogy between human nature and Nature, the microcosm and the macrocosm. Inasmuch as man practices the classical virtues of prudence and justice, he observes the "law of nature" in the natural law tradition summarized, for example, by Richard Hooker in the first book of <u>The Laws of Ecclesiastical Polity</u>. Inasmuch as man practices the Christian virtue of charity, he is in tune with the world, for as Allworthy says, charity is "enjoined both by the Christian law and by the law of nature itself" (p. 56, Bk. II, ch. v).[19] Of course classical prudence and Christian charity are harmonious complements, not opposing contraries, as Allworthy the judge and Allworthy the benefactor illustrate. Fielding's truly magnanimous, heroic characters, Mr. Wilson, Amelia, Dr. Harrison, practice both the cardinal virtues of prudence, justice, temperance, and fortitude and the theological virtues of faith, hope, and charity.[20] Thus to be, like Capt. Blifil or Blifil, coldly intellectual, calculating, falsely prudent without a good heart or pure intentions destroys the harmony of reason and will, the union of the head and heart. To be, like Tom, good-hearted or good-natured, without true prudence or right reason, also untunes the soul and violates the golden mean. In both cases, either when mathematical reckoning replaces right reason and calculation for one's self-interest is substituted for foresight on behalf of others--prudence devoid of charity--or when will or instinct dominates right reason to create a good-natured but imprudent benevolist, then discord follows, the confusion brought on by the "insults of Fortune" which are actually provoked either by Blifil's or Tom's type of folly--the proud assumption that Fortuna is a weak goddess that can be raped or the naive belief that Fortune is a kind mother who will do everything.

In many ways Tom's misfortunes, the discord in his life, stem from the intemperance in his soul, the various ways he deviates from the harmony of the golden mean. The Fortune who seldom does things by halves suddenly deals Tom several blows all at once, all of them precipitated by Tom's own folly. After hearing of Allworthy's recovery, Tom's "violent animal spirits" lead him to get drunk, to sleep with Molly, and to have a fight with Thwackum, all on the same night--the intemperances of gluttony, lust, and wrath in the scheme of the seven deadly sins. When Blifil eventually discloses these matters to Allworthy, it leads to the misfortune of Tom's banishment from Paradise Hall, his sudden fall from high to low. Tom, in his imprudence, even adds more to his bad luck. In his despair at the loss of Allworthy's favor and in his grief at parting from Sophia, Tom rushes to a brook where he grovels in sadness, tearing his hair and throwing away his possessions--including the £500 note he received from Allworthy. At this point Tom's life is total chaos. Penniless, he leaves Somersetshire in a condition of virtual nakedness. Exiled from Paradise like Milton's Adam, to whom Fielding compares Tom, "the world lay all before him," which Fielding explains as "the prospect was all a melancholy void" (p. 270, Bk. VII, ch. ii). Like Adam, Tom loses Paradise because he fails to exercise right reason and causes his own misery.

The histories of the man of the hill and Mrs. Fitzpatrick also illustrate how the misfortunes and confusion in their lives follow from their own folly. In his sudden fall from high to low, the man of the hill relates his descent from the life of a scholar to the profligacy of a debauchee. Corrupted by a young rake, Sir George Gresham, the man of the hill quits Oxford, loses his fortune, considers suicide, and finally goes to jail. All this disorder results from his own imprudence: in his mention of the "miscarriages" of his youth, the hermit refers to "the misfortunes which I brought on myself" (p. 385, Bk. VIII, ch. xi). Likewise, Mrs. Fitzpatrick causes all her own marital problems by her unfortunate choice of husband. Admitting that she married a fool, Mrs. Fitzpatrick confesses: "To rival my aunt delighted me; to rival so many other women charmed me. In short, I am afraid I did not behave as I should do . . ." (p. 504, Bk. XI, ch. iv). Thus, rather than viewing Fortune as a blind, irrational force or as cruel fate or as some form of cosmic determinism, Fielding sees a mysterious, hidden connection between luck and moral choice. He respects both the logic and mystique of Fortune:

> Notwithstanding the sentiment of the Roman satirist, which denies the divinity of Fortune, and the opinion of Seneca to the same purpose; Cicero, who was, I believe, a wiser man than either of them, expressly holds the contrary; and certain it is, there are some incidents in life so very strange and unaccountable, that it seems to require more than human skill and foresight in producing them. (p. 678, Bk. XIV, ch. viii)

The man of the hill's history depicts the two kinds of folly that provoke the insults of Fortune: the excesses and intemperance of Tom's type of folly and the false prudence of the "rape Fortune" psychology of a Blifil. After confessing the errors of his youth, the hermit realizes his wildness, his violation of the golden mean: "for I was high-mettled, had a violent flow of animal spirits, was a little ambitious, and extremely amorous" (p. 379, Bk. VIII, ch. vii). However, after he leaves prison, the man of the hill also learns that ill fortune occurs when man tries to rape Fortune in the game of dice. Watson, for example, who introduces him to gambling, one day accosts his friend and complains, "I find luck runs so damnably against me, that I will leave off play for ever" (p. 402, Bk. VIII, ch. xiv). Because of the "tide of ill luck" that has plagued him at the gambling table, Watson ponders suicide. Having pursued the life of a gambler for two years, the man of the hill knows the absurdity of trying to climb the wheel of Fortune and the impossibility of outmaneuvering fickle Fortune with "all the freaks which Fortune, or rather the dice, played in this her temple" (p. 392, Bk. VIII, ch. xii). In other words, these two causes of misfortune, imprudence and false prudence, indicate that Fortune is an <u>intelligible mystery</u>: neither so elusive or irrational as to be without any explanation nor so clear or predictable as to be without all wonder. The misfortunes in the histories of Tom, the man of the hill, and Mrs. Fitzpatrick all indicate a reason for bad luck, a correlation between imprudence and ill fortune. That is, Fortune is partly "intelligible" and not totally obscure or illogical in her workings. On the other hand, the ravishers of Fortune, Blifil, Watson, Mr. Fitzpatrick (who marries his wife "to rob a lady of her fortune by way of marriage"), discover that Fortune is partly "mysterious" and can never be figured out or predicted by man's cunning mind. As Sophia's sudden flight and Mrs. Fitzpatrick's surprising escape illustrate, the fickleness of woman resembles the mutability of Lady Luck. For example, just when Blifil enjoys the victory of Sophia's submission--at the very moment the proposed match appears decided--the unexpected accident of Sophia's "strange resolution" to run away foils Blifil's designs to seize her fortune. Just when Mr. Fitzpatrick congratulates himself upon overpowering his perverse wife and breaking her stubborn will by confining her to a room until she consents to sell her inherited estate--"by the greatest good fortune in the world, an accident happened" (p. 520, Bk. XI, ch. vii): Mrs. Fitzpatrick bribes the guard and escapes her husband's attempts to ravish more of her inheritance. As Fielding said, "nothing more aggravates ill success than the near approach to good":

> The gamester, who loses his party at piquet by a single point laments his bad luck ten times as much as he who never came within a prospect of the game. So in a lottery, the proprietors of the next numbers to that which wins the great prize are apt to account themselves much more unfortunate than their fellow sufferers. In short, these kind of hairbreadth missings of happiness look like the insults of Fortune, who may be considered as thus playing tricks with us, and wantonly diverting herself at our expense. (p. 602, Bk. XIII, ch. ii)

Fortune, like Sophia and Mrs. Fitzpatrick, refuses to be forced and asserts a mind and will of her own.

Although Fortune defies all man-made systems and transcends simplistic ideas--the attempts to control or dominate or reduce her--although she exercises the caprices of a woman who is privileged to change her mind, Fortune is not merely erratic. She shows an unmethodical logic of her own. She is neither formal (predictable) nor formless (illogical). Fortune's intelligible mystery reveals both its logic and mystique in the strange way it favors the good-natured man. More often than not, luck is a corollary of charity, a consequence of giving without expecting to receive, the result of a bold generosity that does

not count the cost or fear the dangers. The man
of the hill knows good fortune in the same way
that Allworthy and Tom experience the boon of
luck. Just as Allworthy adopts a foundling only
to find later an heir and a nephew, just as Tom
rescues a distressed lady only to realize afterwards that he has fallen in love with her, so too
the man of the hill helps a needy man only to discover his long-forgotten father. All three characters give without expecting to receive, yet they
all receive in <u>marvellous</u>, unforeseen ways. One
night, seeing a man beaten and robbed, the man of
the hill plays the role of the good Samaritan. In
the same way Allworthy invited calumny when he
welcomed a bastard into his home, in the same way
Tom broke his arm in his rescue of Sophia, the man
of the hill takes a chance and gives all. By
practicing charity toward another man, by obeying
the natural law of justice--"enjoined both by the
Christian law," to recall Allworthy's words, "and
by the law of nature herself"--the hermit was in
tune with the world and received the unexpected
blessing of luck, an experience of the wonderful.
That Fortune favors the just or generous characters who follow the law of Nature or practice
charity seems to be the logic behind her prefer-
ences. That Fortune does not always smile on
these characters is the mystique behind her actions. Fielding does not intend the intelligible
mystery of luck to reduce itself to any clear idea
like the "virtue rewarded" formula. Although
charity sometimes or often invites luck, it does
not guarantee it or work according to any contrac-
tual agreement. Indeed the man whom the man of
the hill saved from drowning, Watson, is the same
man who later betrays him to the enemy when they
both join the uprising in favor of the Duke of
Monmouth: "This Mr. Watson, this friend, this
base, barbarous, treacherous villain, betrayed me
to a party of horse belonging to King James, and
at his return delivered me into their hands" (p.
405, Bk. VIII, ch. xiv). Likewise, Tom's good-nature toward Black George, the selling of the pony
and the Bible to provide for the Seagrim family,
results in ingratitude, for Black George finds

Tom's £500 note and keeps it for himself. Hence Fielding objects to the moral doctrine that "virtue is the certain road to happiness": "namely, that it is not true" (p. 690, Bk. XV, ch. i).

To reconcile these two notions, first, the fact that the virtuous characters in Fielding's novels are rewarded or favored by Fortune and, second, the fact that Fielding abhorred the "virtue rewarded" platitude of Richardson and said that "in pursuing the good of others . . . I cannot so easily agree that this is the surest way to human happiness" (p. 690, Bk. XV, ch. i)--it is necessary to examine further Fielding's concept of harmony, the notion of two or many becoming one. The order of love (<u>ordo amoris</u>) has its own musical laws, and the paradox of the good-natured man's giving and receiving has an unsystematic logic of its own--an order as unmethodical as Nature's art of creation or Fortune's feminine mystique. To be sure, the riddle of charity as both disinterested and rewarded is not a simple "clear idea." It strikes the purely rational mind in the same way that Christianity appeared to the ancient Greeks or to the eighteenth-century deists, as nonsense. As Square explains in his letter: "The pride of philosophy had intoxicated my reason, and the sublimest of wisdom appeared to me, as it did to the Greeks of old, to be foolishness" (p. 831, Bk. XVIII, ch. iv). M. C. D'Arcy, quoting Etienne Gilson, comments on the riddle or paradox of Christian <u>agape</u> in <u>The Mind and Heart of Love</u>:

> Love seeks no recompense; did it do so it would at once cease to be love. But neither should it be asked to renounce joy in the possession of the thing loved; love would no longer be love if it renounced its accompanying joy. Thus all true love is at once disinterested and rewarded, or let us say rather that it could not be rewarded unless it were disinterested, because disinterestedness is its very essence.[21]

When Tom saves Mrs. Waters from death at the hands of Northerton, he seeks no recompense. When Tom helps Mrs. Miller's pregnant daughter, Nancy, by finally convincing Nightingale to marry her, he wants no reward. Tom especially reveals his disinterestedness or unselfishness toward Sophia when he resolves to leave her rather than ruin her. As he says in his farewell letter to Sophia before leaving for London: "Think I never loved you; or think truly how little I deserve you; and learn to scorn me for a presumption which can never be too severely punished" (p. 256, Bk. VI, ch. xii). When they are in London, Tom again offers to sacrifice his own happiness for Sophia's peace of mind. In a letter he writes, "and if there be no way left to reconcile your father, and restore the peace to your own mind, but by abandoning me, I conjure you, drive me for ever from your thoughts . . ." (p. 749, Bk. XVI, ch. iii). In all these magnanimous acts toward Mrs. Waters, Mrs. Miller, and Sophia, Tom freely gives from pure disinterested motives without expecting to receive.[22] Yet unselfish as Tom's charity is, it is rewarded. Although he gave without the intention of receiving, all three women reciprocate and provide Tom the miracles of Lady Luck that rescue him from tragedy at the end of the novel.

The order of love involves the harmony of mutual giving and receiving as symbolized by the spontaneous flow of Tom and Sophia's love, not the political arithmetic of giving-in-order-to-receive as represented by Blifil's "formal courtship" of Sophia or by Lady Bellaston's liaison with Tom. Love is an art that can begin or proceed by infinitely various and subtle ways, such as an old muff; love is not a methodology that follows a rigid procedure, such as Capt. Blifil and Bridget Allworthy's mechanical courtship: ". . . the captain made his advances in form, the citadel was defended in form, and at length, in proper form, surrendered at discretion" (pp. 33-34, Bk. I, ch. xi). Love's law transcends the fixed customs and established formalities of a society, such as "the proper match" alliance. Rather than a union of equals in fortune, rank, and heredity, Fielding's match between Tom and Sophia pairs a putative bastard and the daughter of a squire, a penniless vagabond and a wealthy lady. Love's law does not balance scales or reckon profits in the way that Black George and Mrs. Honour weigh consequences: Black George deciding to keep Tom's £500 note because it was "a matter of very little hazard" but choosing to return Sophia's sixteen guineas because of "the utmost danger of discovery" (p. 263, Bk. VI, ch. xiii); Mrs. Honour agreeing to escape with Sophia rather than betray her to Squire Western--"as she knew Sophia to have much more generosity than her master, so her fidelity promised her a greater reward than she could gain by treachery" (p. 291, Bk. VII, ch. viii). Thus the law or logic of love transcends all closed, rigid systems; it defies all the mathematical, economic, or formal techniques and methods which eliminate the wonderful, the sense of the Marvellous that Fielding associates with love. Tom and Sophia's love occurs naturally or spontaneously, without calculation or premeditation on either side. It could not be foreseen or predicted--as Mrs. Western's shock indicates. Rejecting the economic considerations of false prudence or worldly wisdom, Sophia prefers the poverty of Tom to the inheritance of Blifil. Overstepping the narrow views and conventional attitudes epitomized in Mrs. Western's "doctrine of Amour"--the observance of "manners, customs, ceremonies, and fashions" (p. 217, Bk. VI, ch. ii)--the true order of love obeys a higher law. To define further this boundless, transcendent quality of goodness or love, Fielding quotes Prior; true charity goes

> Beyond the fix'd and settled rules
> Of vice and virtue in the schools,
> Beyond the letter of the law. (p. 729, Bk. XV, ch. x)

In the same vein, like the art of love, Fielding's art of history, which sometimes stands still and sometimes flies, transcends systematic chronologies and formal histories. Fielding's idea of plot, based upon Nature's art of contrast and variety, goes beyond neo-classical unities and formalist rules. Fortune in Tom Jones, which never does anything by halves, defies all mathematical laws of predictability. The goodness of Allworthy and Tom with its quality of "numberless benefits" exceeds fixed boundaries and limits. The constant variations, the endless subtleties, and unceasing surprises that distinguish the art of Nature, woman, Fortune, history, and love from a system or method provide causes of wonder and create a sense of the Marvellous because of their inexhaustible possibilities.

Fielding especially provides this sense of prodigious variety at the end of the novel, for in the finale he summarizes and synthesizes the concept of Fortune, in all its fullness, into a harmony of the one and the many. All the individual aspects of Fortune presented earlier in the novel are integrated to form, not a clear idea of mathematics, but the true sublimity of wonder. First, like the opening scene of the novel in Allworthy's bedroom where chance and choice interact, again Fortune proposes and man disposes. When Tom takes lodgings at Mrs. Miller's boarding house, he involves himself with the problems of Nightingale, Nancy, and Mrs. Miller. The goodness he shows in trying to reconcile Nightingale's father to his son's marriage, in doing all in his power to effect the marriage of Nightingale and Nancy, in overcoming the plight of Nancy the unwed mother and Mrs. Miller the disgraced parent all reflect his true charity, his pure disinterested motives. Like Allworthy who risked the censure of the world when he adopted Tom, Tom too neglects his own self-interest: "while Mr. Jones was acting the most virtuous part imaginable in labouring to preserve his fellow creatures from destruction, the devil . . . one perhaps clothed in human flesh, was hard at work to make him completely miserable in the ruin of his Sophia" (p. 629, Bk. XV, ch. i). Like Allworthy, Tom responds to chance and acts as a providential agent in the lives of his friends--"a child sent by Fortune to my care" (p.

829, Bk. XVIII, ch. iii), as Mrs. Miller says. By following the motto of Terence that Fielding cites in Tom Jones (p. 721, Bk. XV, ch. viii), "Homo sum; humani nihil a me alienum puto" (I am a man; nothing human is foreign to me), Allworthy and Tom accidentally find themselves surprised by joy to discover their own miraculous good fortune. Like Allworthy's beneficence, Tom's goodness to his friends brings unforeseen returns: Mrs. Miller restores Tom's reputation in the eyes of Sophia and Allworthy, and Nightingale uncovers all of the circumstances that have implicated Tom in his duel with Fitzpatrick.

Second, since good fortune often conceals itself as bad luck, since good often grows out of evil in the way that the wheat mixes itself with the chaff--as seen in the episode where Tom both suffers the misfortune of breaking his arm and enjoys the blessing of falling in love with Sophia--this notion of Fortune as a bittersweet recurs again in the conclusion of the novel. In London Tom experiences the bitterness of poverty and persecution; he suffers the conspiracy of all his inveterate enemies en masse--Blifil, Lady Bellaston, Fitzpatrick. However, he also knows the sweetness of friendship and love, the consolation of all his well-wishers, Sophia, Allworthy, Mrs. Miller. Especially during his sojourn in prison Tom undergoes the ups and downs of Fortune. One moment he fears that he has fatally wounded Fitzpatrick and stands a good chance of being hanged; the next moment he hears the good news brought by Mrs. Waters that Fitzpatrick's condition is not serious and that Fitzpatrick has acknowledged his own guilt in provoking the duel. Just as quickly as Tom goes from low to high, he falls just as suddenly from high to low. For the following moment Tom learns from Partridge that Mrs. Waters is Jenny Jones and thus believes that he has committed incest by sleeping with his own mother at the inn at Upton. During this interlude in jail, the wheat and the chaff in Tom's history mix in another way: out of the evil in his life at London, which forces Tom to call himself "the most unfortunate man in the world" arises the good that raises Tom to be, in Sophia's words, "the most fortunate man in the world." Out of evil--his poverty, his liaison with Lady Bellaston, his persecution by Blifil, his quarrel with Fitzpatrick--which all culminates in Tom's imprisonment, the nadir in his life, arises the good--the discovery of Tom's real parents, Tom's inheritance of Allworthy's estate, the revelation of the whole truth concerning Blifil's villainy and Tom's virtue, and the marriage of Tom and Sophia. According to Fielding, ". . . the greatest events are produced by a nice train of little circumstances" (p. 822, Bk. XVIII, ch. ii). Just as the minor accident of Tom's broken arm and the trifling episode with the muff lead to the revelation of love, so too the small accident of Tom's rescue of Mrs. Waters from Northerton and Tom's casual meeting with Mr. Fitzpatrick as Jones leaves Mrs. Fitzpatrick's lodgings leads to the marvellous discovery of the whole truth behind Tom's history. A great event can arise from a trivial incident; good can grow out of evil; good fortune can exist side by side with bad luck. Such is the logic and mystique of Fortune.

Third, in the conclusion of the novel Fielding again emphasizes the correspondence between imprudence and misfortune. In the same way that Tom's folly, in the form of his drunkenness, lust, and wrath on the evening of Allworthy's recovery, led to his sudden fall from high to low, his imprudence in London also prompts the insults of Fortune. Tom's indiscretion of course is his liaison with Lady Bellaston. This entanglement leads to imbroglios that compare with the discord at the inn at Upton. On one occasion, when Mrs. Honour visits Tom at his lodgings at Mrs. Miller's house to promote the romance of Tom and Sophia, Lady Bellaston suddenly arrives to inquire about her secret lover's health. Forgetting that he is supposed to be playing the part of a sick man to corroborate his excuse for not visiting Lady Bellaston that evening, confused about what to do with Mrs. Honour or how to explain the visit of Lady Bellaston to Sophia's maid--"Jones was certainly at this instant in one of the most disagreeable and distressed situations imaginable" (p. 716, Bk. XV, ch. vii). Another complication that follows from Tom's affair with Lady Bellaston is his marriage proposal to her. Following Nightingale's advice that an offer of marriage is a foolproof way to break off his relationship with Lady Bellaston, Tom writes a letter and proposes marriage--the very letter that Lady Bellaston later gives to Mrs. Western to show Sophia as evidence of Tom's infidelity. Thus Tom's imprudence makes him his own enemy, a felon to himself, a "felo de se," as Fielding says. In Tom's own words, "But why do I blame Fortune? I am myself the cause of all my misery. All the dreadful mischiefs which have befallen me are the consequences only of my own folly and vice" (p. 821, Bk. XVIII, ch. ii).

Fourth, the finale in London reasserts the divinity or mystery of Fortune, a goddess or power with a mind and will of her own who resists man's attempts to manipulate her--in the same way Sophia refuses to be controlled by her father or aunt in her choice of a husband. For example, Squire Western, after finding his daughter in London, insists that Sophia marry Blifil while Mrs. Western demands that Sophia marry Lord Fellamar. Fellamar actually tries to rape Sophia, and Blifil continues to persist in his willfulness or "perseverance" as he euphemistically calls it when he comes to London still expecting to win Sophia's hand. Like Lady Luck, however, Sophia cannot be ruled by schemes like Lady Bellaston's design to have Tom's letter of proposal fall into Sophia's hands, by attacks like Fellamar's attempt to rape her, or by vehemence like Squire Western's confinement of Sophia to her room. Like Fortune, Sophia shows an absolute will of her own, rejecting Blifil with a "more peremptory and resolute refusal than she had ever done before" (p. 740, Bk. XVI, ch. ii).

Likewise, Lady Bellaston's strategems to ruin Jones by having him pressed into the navy, by alienating Tom and Sophia through the clever use

of the letter, and by disposing of Sophia through
a match with Lord Fellamar all result in those
"hair-breadth missings of happiness" that Fielding
calls "the insults of Fortune." Just before Tom
is pressed for the navy, he duels with Fitzpatrick
and finds himself in a prison instead of a ship.
Just when Fellamar is about to ravish Sophia,
Western breaks through the door. Similarly,
Blifil misses his happiness by a hair. Exulting
over Tom's predicament with the law, gloating over
Squire Western's capture of Sophia, Blifil begins
to taste his victory. To deliver the <u>coup de
grace</u>, he hires Dowling to give free legal assistance to Mrs. Waters (whom he assumes to be Mrs.
Fitzpatrick) to insure Tom's prosecution. However, Mrs. Waters is the person who undoes Blifil,
not Tom. She is the grateful woman Tom saved from
the clutches of Northerton, not the irate wife of
the wounded Mr. Fitzpatrick. Being the only other
person besides Dowling and Blifil who knows the
whole truth behind Tom's birth, she reveals all.
To repeat Fielding's words, "The gamester, who
loses his party at piquet by a single point, laments his bad luck ten times as much as he who
never came within a prospect of the game."

    Finally, the paradox of love or charity as
both disinterested and rewarded, the wonder of
giving without expecting to receive yet receiving
in marvellous and unforeseen ways unveils its intelligible mystery when Sophia consents to marry
Tom. Tom does not give in order to receive by doing one favor in return for another--in the manner
that Mrs. Western delivers Sophia from her father's tyranny only to subject Sophia to another
form of authoritarian rule: "'How! madame!' cries
the aunt; 'is this the <u>return</u> you make me for my
kindness in relieving you from your confinement at
your father's?'" (p. 793, Bk. XVII, ch. iv; italics mine). Tom does not count on, demand, or expect Sophia to respond to his love according to
any artificial rules of decorum in the way, for
example, that Squire Western expects his daughter
to agree with his wishes and follow the prescribed
formalities of an arranged match: "But I believe

you will allow me to be her father, and if I be, am I not to govern my own child?" (p. 789, Bk. XVII, ch. iii). Rather Tom <u>hopes</u> that Sophia will requite his love but respects her own wishes and allows her to respond in her own original way instead of according to "due form." As Sophia explains to Allworthy, "'Our inclinations are not in our own power; and whatever may be his merit, I cannot force them in his favour'" (p. 856, Bk. XVIII, ch. ix). Tom treats Sophia as a woman with a reason and will of her own, and he pursues her, to use Allworthy's distinction, by "gentle methods," not by "violent measures." He agrees to heed Allworthy's advice: "to abide entirely by the determination of the young lady, whether it shall be in your favour or no" (p. 865, Bk. XVIII, ch. x). Thus Tom neither pursues Sophia with the rapacity of a Lord Fellamar nor attempts to win her with the "perseverance" of a Blifil; his love is neither sheer willfulness nor cold calculation. Tom refuses to force Sophia or predict her response. Besides, Sophia, like Nature and Fortune, defies man's rational methods to figure her out and acts in astonishing ways. For Sophia resists not only the marriage offers of Blifil and Fellamar and the threats of her aunt and father but also the arguments of Allworthy and Mrs. Miller. Even after expostulating with Sophia and singing praises of Tom, Mrs. Miller sadly admits that Sophia remains adamant in her rejection of Tom: "'I wish I could give you joy on another account, my dear child; but anything so inexorable I never saw'" (p. 866, Bk. XVIII, ch. x). Although Sophia refuses to bend to either force or argument, she responds, however, in her own surprising, original way when she learns of Tom's disinterested love. When she accidentally discovers that the rich and beautiful widow, Mrs. Arabella Hunt, has proposed marriage to Tom, Sophia astonishes Mrs. Miller. As Mrs. Miller describes the scene:

> I heard of it this very morning, and I told it to Miss Western; nay, I went a little beyond the truth again; for I told her you had refused her; but indeed I

knew you would refuse her. And here I
must give you a little comfort; when I
mentioned the young lady's name, who is
no other than the pretty widow Hunt, I
thought she turned pale; but when I said
you had refused her, I will be sworn her
face was all over scarlet in an instant;
and these were her very words: "I will
not deny but that I believe he has some
affection for me." (pp. 866-867, Bk.
XVIII, ch. x)

Sophia is suddenly influenced more by this one
particular proof of Tom's love than all the other
evidence. Turning pale and turning red, she responds in her natural, spontaneous way, not according to the empty forms of custom and ceremony.
Using her own mind, not the opinions of the town
or the views of her aunt, Sophia discovers the
real truth: "I will not deny but that I believe
he has some affection for me." Exercising her own
free will in the choice of a husband, Sophia
yields to Tom--but not because of the influence or
authority of her elders. In short, Sophia <u>rewards</u>
Tom's love only when she feels convinced of its
<u>disinterested</u> quality, when she is assured by "the
strongest proof of its sincerity" (p. 876, Bk.
XVIII, ch. xii).

When Sophia realizes that Tom rejected a marriage proposal from the wealthy Mrs. Hunt because
of his devotion to her, she recognizes this disinterested quality, what Tom calls "the sincerity of
the purest passion that ever inflamed a human
heart" (p. 876, Bk. XVIII, ch. xii). At a crucial
time when Tom was destitute, at an opportune moment when "this lady's fortune would have been exceedingly convenient to him," during a state of
despair when he had nearly given up all thoughts
of Sophia, "since it was plain she could not be
his" (p. 733, Bk. XV, ch. xi)--Tom sacrifices his
own prosperity because of the purity of his love
for Sophia; he gives up a fortune without expecting to receive anything in its place. As Etienne
Gilson said, "Love seeks no recompense." Nor does

Tom give-in-order-to-receive. That is, Tom never intended that a report of his magnanimity should reach Sophia's ears or provide some spectacular testimony of his attachment. Tom, like Allworthy, follows the maxim of Pope cited by Fielding in his dedication to George Lyttleton: "Do good by stealth, and blush to find it fame." For Mrs. Hunt's letter expressed the wish that her marriage proposal remain a secret, and Tom promised to respect that wish: "Be assured that your secret was not more safe in your own breast than in that of your most obliged and humble servant, T. Jones" (p. 734, Bk. XV, ch. xi). Thus as Gilson's quotation on Christian love states, love "could not be rewarded unless it were disinterested, because disinterestedness is its very essence."

In a conclusion full of wonder and "surprising discoveries," Sophia's love for Tom, like the beauty of Sophia, like the majesty of Nature, like the mystery of Fortune, is another example of the Marvellous--a matter too great for the human mind or man's eyes to comprehend or exhaust. Sophia's love for Tom comes as a miracle of luck--explainable only in terms of the paradox or "folly" of Christian love as both disinterested and rewarded, not in terms of any simplistic idea like the "virtue rewarded" formula. As Tom himself acknowledges to Sophia, "'Alas! madame,' answered he, 'it is mercy, and not justice, which I must implore at your hands. Justice I know must condemn me'" (p. 875, Bk. XVIII, ch. xii). Like Tom's goodness in refusing Mrs. Hunt's offer, a magnanimity which went, to cite again Fielding's quotation of Prior, "beyond the fix'd and settled rules," Sophia's virtue, her mercy and forgiveness, transcend "Beyond the letter of the law." The order of love or charity, then, oversteps narrow rules and closed systems and moral platitudes. Like Fortune, love seldom does things by halves; rather its cup runs over. As Tom remarks of Allworthy's generosity, "'Oh, sir, you are too good to me'" (p. 81, Bk. III, ch. ii; italics mine). And as Fielding comments about Fortune: "But Fortune, who is a tender parent . . . often doth more for her favourite

offspring that neither they deserve or wish
. . ." (p. 32, Bk. I, ch. xi). Tom's luck, the
gift of Sophia from Fortune--the Alma Mater who
is too good to him--is more than he deserves.
Thus the goodness or generosity of men, like the
abundance of Nature or the blessings of Fortune,
is a matter of true astonishment for Fielding, another example of the wonder-full.

    Hence the art of Tom Jones, with its harmony
of the one and the many which the conclusion of
the novel reveals, imitates the copious variety of
Nature's art as epitomized at Allworthy's estate.
The surprises of Fortune, its sudden ups and
downs, compare with the unexpected turns of the
land and the water, the irregular undulations of
the countryside and the subtle meanderings of the
water. The whole range of vicissitudes and possibilities that Fortune provides in the story, which
prompts Tom to say "but while there is life there
are hopes" (p. 713, Bk. XV, ch. vii), relates to
the broad vistas or open prospects which Somersetshire affords. The cooperation of man's art and
Nature's provisions in Somersetshire (the interspersion of human artifacts--the abbeys and buildings--with Nature's creations--landscape and mountains) resembles the interaction between man and
Fortune, chance and choice, in the novel: man can
shape history as well as improve Nature. The various combinations of land and water or meadow and
woods which create the pied beauty of contrast are
analogous to Fortune's love of motley, her blend
of the Marvellous with the natural, her mixture of
good with evil, her distaste for "clear and distinct ideas." Just as Nature reveals herself as
both beautiful and useful, as decorative and purposive, so too Fortune shows herself to be both
playful and serious, as capricious yet wise. Just
as Nature is unmethodized but not without intention or telos, so too the plot of the novel, the
life of Tom Jones, is unsystematic, episodic, chaotic but not without form or purpose. The form or
purpose or intelligibility, however, of Nature's
plan, behind Fortune's actions, in Tom Jones' life
is modestly camouflaged or semi-hidden and thus

does not appear self-evident or transparent.
<u>Form</u>, like Sophia the woman or <u>sophia</u> as truth or wisdom, needs to be sought and pursued. Yet it is an open secret. Although Sophia's lips are closed and her love for Tom is part-concealed, her looks and blushes also make it part-revealed. Although Fortune appears mysterious and fickle, she also is intelligible and constant--as the histories of Tom, the man of the hill, and Mrs. Fitzpatrick all point to the same universal truths about luck. When <u>form</u> or truth is discovered, it does not provide any "final answer" to a problem that has been solved once and for all, but it creates a sense of wonder at the miracle of Being--Nature's glory, Sophia's beauty and goodness, Fortune's blessings, Allworthy's greatness--a wonder which is the "beginning" of philosophy (<u>Philo-Sophia</u>), the first step toward knowledge in the classical-Christian tradition which Fielding reasserted through his idea of the Marvellous in an age that saw the wane of wonder.

NOTES TO CHAPTER TWO

[1] A. O. Lovejoy, The Great Chain of Being (New York: Harper Torchbooks, 1960), p. 181.

[2] Lovejoy, p. 154.

[3] Lovejoy, p. 169.

[4] John Locke, An Essay Concerning Human Understanding, III, ch. 6, 12; as quoted by Lovejoy, p. 184.

[5] Dennis Quinn, "Donne and the Wane of Wonder," A Journal of English Literary History, XXXVI, No. 4 (Dec., 1969), 641.

[6] Works, ed. Henley, XIV, 284.

[7] Leo Spitzer, Classical and Christian Ideas of World Harmony (Baltimore: The Johns Hopkins Press, 1963), p. 79.

[8] William F. Lynch, Christ and Apollo (New York: Mentor-Omega, 1963), p. 143.

[9] John D. Bury, The Idea of Progress (New York: Macmillan, 1933), p. 79.

[10] Quinn, p. 642.

[11] Quoted by J. V. Cunningham, Woe or Wonder (Denver: Swallow Paperbacks, 1964), p. 78. The history of the idea of wonder, from ancient, medieval, and Renaissance sources, is thoroughly documented and traced in this book. For our purposes the following passages from Aristotle, Fielding's primary source for the idea of the Marvellous--as seen in the first chapter of Book VIII of Tom Jones--are especially pertinent:

> The marvellous is certainly required in tragedy. Epic, however, offers more opening for the improbable, the chief factor in the marvellous, be-

cause in it the agents are not visibly before us . . . . The marvellous, however, is a cause of pleasure, as is shown by the fact that we all tell a story with additions, in the belief we are doing our hearers a pleasure. (Poetics, 1460a 11-17)

For it is owing to their wonder that men both now begin and at first began to philosophize . . . . And a man who is puzzled and wonders thinks himself ignorant (whence even the lover of myth is in a sense a lover of Wisdom, for the myth is composed of wonders) . . . (Metaphysics, 1.2. 982b 11-19)

Again, since learning and wondering are pleasant, it follows that such things as acts of imitation must be pleasant--for instance, painting, sculpture, poetry--and every product of skilful imitation; this latter, even if the object imitated is not itself pleasant; for it is not the object itself which here gives delight; the spectator draws inferences ('That is a so-and-so') and thus learns something fresh. Dramatic turns of fortune and hairbreadth escapes are pleasant, because we feel all such things are wonderful. (Rhetoric, 1. 11. 1371b 4-12)

[12]Criticism: The Major Texts, ed. W. J. Bate (New York: Harcourt, Brace, & World, 1952), p. 210.

[13]Criticism: The Major Texts, p. 210.

[14]Jacques Maritain, in one of his own footnotes to Art and Scholasticism and the Frontiers

of Poetry (New York: Scribner, 1962), p. 28, explains the correlation between form and wonder or mystery:

> By "radiance of the form" must be understood an ontological splendor which is in one way or another revealed to our mind, not a conceptual clarity. We must avoid all misunderstanding here: the words clarity, intelligibility, light, which we use to characterize the role of "form" at the heart of things, do not necessarily designate something clear and intelligible for us, but rather something clear and luminous in itself, intelligible in itself, and which often remains obscure to our eyes, either because of the matter in which the form is buried, or because of the transcendence of the form itself in the things of the spirit. The more substantial and the more profound this secret sense is, the more hidden it is for us; so that, in truth, to say with the Schoolmen that the form is in things the proper principle of intelligibility, is to say at the same time that it is the proper principle of mystery. (There is in fact no mystery where there is nothing to know: mystery exists where there is more to be known than is given to our comprehension.)

[15] W. J. Bate, From Classic to Romantic (New York: Harper Torchbooks, 1961), p. 41.

[16] Works, XV, 87-90.

[17] Works, XV, 88.

[18] R. S. Crane, "The Concept of Plot and the

Plot of Tom Jones," in Critics and Criticism, abridged edition, ed. R. S. Crane (Chicago and London: Univ. of Chicago Press, 1957), p. 84.

[19] Leo Spitzer's Classical and Christian Ideas of World Harmony alludes to the following quotation from St. Paul to indicate how charity is a form of music in tune with the harmony of the world: "If I speak in the tongues of men and of angels, but have not love, I am a noisy gong or a clanging symbol" (I Cor. 13:1). Spitzer thus comments: "Only through charity can man reach true music" (p. 19).

[20] Fielding shows considerable interest in the cardinal virtues. For example, he writes in Covent Garden Journal (No. 24), an essay that argues in behalf of the natural virtues during a time when they were defamed:

> It may perhaps be objected to what I have hitherto advanced that I have only mentioned the cardinal virtues, which (possibly from the Popish epithet assigned to them) are at present held in so little repute, that no man is conceived to be better for possessing them, or the worse for wanting them. (Works, XIV, 152)

Fielding devotes one of the articles in The Champion (Apr. 5, 1740) to a discussion of the theological virtues. Commenting upon St. Paul's famous letter on faith, hope, and charity (I Cor. 13), Fielding devotes this essay to a study of the qualifications of clergymen.

> Ninthly, "charity believeth all things, hopeth all things." It is inclined to maintain good and kind thoughts of men. It is a stranger to all sourness and bitterness of mind, that moroseness of temper which seduces us to think evil of others; whereas, charity always

turns the perspective, with a friendly care to magnify all good actions, and lessen evil. (Works, XV, 272)

[21]M. C. D'Arcy, The Mind and Heart of Love (Cleveland and New York: Meridian Books, 1964), p. 113.

[22]Fielding's concept of good-nature relates to the Greco-Roman idea of natural law and to Christian agape; it is not a version of Shaftesbury's benevolism. As Fielding explains the term good-nature in one of the papers of The Champion, he compares it to the Greek notion of φιλανθρωπία and to the Roman ideals of comitas, benignitas, benevolentia, and humanitas: "Indeed, the ancients seem to have looked on what we call good-nature as a quality almost inseparable from nature, as appears in the motto of this paper ("Natura propensi sumus ad diligendos homines") and several other passages of the same and other authors, particularly in that famous Stoic rant (as a modern writer calls it) wherein ill-nature is represented magis contra naturam quam mors quam paupertas quam cetera omnia &c. And whoever reads the works of Plato will be very little inclined to imagine that the ancients either wanted the idea of good nature, or words to express it." (Thurs., Mar. 27, 1740; Works, XV, 256)

Fielding relates his idea of good-nature to Christian agape in his distinction between "good-humour" and "good-nature"; good-nature has nothing in common with the smiling countenance of good-humor. As Fielding explains in "An Essay on the Knowledge of the Characters of Men":

> But how alien must this countenance be to that heavenly frame of soul, of which Jesus Christ Himself was the most perfect pattern; of which blessed person it is recorded, that He never was once seen to laugh, during His whole abode on earth.

And what indeed hath good-nature to do with a smiling countenance? (<u>Works</u>, XIV, 286)

CHAPTER III

THE HEROIC AND THE MARVELLOUS: VIRTUE OR MAGNANIMITY AS A SOURCE OF WONDER IN AMELIA

> "I do not remember a more noble sentiment preserved to us in the records of all antiquity, than what is contained in a short sentence of Plato, which I have often seen quoted. 'That could mankind behold virtue naked, they would all be in love with her.'"
> --Fielding The Champion (Thurs., Jan. 24, 1739-40)

It has been mentioned in the first two chapters that Fielding associates the great with the small, the marvellous with the natural: wisdom with folly (Parson Adams), divine miracles with commonplace incidents (Wilson's discovery of his son through a casual meeting with Adams), epic events with minor episodes (the revelation of Tom and Sophia's love through a simple muff), Christianity with folly, and strength with weakness. Likewise, Fielding's conception of the truly great man, the magnanimous hero, views greatness in the form of lowliness or humility--Christian meekness as opposed to pagan vainglory. Fielding cites an example from history of greatness in the form of lowliness, the life of Oliver Cromwell. Fielding observes in The Champion (Dec. 6, 1739): "Fortune often picks a great man, in jest, out of the lowest of people." In his youth Cromwell showed no signs of his potential greatness:

> He is reported, in his youth, to have
> ruined his paternal estate by his vicious
> and disorderly courses; nor did he, at
> his first appearance in parliament, make
> any extraordinary figure, nor discover
> any of those talents, which generally
> gain applause, and work on the affections
> of the hearers.[1]

The greatest among men will be the least. According to the Bible, "He who is greatest among you shall be your servant; whoever exalts himself will be humbled, and whoever humbles himself will be exalted" (Matthew 23:11, Revised Standard Version). It is this paradox of Christianity that informs Fielding's idea of greatness. As he explains in his essay on clergymen in the Champion (Sat., Mar. 29, 1740), the first duty of a Christian disciple is to imitate the humility of Christ:

> The first I shall name is humility; a
> virtue of which He himself was so perfect
> a pattern, and which he so earnestly rec-
> ommended to His disciples, that He re-
> buked them when they contended who should
> be reckoned the greatest; and in another
> place exhorted them 'to beware of the
> scribes which desire to walk in long
> robes, and love greetings in the markets,
> and the highest seats in the synagogues
> . . .', &c.
>   Luke xx. 46,47.

Fielding goes on to cite the authority of St. Paul[2], who warns against vainglory and boastfulness, greatness in the form of worldly possessions, St. Paul "forbidding any to think high of himself, for which he gives them this reason, that very few wise, or mighty, or noble, in a worldly sense, were called to the ministry, but such as were reputed to be the filth of the world and the offscouring of all things." Finally, in the same essay, Fielding views Christ's whole life as an example of humility, a great man associating Himself with small things and lowly people, a divine person hiding Himself in the commonplace:

> Our blessed Saviour Himself, instead of introducing Himself into the world in the houses or families of what we call the great, chose to be born of the wife of a carpenter, His disciples were poor fishermen, and Paul himself no more than a tent-maker; He everywhere practised and taught contempt of worldly grandeur and honours, often inculcating in His excellent discourses that His kingdom was not of this world . . . .³

In contrast to this ideal of Christian humility as a characteristic of true greatness, which does good by stealth, Fielding comments on the vainglory of ancient heroes like Alexander the Great and Julius Caesar, who do evil for fame. False greatness, according to Fielding in <u>Jonathan Wild</u>, "consists in bringing all manner of mischief on mankind" (p. 22, Bk. I, ch. i): Alexander destroyed countless innocent lives in his expeditions to conquer the world and win glory; Caesar corrupted the Roman populace with bribery in his ambition to rule the empire and possess the title of emperor. Whereas Christianity relates greatness to goodness and humility, as exemplified in a character like Allworthy--"what, do you know that <u>great and good</u> Mr. Allworthy then," Tom Jones exclaims at one point in the novel (p. 341, Bk. VII, ch. ii; italics mine)--the ancient pagan conception and the vulgar eighteenth century view separate greatness and goodness and relate greatness to fame or notoriety. Fielding, parodying the rogue's biography, the life of Jonathan Wild as the celebrated hero of an age that lionized criminals executed at Tyburn, comments on this divorce of heroism from virtue: ". . . as we are to record the actions of a GREAT MAN, so we have nowhere mentioned any spark of goodness . . . but as a meanness and imperfection" (p. 23, Bk. I, ch. i). In a more serious tone, however, Fielding in <u>Inquiry into the Causes of the Late Increase of</u>

Robbers laments the apotheosis of the rogue on the day of his hanging:

> The day appointed by law for the thief's shame is the day of glory in his own opinion. His procession to Tyburn, and his last moments there, all are triumphant; attended with applause, admiration, and envy, of all the bold and hardened.[4]

In short, this perversion of heroism, this separation of goodness from greatness leads to the equation of evil with good, of ugliness with beauty, of the worst with the best, of the Monstrous with the Marvellous. According to Fielding's "A Modern Glossary" in Covent-Garden Journal No. 4, a dictionary of eighteenth century cant terms, "great," when applied to a man, signified "littleness or meanness." On the other hand, "modesty" or humility means "awkwardness, rusticity."[5] Instead of, in the tradition of classical biography and Christian saint's lives where the poet as custodian of fame moves men, to use Fielding's phrases, to love and admire the "true beauty of virtue" and to hate or loathe the "deformity of vice," the corrupt eighteenth century idea of greatness, as seen in the lives of rogues and whores[6], blames virtue and praises vice. In Jonathan Wild Fielding's discussion of the shift in meaning of the idea of honor emphasizes this reversal of values:

> Do not some by honour mean good nature and humanity, which weak minds call virtues? How then! Must we deny it to the great, the brave, the noble, to the sackers of towns, the plunderers of provinces, and the conquerors of kingdoms! Were not these men of honour? (p. 61, Bk. I, ch. xiii)

Instead of greatness humbling itself to become the servant of man in imitation of Christ, meanness exalts itself by arrogating power and exploiting mankind in imitation of Alexander, Caesar, or Jonathan Wild.

Using Christ's humility and service as the model of true greatness, Fielding summarizes this ideal of Christian magnanimity in the line he quotes from Pope's Epistle to the Satires in the dedication to Tom Jones: "Do good by stealth, and blush to find it fame." He honors George Lyttleton, his patron, for both his "truly benevolent mind" and his "dislike of public praise." This ideal permeates Fielding's work in general. For example, Fielding's "Essay on Conversation" contrasts the vain Cenodoxus and the modest Sophronius. Sophronius, as his name implies, is a learned man; however, he conceals his erudition: "nor had ever any one, who was not himself a man of learning, the least reason to conceive the vast knowledge of Sophronius, unless from the report of others." In Covent-Garden Journal No. 58 Fielding criticizes a woman's violation of good-breeding because of her lack of modesty:

> so far from running away from, she runs after, the men; and instead of blushing when a modest man looks at her, or speaks to her, she can bear, without any such emotion, to stare an impudent fellow in the face . . . .

Thus a generous patron, a wise man, and a beautiful woman all reflect this quality of humility--an essential ingredient of Christian magnanimity. The following quotation provides one of Fielding's most complete statements on how humility constitutes a sine qua non of true greatness and also shows how true greatness comprises an aspect of the sublime, the wonderful or the marvellous, in the way it reflects a transcendent beauty, goodness, or power:

> Nothing can, in fact, be more foreign to the nature of virtue than ostentation. It is truly said of Virtue, that could men behold her naked, they would be all in love with her. Here it is implied,

> that this is a sight very rare or difficult to come at; and, indeed, there is always a modest backwardness in true virtue to expose her naked beauty.[7]

Indeed this "modest backwardness in true virtue to expose her naked beauty" characterizes all of Fielding's truly great heroes and heroines. They all "Do good by stealth, and blush to find it fame." For example, when Allworthy banishes Tom from Somersetshire, he also quietly provides his adopted son with a sum of money, a little "something which may enable you, with industry, to get an honest livelihood" (p. 254, Bk. VI, ch. xi). Wilson also does good by stealth when he conceals a purse of money in the package of food he gives Adams and company for the remainder of their journey. Likewise, Amelia too performs a noble act in an unobtrusive way when she, without consulting her husband, decides to pawn her picture and feed her hungry children. Thus true greatness does good works, performs humble acts, serves others, in short, imitates Christ--the ideal of Christian magnanimity epitomized in Fielding's description of Allworthy: "a human being replete with benevolence, meditating in what manner he might render himself most acceptable to his Creator, by doing most good to his creatures" (p. 10, Bk. I, ch. iv).

On the other hand, the false greatness symbolized by Jonathan Wild does evil rather than good, serves self rather than others, seeks fame or notoriety rather than anonymity, and exemplifies the Monstrous or false sublime rather than the Marvellous or true sublime. For example, Fielding depicts Alexander in "A Dialogue between Alexander the Great and Diogenes the Cynic" as the embodiment of all these traits of vulgarized greatness. Instead of exemplifying good works or public service, Alexander's famous deeds lack all virtue. As Diogenes says, instead of helping his fellow man, the Macedonian has been guilty of "ravaging countries, burning cities, plundering and massacring mankind." Instead of seeking anonymity or practicing humility, Alexander thirsts after "honour, glory, and fame" in the sense of notoriety rather than praise--the ignorant applause of the mobs who flatter Alexander's pride rather than the judicious praises of true judges like Diogenes who speak the truth. Diogenes calls Alexander's notion of glory "the applause of . . . slaves and sycophants," "superiority on the backs of a multitude of armed slaves," "the suffrages of such wretches." Or, as Fielding comments on Jonathan Wild's type of "honor": an encomium bestowed upon him, not because of the merit of service or virtue, "but because men, I mean those of his own party or gang, call him a man of honour . . ." (p. 61, Bk. I, ch. xiii). Instead of letting honor or glory accrue as an incidental, unintended effect of "doing good by stealth," as the shade of virtue, pseudo-greatness pursues this love of fame with a monomania and worships glory as the be-all and end-all. As Alexander testifies:

> . . . . What other reward than this [fame] have all those heroes proposed to themselves, who rejected the enjoyments which ease, riches, pleasure, and power, have held forth to them in their native country, have deserted their homes, and all those things which to vulgar mortals appear lovely or desirable . . . .

Thus Alexander destroys rather than creates; he seeks self-glory rather than the happiness of others; and he depends on the ignorant opinions of hoi polloi rather than the intelligent judgments of wise men. For all these reasons Diogenes abhors Alexander and detests his greatness: "for now I despise and curse thee more than I do all the world besides." Evoking loathing, Alexander's greatness is a species of the Monstrous. Indeed Diogenes compares it to the ugliness and evil of death and disease: they too deserve the title of "great" since they can boast with Alexander that they have slaughtered millions. Thus, calling the conqueror's great soul "contemptible" and exposing his folly and vice as ugly or monstrous, Diogenes appears in the dialogue as a true critic and wise judge, a custodian of fame who only praises virtue and always blames vice. He epitomizes the classical view of comedy as justice that Fielding summarized in his "Author's Perface" to Joseph Andrews: folly deserves ridicule or laughter and vice detestation or hatred. Diogenes the Cynic, snarling and biting, blaming and ridiculing, hopes to attract men to the beauty of virtue and to repel men from the ugliness of evil: "My snarling is the effect of my love, in order, by my invectives against vice, to frighten men from it, and drive them into the road of virtue."[8]

The roles of the rogue and the thief-catcher in eighteenth century England also illustrate the difference between true and false greatness. In the Inquiry Fielding describes the thief-catcher's traditional role as a noble, heroic calling. Comparing him to the famous men of antiquity--Pompey, Hercules, and Theseus--Fielding comments: "Were they not the most eminent of thief-catchers?" However, the apprehender of criminals in Fielding's London is loathed rather than admired; he is regarded, not as "the first and highest officer in the state," but as a kind of devil: "and the thief-catcher is in danger of worse treatment from the populace than the thief." Whereas the informer, the constable, and the hangman, the agents of justice, are detested, the representatives of evil, the thief and the felon, are honored. Fielding refers to this condition in England when he writes in the Vernoniad, a parody of greatness in the vein of Jonathan Wild: "Virtue looks black, and vice resembles snow." Especially on the day of his execution the rogue is hailed as a celebrity and surrounded with glory, "spoken of by many with honour, by most with pity, and by all with approbation."[9] Nevertheless, the thief-catcher, though unpopular, is still the magnanimous man, just as Diogenes, though relatively unknown in comparison to Alexander, is the real hero in "A Dialogue between Alexander the Great and Diogenes the Cynic." As Fielding says in the Champion (Tues., Mar. 4, 1739-40), "True virtue is of a retired, quiet nature, content with herself, not at all busied in courting the acclamations of the crowd."[10]

In short, Christ's humility and charity, the ideal of doing good by stealth, the personification of virtue as a beautiful, modest woman, the love of justice epitomized in Diogenes and the thief-catcher--all these aspects of true greatness not only contrast Christian magnanimity with pseudo greatness but also relate it to the multi-faceted splendor of the sublime or Marvellous: the harmony of the true, the good, and the beautiful found in a heroine like Sophia, for she reflects a variety of virtues, a mosaic of many parts. She discerns the <u>truth</u> about Tom and Blifil and is not deceived like Allworthy. She reflects physical <u>beauty</u> and moral <u>goodness</u>. She shows a heroic greatness of soul in her forgiveness of Tom's infidelity. Hence when Fielding introduces his heroine in <u>Tom Jones</u>, he entitles the chapter, "A Short Hint of What We Can Do in the Sublime . . . " (p. 109, Bk. IV, ch. ii). As a heroine Sophia is an example of the wonderful, the true sublime, the magnanimous--"the great and good" that Fielding discusses in his "Preface to the Miscellanies and Poems." In the following passage that describes the ideal of "the great and good," Fielding explicitly relates the heroic to the Marvellous:

> The last of these is the true sublime in human nature. That elevation by which the soul of man, raising and extending itself above the order of this creation, and brightened with a certain ray of divinity, looks on the condition of mortals. This is indeed a glorious object, on which we can never gaze with too much praise or admiration. A perfect work! The Iliad of Nature! ravishing and astonishing, and which at once fills us with love, wonder, and delight.[11]

Just as Christ exhorted man to combine disparate

virtues, such as the wisdom of the serpent and the gentleness of the dove--a text that Fielding cites in the *Inquiry* to show the need for the caution of prudence along with the impetuosity of good-nature --so too Fielding's heroic characters unite different virtues. For example, Allworthy integrates the classical cardinal virtues and the Christian theological virtues or mixes justice and mercy. Wilson blends the active and the contemplative life. Amelia is as prudent as the serpent and as gentle as the dove. Like Sophia she is wise, beautiful, and good. As "the Iliad of Nature," the "great and good" hero reflects the idea of the one and the many, the copious variety, of the epic --what Fielding in *Amelia* calls "the Art of Life" (p. 4, Bk. I, ch. i). Just as Parson Adams in *Joseph Andrews*, rapt with wonder at the inexhaustible beauties of the *Iliad*, cannot praise Homer's epic enough, exclaiming "This is sublime! This is poetry!" (p. 231, Bk. III, ch. ii)--so too the innumerable virtues and the extraordinary excellence of the hero evoke the kind of admiration that belongs to the true sublime. Whereas the sublimity or brilliance of true greatness shows many colors and reflects different facets, such as wisdom, beauty, and goodness, false greatness lacks this variety or harmony of the one and the many. Rather false greatness excludes all goodness in order to preserve a pure univocal idea of greatness; it does not mix opposites or complements like greatness and humility or prudence and charity. As Fielding ironically states it in *Jonathan Wild*, any attribution of goodness to "great" men like Alexander, Caesar, or Jonathan Wild would taint their unblemished reputations and violate "the great perfection called uniformity of character" (p. 22, Bk. I, ch. i). Commenting on their "uniformity," Fielding sees in these famous men a one-sidedness, a monomania that fixes on one predominant passion, a lust for glory. In their mad pursuit of fame at any cost, they sacrifice the many sources of happiness, the variety of life's pleasures, for the sake of a ruling passion. In "A Dialogue between Alexander the Great and Diogenes the Cynic," Alexander admits that he has rejected the enjoyments of "ease, riches, pleasure, and power" in order to pursue glory. Likewise, the great Tom Thumb, obsessed with fame, stops at nothing to achieve distinction; he vows to tear away the book of fate if it obstructs his will: "We fall contented, if we fall renowned."[12] Fielding's well-known distinction between wisdom and folly points to the difference between true and false greatness: "The wise man gratifies every appetite and every passion, while the fool sacrifices all the rest to pall and satiate one" (Tom Jones, p. 226, Bk. VI, ch. iii).

Thus true greatness not only consists of a mosaic of many virtues as seen in a Sophia but also in a love of the variety of life's blessings as reflected in Mr. Wilson or Allworthy. Allworthy, for example, along with his love of wisdom and justice, also enjoys the blessing of riches, his magnificent estate, and at one time delighted in the pleasure of marriage, having been united to a "very worthy and beautiful woman" (p. 4, Bk. I, ch. ii). The wholeness of "the great and good" not only opposes the narrowmindedness of "the great" but also distinguishes them from "the good." Fielding explains the difference between "the great and good" and "the good" in the "Preface to the Poems and Miscellanies" as a matter of completeness. The good need other virtues besides "benevolence, honour, honesty, and charity"; they lack the "parts" or complementary virtues such as courage that characterize the great and good. The good do not arouse the wonder or admiration which the great and good elicit: "Our wonder ceases; our delight is lessened, but our love remains."[13] That is, the more elements or characteristics which are harmonized, the greater the diversity that becomes unity either in a woman like Sophia or in landscape like Somersetshire--the greater the sublimity or wonder. As Fielding remarked in Tom Jones (p. 161, Bk. VI, ch. i), contrast or variety is a universal quality that "runs through all the works of the creation" to provide the idea of beauty, a species of the wonderful. "The good," then, hardly astonish because they lack the "parts," the many-colored, multi-faceted virtues of "the great and good."

Throughout his work Fielding portrays the merely good-natured characters ("the good") as incomplete. Heartfree, Parson Adams, Tom Jones, and Booth all require the cardinal virtue of prudence or right reason. One of Fielding's plays, The Fathers or The Good-Natured Man satirizes the folly of the good-hearted man who lacks sound judgment. As Sir George Boncourt says to his brother, "the good" Mr. Boncourt:

> You have acted very wrong in doing good to a parcel of rogues and rascals, who with the tenth part of your understanding have called you fool for serving them; have privately laughed at you in your prosperity, and will publicly despise you in your adversity--a good-natured man! Oh! 'tis a precious character.[14]

Likewise, in the Inquiry Fielding warns against the danger of mercy without justice, a form of goodness that falls into sentimentality:

> and since our king . . . is of all men the truest image of his Maker in mercy, I hope too much good-nature will transport no noblemen so far as it did once a clergyman in Scotland, who in the fervour of his benevolence prayed to God that he would graciously be pleased to pardon the poor devil.[15]

As Fielding's poem "Of True Greatness" indicates, a magnanimous man like George Dodington combines many heroic traits like wisdom, justice, and courage. The great and good, like Argyle, unite the virtues of the statesman and the soldier: "Supreme in all the arts of peace and war." The great and good hero fuses dissimilar virtues like the ability to be both warlike and civil: "Fierce to his foes, and faithful to his friends." Unlike the benevolist whose pure goodness divorces justice from mercy to pardon the devil, a truly great man like Lee blends severity with gentleness: "Greatness with learning deck'd in Cartaret see,/ With Justice, and with clemency in Lee." Fielding's tribute to Dodington, then, summarizes the ideal of "the great and good," the marvellous hero of many virtues who arouses "love, wonder, and delight," the effects of the true sublime:

> Lives there a man, by nature form'd to please,
> To think with dignity, express with ease;
> Upright in principle, in council strong,
> Prone not to change, nor obstinate too long:
> Whose soul is with such <u>various talents</u> bless'd . . .16
> (italics mine)

Likewise Fielding honors the Duke of Richmond in "Of Good-Nature" as a man of parts. As a good-natured man, however, Richmond is not another Boncourt whose good heart outweighs his common sense. Richmond's good-nature is not "a foolish weakness in the breast" but a part of "the mighty whole": "Full composition of a virtuous soul."17

 Although the topos of goodness and greatness recurs throughout Fielding's work, <u>Amelia</u> especially distinguishes vulgarized greatness from Christian magnanimity. The novel shows how folly, corruption, and depravity are often honored with the title of "great" or encouraged by the prize of the reward; <u>Amelia</u> also portrays how merit, service, and virtue are not given their due in the form of praise, admiration, or recompense. For example, Fielding criticizes the eighteenth century custom of duelling, a gentleman or soldier's idea of honor, as a barbarous practice inconsistent with Christian magnanimity. In the chapter ironically entitled "Containing much heroic matter" (p. 229, Bk. V, ch. v), Fielding describes the absurd duel between Booth and Colonel Bath. Supposedly Bath is defending the "honor" of his brother-in-law, Colonel James, whom Booth has offended by his affair with Miss Matthews--the promiscuous woman whom James, a married man, wants to enjoy as his mistress. Miss Matthews also feels outraged at Booth's affront to her honor because, after their brief liaison in prison, Booth repents, ignores his temptress, and devotes himself to his wife Amelia--a preference that Miss Matthews interprets as an insult to her womanhood. Thus an adulterer like James and a wanton like Miss Matthews promote the duel between Booth and Bath because their "honor" has been violated. Bath's own reasoning on this matter is equally ridiculous. He offers the following <u>non sequitur</u> to Booth as a rationale for the duel, <u>as if his only</u> options were either to fight his brother-in-law or clash with Booth or stand to lose his "honor": "I must either have given him the lie, and fought with him, or else I was obliged to behave as I did, and fight with you" (p. 236, Bk. V, ch. vi). Thus when Booth speaks of Colonel Bath as a hero "of great honour and good-nature," Amelia contradicts her husband: "'Tell me not,' replied she, 'of such good-nature and honour as would sacrifice a friend and a whole family to a ridiculous whim'" (p. 234, Bk. V, ch. vi). Thus honor, when it is perverted in meaning, often means no more than revenge--the very antithesis of the heroic spirit: ". . . the greatest heroes are the backwardest to revenge . . . ," Fielding observes in the <u>Champion</u> (Tues., Jan. 1, 1739-40).[18] Later in the novel, when Dr. Harrison and Amelia discuss the issue of honor, Harrison argues that the duel has no basis in nature, religion, or custom: "It is not the opinion of the world; it is the opinion of the idle, ignorant, and profligate." As a clergyman defending the ideal of Christian magnanimity, Harrison asserts that the acceptance of a duel is not a matter of obligation or duty but a violation of conscience and the commandments of God:

> Honour! nonsense! Can honour dictate to him to disobey the express commands of his Maker, in compliance with a custom established by a set of blockheads, founded on false principles of virtue,

> in direct opposition to the plain and
> positive precepts of religion . . . ?
> (p. 278, Bk. XII, ch. iii)

As a proof of male chivalry, Dr. Harrison explains, the duel has been glorified, not by admirable, heroic women like Homer's Andromache, who grieved when Hector entered battle, but by vain, selfish women who demand foolish exhibitions of bravado as tokens of flattery. Such women he compares to the Furies. In short, both a woman's false sense of honor, as seen in Miss Matthews' instigation of a duel, and a soldier's mistaken concept of manhood, as reflected in Bath's eagerness to offer a challenge, are responsible for the prevalence of duelling, a menace to society. So widespread is this practice in the eighteenth century that Fielding's "A Modern Glossary" defines <u>honour</u> simply as "duelling."

    <u>Amelia</u> not only shows how the true meaning of honor has been distorted to signify revenge and duelling but also reveals how real greatness has come to be associated only with a certain social class, the rank of lords, nobles, and aristocrats. Lloyd W. Brown's article, "The Person of Quality in the Eighteenth Century," discusses this kind of pseudo honor as "a quality of birth to the exclusion of moral or intellectual excellence . . . where the forms of ideal morals and polite manners are aped without regard for the very values on which they are traditionally based."[19] In other words, honor to the person of quality is a matter of manners rather than morals, a question of style or social status rather than noble deeds. Hence Fielding ironically defines <u>worth</u> in "A Modern Glossary" as "power, rank, wealth," not as virtue, service, or humility. In the opening scene of the novel Fielding treats this prejudice of his age through his portraits of the constable and the magistrate. Both characters judge worth by estimating wealth; they determine guilt or innocence according to the poverty or wealth respectively of the defendant. The constable apprehends the thieves who attacked the man Booth was trying to

rescue. However, the rogues are soon discharged as they were "men of fortune" who bribed the constable for their freedom--a prerogative that Booth, "having no money in his pocket, was unable to obtain." Likewise, the magistrate, noticing Booth's shabby clothes, prejudges him as guilty: "In short, the magistrate had too great an honour for truth to suspect she ever appeared in sordid apparel" (p. 10, Bk. I, ch. ii). Thus the law officers, equating nobility with riches rather than with virtue, cannot relate magnanimity to poverty and hence fail to grasp the paradox of Christian heroism--greatness in the form of lowliness. In another minor episode Fielding offers a similar kind of social criticism. Just as Booth, in the incident previously mentioned, played the part of the good Samaritan and the lover of justice only to be scorned as a poor, contemptible wretch, so too Sergeant Atkinson, reflecting Christian magnanimity through his friendship and generosity to Booth in prison, is despised as a low creature. When Booth praises the goodness and greatness of Atkinson, Miss Matthews appears shocked to hear the word honor associated with a man of humble origins: "Good heavens!" cries Miss Matthews, "how astonishing is such behaviour in so low a fellow!" Her comments prompt Booth to assert the values of Christian magnanimity: he tells her that "greatness of mind" is not limited to "one degree or rank of life"; heroic virtues may reside "in a beggar as well as in a prince"; honor dwells in "lower" as well as "upper life." He concludes, " . . . so I apprehend that examples of whatever is really great and good have been sometimes found amongst those who have wanted all such advantages" (p. 125, Bk. III, ch. vii). Hence by portraying the poor Booth and the low Atkinson as unacknowledged heroes who show a love of their fellow man, who give without expecting to receive in the form of a reward or fame, Fielding affirms the classical-Christian ideal that "virtue is the true nobility," not wealth or rank.

The best example of a person of quality in <u>Amelia</u> is the lord who debauched Mrs. Bennet and who tries to seduce Amelia. As another example of pseudo honor the lord is a parody of greatness, a mockery of what Fielding calls the true sublime in human nature, the man of parts he honors in "Of True Greatness." The lord seems to reflect the many virtues and varied talents of "the great and good." To Mrs. Bennet he appeared full of wonderful traits like generosity, civility, and kindness. "I thought he discovered good sense, good nature, condescension, and other good qualities . . . ," she confesses to Amelia. The lord's apparent infinite goodness and boundless generosity astonished both Mr. and Mrs. Bennet, for the lord not only promised Mr. Bennet, a poor clergyman, a living but also offered to pay Mr. Bennet's debt at Oxford. Moreover, the lord brings presents to their child and seems to love the boy as his own son. Moved by the ostensible sublimity of such unparalleled magnanimity, Mr. Bennet is rapt in wonder: "Your lordship overcomes me with generosity. If you go in this manner, both my wife's gratitude and mine must be bankrupt" (p. 34, Bk. VII, ch. vi). However, as the rest of Mrs. Bennet's history illustrates, the lord is an example of the Monstrous rather than the Marvellous. His ostensible goodness has been a subtle stratagem to carry out his premeditated design to ravish her. Thus, just as a soldier like Colonel Bath distorts the idea of honor to make it comparible with revenge, so too a gentleman like the lord perverts the meaning of honor to make it consistent with adultery and cunning. Honor, thus, stands, not for virtue or service, but success--what Fielding in "The Characters of Men" calls "the Art of thriving." The lord succeeds or thrives in this sense, for he eventually seduces Mrs. Bennet at a masquerade, inebriates her after the party, and commits adultery with her. As Fielding defines the rogue's version of honor in <u>Jonathan Wild</u>: "Think not anything a man commits can forfeit his honour. Look abroad into the world; the prig, while he flourishes, is a man of honour; when in jail, at the bar, or the tree, he is so no longer" (p. 61, Bk. I, ch. xiii). As a successful rake who "thrives" in winning the object of his lust, the lord as a person of quality maintains his rogue's sense of honor.

To show the prevalence of the lord's type of pseudo honor, the synonymity of honor with adultery and cunning, Fielding shows how Colonel James attempts to corrupt Amelia in the same artful way the lord debauched Mrs. Bennet. Evil again disguises itself as goodness, as James' hypocrisy matches the deceit of the lord. That is, Colonel James poses as a truly magnanimous friend whose generosity and goodness overstep all limits. He promises to pay all of Booth's debts, he vows to find a commission for him in the West Indies, he offers his home and protection to Booth's wife and children. "Sure never man had such a friend; for never was there so noble, so generous a heart--I cannot help this ebullition of gratitude, I really cannot," Booth exclaims (p. 124, Bk. IX, ch. iv). However, James' professed good-nature merely hides his lust, the sexual appetite that hopes to ravish Amelia once Booth leaves for a foreign country. It is this vice of hypocrisy, an endemic problem in eighteenth century London, that Fielding attacks in "An Essay on the Knowledge of the Characters of Men," a work devoted to explain "the several methods . . . by which we may frustrate all the cunning and designs of hypocrisy."[20] Fielding purports in this treatise to alert the unsuspicious good-natured person, people like the naive Mrs. Bennet and the overtrusting Booth, to the various disguises and masks of vice, such as the facade of the flatterer, the professor, and the promiser. Just as the laws of duelling promote revenge, the idea of honor as success of "thriving" encourages deceit since the end justifies the means. Fielding attributes the prevalence of hypocrisy to the social milieu of the eighteenth century rather than to the innate depravity of human nature. In "The Characters of Men" he discusses deceit as a trait fostered by the customs of the day, "nourished and improved by education, in which we are taught to conceal vices than to cultivate virtues."[21] Likewise, Dr. Harrison explains the general acceptance of adultery as a practice condoned by the mores of society: "What wonder then if the community in general treat this monstrous crime as a matter of jest, and that men give way to the temptations of a violent appetite when the indulgence of it is protected by law and countenanced by custom?" (p. 132, Bk. IX, ch. v). In short, the social abuses of the day, the unchristian practices of the eighteenth century--revenge, adultery, hypocrisy--can be traced back to the false concepts of honor and greatness that dominated the age. Carefully analyzing this problem in "The Characters of Men," Fielding shows the cause-effect relationship between pseudo greatness and moral corruption--how the heroic ideals of an age influence the conduct of society:

> the Art of thriving being the very reverse of that doctrine of the Stoics, by which men were taught to consider themselves as fellow citizens of the world, and to labour jointly for the common good, without any private distinction of their own: whereas this, on the contrary, points out to every individual his particular and separate advantage, to which he is to sacrifice the interest of all others; which he is to consider as his Summum Bonum, to pursue with the utmost diligence and industry, and to acquire by all means whatever. Now when this noble end is once established, deceit must immediately suggest itself as the necessary means.[22]

In other words, once Hobbes' notion of self-love replaces Cicero's ideal of public service as the norm; once natural law is founded on mere custom, what men do, rather than on the immutable idea of justice, what men ought to do; once the Machiavellian "Interest Will Not Lie" political maxim replaces the Roman "I am a man myself, and my heart is interested in whatever can befall the rest of mankind" cited by Amelia (p. 214, Bk. X, ch. ix)-- then social evils abound as the unethical hero, the corrupt politician, and the lives of rogues and whores become models for emulation.

As mentioned earlier, Fielding's anatomy of eighteenth century London does not view the problems of the age as simply a manifestation of man's fallen nature but as a consequence of the mores and institutions of society; he attributes the blame as much to education, government, and the church as he does to man. When Amelia shows her disgust at Colonel James' villainy and denounces nearly the whole human race, Dr. Harrison corrects her indictment of mankind:

> Do not make a conclusion so much to the dishonour of the great Creator. The nature of man is far from being in itself evil; . . . . Bad education, bad habits, and bad customs debauch our nature, and drive it headlong into vice. The governors of the world, and I am afraid the priesthood, are answerable for the badness of it. (pp. 131-132, Bk. IX, ch. v)

When public leaders in positions of authority provide bad examples; when virtue is defamed, ridiculed, or goes unacknowledged; when vice is glorified or goes unpunished; when honor is not based on merit or virtue but on wealth and rank--then the customs of society frustrate man's innately moral nature, his inherent love of truth and justice; man's potential goodness is not nourished or encouraged by praise, admiration, or reward. In the chapter "Matters Political" (p. 225, Bk. XI, ch. ii), a noble and Dr. Harrison discuss man's potentiality for goodness. The lord views human nature from Mandeville's point of view, as incapable of virtue or religion. Comparing the depravity of English society to the decadence of Rome, the lord finds mankind ungovernable and uneducable: "And would you think of governing such a people by the strict principles of honesty and morality?" Rather than reform society or use the ideal of justice as a norm, the lord asks Dr. Harrison to accept the customs of the status quo, the unruliness of human nature, the malpractices of politicians, and the inefficiency of government. In a word, he neither trusts the moral nature of man nor believes in the art of government to improve nature; man is indocile and government is powerless. On the other hand, Dr. Harrison sees the co-operation of nature and art--the moral education of man through the institutions of society. Instead of blaming the incapacity of human nature or despairing at the innate evil of mankind, the clergyman criticizes the leaders of society, the so-called great men whose uninspiring examples do not attract men to love the true, the good, and the just to which all men potentially aspire. "Wherever true merit is liable to be superseded by favour and partiality, and men are entrusted with offices without any regard to capacity or integrity, the affairs of that state will always be in a deplorable situation" (p. 229, Bk. XI, ch. ii), Harrison explains in his diagnosis of the ills of society. As long as men are honored for mediocrity or rewarded for vice--like the bailiff in prison who receives what Booth calls "incivility-money" or "fees due for rudeness" for treating prisoners, in Harrison's words, "in an unchristian and inhuman manner" (pp. 105-106, Bk. VIII, ch. x) --then it becomes virtually impossible for men to fall in love with the sublime beauty of Virtue as they never behold her. Rather they merely see the harlot Vice and become enamoured of the Monstrous instead of the Marvellous. Virtue as a woman needs to be visible before she can be admired and hence attract men. Society needs to provide models of excellence for men to imitate before they can be educated to the good.

Booth's misfortunes, then, are not only caused by his own imprudence and naivete, his lack of "The Knowledge of Characters of Men," but also result from the many uncivilized, immoral customs of the day tolerated by society. The eighteenth century habit of duelling threatens Booth's life on two occasions as he is challenged once by Colonel Bath and another time by Colonel James. The adulterous practices of the age nearly corrupt his wife as Monsieur Bagillard, a lord, and Colonel

James all want to ravish Amelia. The rampant hypocrisy of the time, the deceit of such types as the flatterer, the promiser, and the professor mentioned in "The Characters of Men," often beguiles Booth, for he is duped by the various disguises of men. For example, Miss Matthews qualifies as the "flatterer" in the way she seduces him in prison: "'O Mr. Booth! could I have thought, when we were first acquainted, that the most agreeable man in the world had been capable of making the kind, the tender, the affectionate husband . . .'" (p. 159, Bk. IV, ch. i). The lustful lord exemplifies the "professor" in the artful way he professes his affection and friendship for the Booth family: upon the slightest acquaintance he suddenly brings rich gifts to the children to ingratiate himself with Amelia and disarm Booth. Fielding's maxim in "The Characters of Men"--"Fear the professions of your friends"--refers to this instantaneous kind of friendship that has not resulted from the gratitude and esteem of true philia, which grows only "by small and almost imperceptible degrees."[23] Colonel James epitomizes the "promiser" as his actions belie his words, James professing friendship but thinking adultery, promising to protect Amelia but intending to seduce her.

In addition to the barbarous customs of duelling, adultery, and hypocrisy that are the bane of eighteenth century society, there are other social conditions which precipitate the tragedy in Booth's life. His poverty, for example, stems from the state of society rather than from his own sloth. As Fielding commented in the Inquiry, "It must be a matter of astonishment to any man to reflect, that in a country where the poor are, beyond all comparison, more liberally provided for than in any other part of the habitable globe, there should be found more beggars, more distressed and miserable objects, than are to be seen throughout all the states of Europe." Of the three types of poverty that Fielding enumerates in the Inquiry--(1) "Such poor as are unable to work"; (2) "Such as are able and willing to work";

(3) "Such as are able to work, but not willing"[24] --Booth of course belongs to the second category although there is a period when his wounded condition makes him "unable to work." During his first sojourn in prison, when Booth narrates his life's history to Miss Matthews, he describes his dangerous exploits as a sea captain defending his country. Once he nearly drowned at sea in a storm; another time he was almost fatally wounded by a musket shell; on yet another occasion he was hit by an explosive that again threatened his life. Surrounded by death and danger and absent from his wife and family for extended periods of time, Booth both risks his life and sacrifices his happiness. However, Booth's magnanimous spirit that offers his life to his country and his heroic deeds at sea that are inspired by a sense of public service rather than vainglory go unrewarded and unremembered. Recovering from his wound and incapacitated for work, Booth does not receive adequate pay and must borrow money from friends:

> This was the first time I had ever felt that distress which arises from the want of money; a distress very dreadful indeed in a married state; for what can be more miserable than to see anything necessary to the preservation of a beloved creature, and not be able to supply it?
> (p. 124, Bk. III, ch. vii)

Booth as a wounded officer belongs to the class of "Such poor as are unable to work." However, after Booth convalesces and becomes one of "Such as are able and willing to work," even then the state of society, the "great men" who grant commissions to officers, balk at his attempts to find work. When Dr. Harrison petitions a noble peer to acknowledge Booth's true merit and service to his country by some reward or commission that will help him support his needy family, the lord rejects the criterion of true greatness or real worth as the basis for preferments: "My dear, dear sir," cries the other, "what is the merit of a subaltern officer?" He offers other rationalizations:

> And there are abundance with the same merit and the same qualifications who want a morsel of bread for themselves and their families.
>
> Do you think it is possible to provide for all men of merit? (p. 227, Bk. XI, ch. ii)

Thus, given the lack or reward, praise, or admiration for excellence and given the lack of pity for the poor, Booth becomes an easy prey to the vice of gambling, which Fielding also regards as another vile custom of the age. As he points out in the Inquiry, this "great evil" presents a formidable danger to "the more thoughtless and giddy part of mankind,"[25] a title that certainly applies to Booth. Lured to the gaming table by Colonel Trent, Booth loses his small fortune and even goes into debt. Owing his friend the fifty pounds he borrowed on his gambling spree--a sum that Trent soon exacts--Booth now finds himself bound by the code of the gambler, another one of the ideas of false honor in the eighteenth century: " . . . the most dishonourable of all things is not to pay a debt, contracted at the gaming-table, the next day, or the next time at least that you see the party" (p. 200, Bk. X, ch. vii). At this point in the novel Booth reaches the nadir in his life. All kinds of forces conspire against him--the whims of Fortune, his own imprudence, the malice and hypocrisy of his enemies, and the customs and laws of his nation. Booth is imprisoned because he cannot pay his gambling debt to Trent; he is disgraced because of his poverty; he is ashamed because Miss Matthews threatens to disclose his infidelity to Amelia; and Colonel James is prepared to challenge him to a duel. This brief summary of the major events in Booth's history shows how his fall from high to low--from sea captain to half-pay officer to unemployed veteran to pauper--stems, to a large degree, from the corrupt merit system and the accepted mores of the age. Society's failure to recognize greatness in the form of valor or virtue, to measure heroism in terms of a love of humanity--Christian <u>agape</u> or Stoic <u>humanitas</u>--leads to a host of evils from poverty to gambling. While the unjust laws of the country and the degenerate politicians of the time almost reduce Booth to nothing, the popular code of the duel and the gambling table deal the <u>coup de grace</u>. That is, while the lords reflect apathy toward Booth's merit and poverty, the pseudo honor of Trent's gambler's code and Colonel James' duel ethic exacerbate Booth's condition of poverty with the additional woes of a prison sentence and the threat of death. Thus the false greatness of lords and persons of quality, the pseudo honor of military men, and the lack of integrity in sexual mores and marriage customs, as seen in Colonel and Mrs. James' readiness to pimp for one another or in Colonel Trent's willingness to prostitute his own wife for the lord--these are the root causes of the social evils that afflict Booth and Amelia.

As victims of the abuses of greatness and the violations of honor Booth and Amelia are delivered from their oppression by the actions of true greatness, by noble deeds that reflect the Stoic ideals of <u>humanitas</u> or <u>comitas</u> as well as the Christian virtues of charity and humility. Good-Nature, as fully explained by Fielding in the <u>Champion</u> (Thur., Mar. 27, 1740) and in "Of Good-Nature," synthesizes both classical and Christian virtues--a combination of Greek φιλανθρωπία, Roman <u>benignitas</u>, and Christian love; a union of the cardinal virtue of justice and the theological virtue of charity.[26] Thus Fielding defines good-nature in his poem:

> What by this name, then shall be understood?
> What? but the glorious lust of doing good?
> The heart that finds its happiness to please
> Can feel another's pain, and taste his ease;
> The cheek that with another's joy can glow,

> Turn pale and sicken with another's woe;
> Free from contempt and envy, he who deems
> Justly of life's two opposite extremes,
> Who to make all and each man truly bless'd
> Doth all he can and wishes all the rest?[27]

Dr. Harrison and Amelia especially embody this classical-Christian principle of magnanimity which Fielding's "Of Good-Nature" encompasses. At the end of the novel, when Booth is imprisoned and Amelia and her children are left destitute, Dr. Harrison exercises "the glorious lust of doing good" and "doth all he can." Pitying the poor rather than regarding them as objects of contempt --a common attitude in the eighteenth century reflected in the use of the word <u>creature</u> ("a quality expression of low contempt, properly confined only to the mouths of ladies who are Right Honorable," according to Fielding's "A Modern Glossary")--Dr. Harrison offers them his parsonage. When the clergyman hears of Colonel James' challenge of a duel to Booth, he again shows his true magnanimity by defending the Christian idea of honor: he persuades James to forgive his enemy rather than to take revenge. Defending the sacrament of marriage and the ideal of chaste love from the sensuality of the age, Harrison challenges the vulgarized view of love defined in "A Modern Glossary" as "delight in particular kinds of food" and "the favourite objects of all our appetites"--love as a purely physical gratification. Hoping to protect Amelia from the lust of Colonel James, Dr. Harrison circulates his sermon on adultery at, of all places, a masquerade--the scene of rendezvous where the beaux ridicule it as "d__ned stuff." However, Dr. Harrison's absurd nonsense ultimately reveals itself as practical wisdom. The sermon, which mistakenly reaches Colonel Bath instead of Colonel James, nevertheless effects its purpose, for it eventually exposes James' infidelity to his own brother-in-law, "who would not only have condemned him equally with the doctor, but would possibly have quarreled with him on his sister's account whom . . . he loved above all things" (p. 286, Bk. XII, ch. iv). Thus Dr. Harrison's genuine good-nature or <u>humanitas</u> does everything possible, in the words of the poem, "to make all and each man truly bless'd." His true greatness saves Booth and Amelia from the imminent dangers of poverty, revenge, and adultery--all effects of pseudo honor. As Fielding remarks in <u>Jonathan Wild</u>, false greatness "consists in bringing all manner of mischief on mankind, and goodness in removing it from them" (p. 22, Bk. I, ch. i).

As the embodiment of Christian magnanimity, as an example of "the great and good," the true sublime in human nature, Harrison's myriad of noble deeds and variety of virtues create the sense of the wonderful that follows from the Marvellous or heroic. His countless acts of generosity transcend narrow limits and know no boundaries. As Booth says of him, "The doctor hath an income of little more than six hundred pounds a year, and I am convinced he gives away four of it" (p. 304, Bk. XII, ch. viii). Harrison reveals his liberality to Booth and Amelia not only at the end of the novel when they are in dire need but also throughout their lives, at the beginning and middle of their history as well as at the end of the novel. As Booth mentions in his history, he owes the beginning of his happiness, his marriage to Amelia, to Dr. Harrison's intervention. When Amelia's mother, Mrs. Harris, opposed the match, Harrison promoted the nuptials and eventually reconciled Mrs. Harris to the fact. Booth and Amelia are further indebted to their friend for the continuation of their happiness as well as the beginning of their marital bliss. At the juncture in their life, when Booth is convalescing from a battle would, receiving only half-pay, and lacking prosspects for another commission, Harrison again shows his magnanimity by offering Booth his parsonage and leading him to the good life on a farm --an interlude in Booth's life which approximates the golden age: "The whole was one continued series of love, health, and tranquility," he recalls (p. 151, Bk. III, ch. xii). Thus, by his timely intervention in the lives of Booth and Amelia during the critical moments of their history, Harrison's constant watchful care of Booth and Amelia, whom he calls his "children," resembles the providence of God for His creatures. His immeasurable liberality imitates the infinite love of God and the supernatural virtue of charity--hence its miraculous, wonderful quality. Unlike pseudo greatness that is motivated by self-love, which confers obligations only to request a favor, which gives-in-order-to-receive--as seen in the way the lustful lord brings presents to the children in order to debauch the wife--Harrison's Christian magnanimity is inspired by charity, good-nature in its deepest sense: giving without expecting to receive and giving beyond measure. In St. Paul's words, cited by Fielding in the Champion (Sat., Apr. 5, 1740), "charity is kind" and "seeketh not her own":

> or, as the Greek signifies, does good offices, behaves kindly; not confined to our wishes merely, but our actions, under which head I shall introduce liberality, a necessary qualification of any who would call himself a successor of Christ's disciples.[28]

However, as a clergyman imitating Christ, Harrison's magnanimity combines the wisdom of the serpent with the gentleness of the dove. Fielding describes his hero's actions as "truly congruous with all the rules of the most perfect prudence as well as with the most consummate goodness" (p. 111, Bk. IX, ch. i). As a character who reflects the spirit of "Of True Greatness," Harrison qualifies as a hero "Whose soul is with various talents bless'd." As a man whose good heart is part of a "mighty whole/Full composition of a virtuous soul," to quote again from "Of Good-Nature," Harrison supplements his good-nature with learning, conversation, and genius--the other attributes of ripened wisdom that Fielding discusses in Tom Jones (p. 413, Bk. IX, ch. i). As an example of "the great and good," then, as opposed to the merely "good," Harrison reflects many virtues or parts. For example, when Harrison has Booth arrested and sent to prison, he illustrates how he can mix justice with mercy, how he can blame folly as well as pity the poor. When Booth lived the life of the farmer, he indulged his vanity by the purchase of an equipage, an unnecessary luxury. Whereupon Harrison reproaches him with sternness: "but I will not suffer my money to support the ridiculous, and, I must say, criminal vanity of any one. I expect, therefore, to find at my return, that you have either discharged my whole debt, or your equipage" (p. 173, Bk. IV, ch. iii). Failing to persuade Mrs. Harris to consent to Amelia's marriage through "soothing methods," Harrison compels her to agree to the match by his authoritative look and voice, "calculated to inspire awe, and even terror" (p. 83, Bk. II, ch. vii). Although Harrison pities the undeserved misfortune of Amelia and her hungry children, he shows no sympathy for Booth's sufferings when they result from his own folly, such as his gambling: "I am sorry, child, for the share you are to partake in your husband's sufferings; but as for him, I really think he deserves no compassion" (p. 277, Bk. XII, ch. iii). Thus Harrison unites the severity of justice with the gentleness of pity. As an exemplar of justice he ridicules folly and detests vice; he is no sentimentalist like the Scottish clergyman who begged God to please pardon the devil.

As a corollary of this harmony of justice and mercy, the synthesis between the wisdom of the serpent and the gentleness of the dove constitutes another characteristic of Christian magnanimity. Unlike Booth, who does not join prudence to goodnature and hence is fooled by hypocrites like Miss Matthews, the lord, and Colonel James, Harrison knows how to read the characters of men and is not deceived by their countenances, words, or external appearances. He detects vanity and hypocrisy in all its forms. For example, he exposes Colonel Bath's profession of honor, his love of the duel, as a kind of butchery: "How, sir!" said the doctor, "would you compensate one breach of the law by a much greater, and pay your debts by committing murder?" (pp. 119-120, Bk. IX, ch. iii). Unlike Amelia, who always tends to sympathize with her husband, Harrison sees the ingredients of vanity and folly that comprise a part of Booth's character. Nor is Harrison fooled by a fellow clergyman's pose of sanctity. When Tom, a young priest, exalts his own profession by blaming society and government for the lack of respect toward clergymen, he fails to detect his own pride or lack of humility. Ironically, he is proud of his low rank: "'It was very justly observed of you, sir,' said he to the doctor, 'that the lowest clergyman in England is in real dignity superior to the nobleman'" (p. 157, Bk. IX, ch. x). In the course of the conversation, however, Harrison blames the conduct of mediocre, incompetent, worldly clergymen--which Tom exemplifies--as well as the bias of society toward the whole profession. Attacking Tom's false honor, his love of prestige and reputation, Harrison finds him unqualified to be a disciple of Christ. In short, as a prudent man who recognizes both the good and the evil in men, Harrison avoids Booth's simple-minded good-nature that naively trusts men. As a wise serpent who neither oversimplifies the goodness of men nor exaggerates the depravity of human nature, Harrison also escapes the cynical distrust of mankind expressed by the lord in the chapter "Matters Political" (p. 225, Bk. XI, ch. ii), the view of Mandeville that also intrigues Miss Matthews--human nature as "a picture of the highest deformity" (p. 114, Bk. III, ch. v).

Dr. Harrison's milti-faceted virtues correspond to the parts of the magnanimous author or teacher cited in Tom Jones: genius, learning, conversation, and a good heart. In addition to liberality or charity ("a good heart"), to a knowledge of the characters of men ("conversation," i.e., the wisdom of experience), to prudence ("genius," i.e., the ability to discern similarities and differences, to see the one and the many, both good and evil), Harrison also possesses learning. Just as Fielding in Tom Jones (p. 413, Bk. IX, ch. i) refers to Homer and Milton as "masters of all the learning of their times," Amelia speaks of Harrison's mind as "the treasury of all ancient and modern learning" (p. 132, Bk. IX, ch. v). In his discussion with Colonel Bath on the concept of honor and the practice of duelling (p. 119, Bk. IX, ch. iii), Harrison reveals a knowledge of Pope and Dryden, Virgil and Homer, and of course the Bible. In his sermon on adultery Harrison studies the vice as a violation of both the classical law of nature and the Ten Commandments as well as a degenerate custom of the eighteenth century. During a conversation with an old friend and this man's clergyman son on the topic of goodness, whether "to do good to everyone" (p. 147, Bk. IX, ch. viii) is a pagan or Christian doctrine, Harrison displays a wealth of classical, Christian, and modern learning. After he alludes to the ancient Agrippa and Phocylides and the modern D'Esprit, he goes on to show a deep familiarity with the sources cited by the young clergyman: Homer, Plato, and Eustathius. Moreover, Harrison reveals the depth of his scholarship when he criticizes the young man for quoting out of context:

> but if you remember the rest of the quotation as well as you do that from Eustathius, you might have added the observation which Mr. Dryden makes in favour of this passage, that he found not in all the Latin authors, so admirable an instance of extensive humanity. (p. 147, Bk. IX, ch. viii)

In other words, Harrison's breadth of learning goes beyond custom, the fashion of the day, "the knowledge of the town," to quote from Fielding's definition of <u>knowledge</u> in "A Modern Glossary," to nature and religion, to the universal first principles. Because there is so much to admire in Harrison, a depth of generosity beyond measure, so many varied virtues from good-nature to learning, such varied kinds of excellence from justice to mercy, he belongs to the type of hero that Fielding calls "the great and good," "the Iliad of Nature," "the true sublime in human nature."

Amelia of course also epitomizes Christian magnanimity; her sense of honor too is based on nature and religion rather than on what Fielding calls "the custom of the world." For example, her decision to marry Booth challenges the worldly custom of the "proper match"; she prefers to marry the man she loves though he is poor than to accept her mother's choice of a rich aristocrat, a Mr. Winckworth with a beautiful equipage and a large estate. She does not estimate worth as "power, rank, or wealth," Fielding's definition in "A Modern Glossary." Secondly, unlike Miss Matthews, whose false sense of honor encourages the duel between James and Booth, a custom Harrison attributes to ". . . the nonsense of women, who, either from their extreme cowardice and desire of protection, or . . . from their excessive vanity, have been always forward to countenance a set of hectors and bravoes" (p. 278, Bk. XII, ch. iii), Amelia does not enjoy her husband's adventures with death. She regards the glory and fame of a military hero as a vanity; she prefers her husband at home than at war: "'But if,' said she, 'my situation, even in health, will be so intolerable, how shall I, in the danger and agonies of childbirth, support your absence?'" (p. 100, Bk. III, ch. ii). Third, in contrast to the hypocrisy of the age, the various disguises and masks seen at the masquerade, the guile of adulterers, flatterers, and promisers, Amelia embodies purity of heart, innocence, and candor. "I may call her an Israelite indeed, in whom there is no guile," Dr. Harrison declares (p. 146, Bk. IX, ch. viii). Amelia shows her love of truth when she objects to Mrs. Atkinson's counterfeiting her at the masquerade and flirting with a lord. Even though Mrs. Atkinson, disguised as Amelia, intends justice--deceiving the same man who betrayed her when she was Mrs. Bennet--even though Mrs. Atkinson has good intentions, the procurement of a commission for her deserving husband, a favor the lord will grant only in exchange for a rendezvous with Amelia, Amelia remonstrates against her dishonest, devious, artful ways; the end does not justify the means. Amelia again illustrates this love of truth in her frank discussion with another friend, Mrs. James, the former Jenny Bath. Amelia, snubbed by her old friend because of Booth's sudden poverty and because of Jenny Bath's recent marriage into wealth, openly asks Mrs. James to explain and justify her snobbery--her distant civility, her cold formal visit to Amelia's dismal lodgings, her lack of correspondence:

> Could I have expected, when I parted the last time with Miss Jenny Bath, to have met her the next time in the shape of a fine lady, complaining of the hardship of climbing up two pairs of stairs to visit me, and then approaching me with the distant air of a new or a slight acquaintance? (p. 227, Bk. V, ch. iv)

In short, Amelia's honesty and straightforwardness reflect the simplicity that Christianity associates with truth: "Let your speech be yea, yea: no, no" (Matthew 5:37). Thus Amelia's sense of honor is based on truth rather than custom, on nature and religion rather than the mores of the time. As Fielding says in "Of True Greatness," "By fashion led not, nor by whim betray'd,/By candour only biass'd . . . ." In contrast to the hypocritical customs and false honor of the day, Amelia's real love of her husband, her sincere desire to see Booth's safety, and her candor toward her friends all reflect the spirit of truth and the purity of Christian honor.

Like Sophia in <u>Tom Jones</u>, Amelia exemplifies the good and the beautiful as well as the true. She reveals this goodness in many overt ways, such as her love of her children, her fidelity to Booth --"for better for worse, for richer for poorer"-- her loyalty to friends like Dr. Harrison, and her compassion for the distressed like Mrs. Bennet. As Fielding commented in "The Characters of Men," general philanthropy begins with the love of one's neighbor or kin: "It is well said in one of Mr. Pope's letters, 'How shall a man love five millions, who could never love a single person?'":

> If a man hath more love than what centers
> in himself, it will certainly light on
> his children, his relations, friends and
> nearest acquaintance.[29]

However, Amelia's profound good-nature expresses itself in more covert and more heroic ways than the visible love of husband, family, and friends. Doing good by stealth, she conceals Colonel James' lust for her from Booth and confides in Dr. Harrison in order to prevent a duel between the two friends. Thus she shows a Christian love of one's enemy instead of the worldly love of revenge. Doing good by stealth, she hides her knowledge of Booth's affair with Miss Matthews. As Booth later comes to discover, Amelia not only has known about his liaison for some time but also has silently forgiven him--displaying a largeness of soul that astonishes Booth: "Amelia never shined forth to Booth in so amiable and great a light" (p. 272, Bk. XII, ch. iii). Likewise her decision to pawn her picture, to sacrifice her precious possessions for the sake of her hungry children--without consulting Booth or Dr. Harrison --exemplifies the humility and charity of Christian greatness.

Another significant aspect of Amelia's goodness, in addition to her good-nature or humanitas and her supernatural agape, the affection for one's fellow man, the love of kin, and the forgiveness of one's enemies, is her fortitude. It will be recalled that Fielding distinguished "the good" from "the great and good" by citing "the parts" and "courage" of the latter. For Fielding a great soul shows its strength by the way it endures adversity, the slings and arrows of outrageous fortune. As Dr. Harrison, echoing Boethius, remarks in his letter to the Booths announcing the death of Amelia's mother: "yet I have long thought there is no calamity so great that a Christian philosopher may not reasonably laugh at it" (p. 141, Bk. III, ch. x). Amelia suffers the accidents of life with Christian patience. Once, as Booth recalls in his history, when Amelia's chaise overturned, her peerless beauty was disfigured because of a broken nose, a misfortune that Booth compares to a general's loss of a victory, a man's loss of a fortune, and a king's loss of a crown. However, Amelia endured this sudden fall from high to low with heroic virtues. She displayed, according to Booth's account, "firmness of soul," "patience and resignation," and a "truly noble heart" (p. 56, Bk. II, ch. i). On another occasion Amelia suffers the bad luck of the loss of an inheritance, her mother's fortune, which is bequeathed to Amelia's sister. Her trials and tribulations as Booth's wife, the constant fluctuations in their financial status, Booth's imprudence and extravagance, also test her great soul. In all these cases Amelia displays the <u>magna anima</u> that Booth attributes to her in his summary comment on her character: "for I am assured that one who can so heroically endure adversity, will bear prosperity with equal greatness of soul" (p. 305, Bk. XII, ch. viii). Or, as Fielding writes in "Of True Greatness": "True greatness lives but in the noble mind;/Him <u>constant</u> through each various scene attends (<u>italics mine</u>).

In addition to the good and the true, Amelia also radiates the beautiful. Booth remarks of his wife, "I knew her in the first dawn of her beauty; and I believe, madame, she had as much as ever fell to the share of a woman" (p. 55, Bk. II, ch. i). She is admired not only by Booth but also sought by men in general. Mr. Winckworth, Monsieur Bagillard, the lord, and Colonel James are all attracted by her beauty. "D__n me, my lord, if she is not an angel," a young rake at Vauxhall comments upon a first sight of Amelia (p. 153, Bk. IX, ch. ix). Both before and after her accident with the chaise, in a state of poverty or wealth, amid the company of older men or young sparks Amelia's universal beauty continues to ravish the male species. Thus Fielding compares her to Milton's Eve, the apotheosis of woman:

--Adorn'd
With what all Earth or Heaven could bestow

To make her amiable.

> Grace was in all her steps, Heaven in her eye,
> In every gesture, dignity and love.
> (p. 258, Bk. VI, ch. i)

Of course Milton's Eve, in her unfallen state, like Fielding's Sophia and Amelia, is both beautiful and good and wise; her body reflects her soul; she personifies the true sublime ("as Milton sublimely describes Eve," Fielding notes, before he cites the passages from Paradise Lost): the multi-splendored, infinitely-various virtues, gifts, and graces that glorify the hero or heroine as semi-divine, an example of the Marvellous. "Art thou really human, or art thou not rather an angel in an human form?" Booth exclaims (p. 195, Bk. X, ch. vi). When Amelia's beauty is superadded to her goodness and wisdom, then the brilliance of the beautiful, the good, and the true create a brightness that dazzles and astonishes, "which at once fills us with love, wonder, and delight," as Fielding says of the emotional effects of the true sublime in "Preface to the Miscellanies and Poems."

Throughout his work Fielding praises the inexhaustible fullness and the transcendent beauty of virtue, the glorious radiance of the true sublime "raising and extending itself above the order of this creation . . . ."[30] From his early plays through his essay-writing period to his last novel the idea recurs. In Don Quixote in England the knight-errant tells his squire, "Virtue, Sancho, is too bright for their eyes, and they dare not behold her."[31] In The Champion (Thur., Jan. 24, 1739-40) Fielding quoting his favorite passage from Plato, writes: "that could mankind behold virtue naked, they would all be in love with her"[32]--a passage that he repeats in "The Characters of Men" and paraphrases in his dedication to Tom Jones ("virtue . . . strikes us with an idea of that loveliness which Plato asserts there is in her naked charms"). Tom Jones' praise of Sophia, in the lines he recites from a poem, reasserts the true sublimity of heroic virtue:

> There's in her all that we believe of heav'n,
> <u>Amazing</u> brightness, purity, and truth,
> (p. 341, Bk. VIII, ch. ii; italics added)

When the true sublime is found in man, then the divine or marvellous has been modestly camouflaged by the commonplace and the natural; greatness has concealed itself in lowliness.

Thus, to summarize, Fielding, like Pope in <u>Peri Bathous</u> and Swift in <u>Gulliver's Travels</u>, ridicules and exposes the various cults of pseudo greatness that prevailed in the eighteenth century: the vainglory of authors like Gulliver and Pope's dunces, the heroism of rogue-politicians like Jonathan Wild, the honor of duellers like Colonel Bath or persons of quality like the rich lords. Fielding, like Pope who mocks "pro<u>fund</u>" authors aspiring to be sublime poets and l<u>ike</u> Swift who satirizes the little, narrow-minded King of Lilliput pretending to be a great, large-souled leader, also censures the mediocrity, presumption, and vanity of incompetent, ignoble, contemptible men, such as Tom Thumb, puffing themselves up as great or good. "'Woe unto them who call evil good and good evil; that put darkness for light, and light for darkness,' &c," as Fielding quotes from Isaiah in "The Characters of Men." To cure this eighteenth century tendency of calling evil good, ugliness beauty, ignominy honor, the worst the best, the bathetic the sublime, and the Monstrous the Marvellous--Fielding reaffirms the classical-Christian ideal of the true sublime or wonderful, greatness that is based on divine archetypes, the actions of gods and heroes ("Sublimity," according to Longinus, "is the echo of a great soul"). True greatness, according to Fielding, transcends temporary customs and models itself upon eternal ideals, such as the imitation of Christ. It does not seek the applause of fickle mobs or crave transient fame; rather it does good by stealth.

As Fielding describes Virtue in The Champion (Tues., Mar. 4, 1739-40), "she is plain and sober in her habit, sure of her innate worth, and therefore neglects to adorn herself with those gaudy colors, which catch the eyes of the giddy multitude."[33] True greatness is not determined by what most men do out of blind habit but by what "the great and good," characters like Dr. Harrison and Amelia, do out of principle. "Nothing should be esteemed as characteristical of a species, but what is to be found among the best and most perfect individuals of that species," Tom Jones remarks to the man of the hill (p. 411, Bk. VIII, ch. xv). Whereas the pride of worldly honor tries to convert base metal, so to speak, into precious gold by the alchemy of hypocrisy, the humility of Christian magnanimity conceals valuable gems among common minerals--camouflaging greatness in the form of lowliness, strength in the form of weakness, and wisdom in the form of folly. Throughout the novel Amelia's true greatness is hidden by her poverty; Mrs. James, for example, scorns her low condition. Amelia's strength of mind and soul is concealed by her modest femininity, her patient resignation--the weakness traditionally associated with women. Monsieur Bagillard, Colonel James, and the lord all assume that Amelia is a vulnerable woman whose lack of will power cannot resist temptation. Dr. Harrison's wisdom appears as folly to the world. Colonel Bath ridicules his idea of honor, the love of one's enemy, as female delicacy: "Women and clergy are upon the same footing. The long-robed gentry are exempted from the laws of honour" (p. 120, Bk. IX, ch. iii). Harrison's old friend calls him "a fool in private life" because he has not yet acquired the fortune or title of a bishop (p. 161, Bk. IX, ch. x). The finale of the novel, Amelia's visit to the pawn shop, illustrates the Christian paradox of greatness in lowliness. Along with the strength concealed as weakness, this incident also shows how wealth is hidden amid poverty. That is, Fielding depicts the riddle of Amelia surrounded by want yet surprised by wealth. Destitute herself, she visits a pawn shop, a symbol of poverty, and accidentally meets Robinson, another emblem of misery. However, the secret of Amelia's great wealth is concealed in this lowly pawn shop. The brightness and sublimity of the truth about her inheritance, a fact that overwhelms Amelia with "love, wonder, and delight," is buried in an inglorious, unattractive man like Robinson. The power of strength is camouflaged in the weakness of a poor woman like Amelia and the helplessness of a prisoner like Robinson: Amelia's visit to the pawn shop and Robinson's confession of the truth dethrone the "great" lawyer Murphy, who forged the will, and exalt the humble, the true heirs of Mrs. Harris's legacy, Amelia and Booth. In the words of St. Paul, which so clearly comment on Fielding's idea of Christian magnanimity: "But God hath chosen the foolish things of the world to confound the wise; and God hath chosen the weak things of the world to confound the things that are mighty" (I Corinthians 1:27).

NOTES TO CHAPTER III

[1] <u>Works</u>, ed. Henley, XV, 89-90.

[2] Maurice J. McNamee's <u>Honor and the Epic Hero</u> (New York: Holt, Rinehart, and Winston, 1960), a study of the history of the idea of magnanimity from Aristotle to the Renaissance, cites the following passages from St. Paul as central texts in the Christian notion of greatness as humility:

> But he that glorieth, let him glory in the Lord. For not he who commendeth himself is approved, but he, whom God commendeth. (II Corinthians 10:17-18)
>
> What hast thou that thou hast not received, And if thou has received, why dost thou glory as if thou has not received it? (I Corinthians 4:7)

[3] <u>Works</u>, XV, 264.

[4] <u>Works</u>, XIII, 122.

[5] <u>Works</u>, XIV, 91.

[6] Donald A. Stauffer's <u>The Art of Biography in Eighteenth Century England</u> (Princeton University Press, 1941) points out the prolific nature of sensational, defamatory lives in the eighteenth century; he quotes from Francis Coventry's <u>History of Pompey the Little</u> (1750):

> The lowest and most contemptible vagrants, parishgirls, chambermaids, pickpockets, and highwaymen, find historians to record their praise . . . (p. 135).

[7] <u>Works</u>, XIV, 268; XIV, 221-222; XIV, 300.

[8] <u>Works</u>, XVI, 79-81.

[9] Works, XIII, 108 ff.; XIV, 56.

[10] Works, XV, 228.

[11] Works, XII, 245.

[12] Works, II, 66.

[13] Works, XII, 245.

[14] Works, V, 210.

[15] Works, XIII, 119.

[16] Works, V, 256-257.

[17] Works, V, 258.

[18] Works, XV, 130.

[19] Lloyd W. Brown, "The Person of Quality in the Eighteenth Century," Dalhousie Review, 48 (1968), 172.

[20] Works, XIV, 304.

[21] Works, XIV, 282.

[22] Works, XIV, 282.

[23] Works, XIV, 292.

[24] Works, XIII, 45; 56.

[25] Works, XII, 37.

[26] Works, XII, 256.

[27] Works, XII, 258-259.

[28] Works, XV, 270-271.

[29] Works, XIV, 302-303.

[30] Works, XII, 245.

[31]_Works_, XI, 32.

[32]_Works_, XV, 166.

[33]_Works_, XV, 228.

CHAPTER IV

THE MIRACLES OF DIVINE PROVIDENCE: GOD AS THE SOURCE OF WONDER

"Now the most hidden cause and the furthest removal from our senses is God who works most secretly in all things."
--Aquinas

"God makes himself known as a revealing God in the works, both equally unreasonable, of miracle and foolishness, and that is how he plays."
--Hugo Rahner, Man at Play

A. Introduction

In an era when strict rationalism, as witnessed in deism, disbelieved in the miracles and mysteries of the Bible; when the new science, as evidenced in Newton's Principia and Opticks, tended to subvert the traditional notion of Providence; when the theory of progress, as seen in the Philosophes, challenged the linear-teleological Christian philosophy of history--attitudes that contributed to the wane of the Wonderful in the eighteenth century--Fielding affirmed the existence of miracles as the real effect of divine Providence, as another species of the Marvellous, as God's intervention in history.

A number of well-known scholarly works all comment on how the rise of the new science and the theory of progress in the age of reason led to a

...concerning the supernatural, a loss of ...dential view of the world. Herbert But-...d writes in The Origins of Modern Science, ...whole tendency of the new philosophes was to ...ve the idea of Providence, which seemed a ca-...icious interference with the laws of nature; and indeed, the new power which was coming to be acquired over material things encouraged the idea that man could, so to speak, play Providence over himself."[1] In The Idea of Progress, J. B. Bury draws a similar conclusion:

> The Cartesian mechanical theory of the world and the doctrine of invariable law, carried to a logical conclusion, excluded the doctrine of Providence. This doctrine was already in serious danger. Perhaps no article was more insistently attacked by sceptics in the seventeenth century, and none was more vital . . . ; for it was just the theory of an active Providence that the theory of Progress was to replace; and it was not till men felt independent of Providence that they could organise a theory of Progress.[2]

Discussing Newton's metaphysics in The Metaphysical Foundations of Modern Physical Science, E. A. Burtt explains how Newton, despite his avowed theism, limits God's role in the universe to that of a mechanic or plumber whose function is "temporal housekeeping": God prevents the stars from falling into space or reforms the world when the mechanism is out of order--a god whose work involves "periodic reformation" rather than "new creative activity."[3]

Thus the trends in scientific, religious, and historical thought in the eighteenth century led to a dislocation in the traditional conception of divine Providence. First, Newtonian physics regarded the deity as the God of Nature and ignored Him as the God of History; it saw His handiwork in the Creation but not in the individual lives or "histories" of men. Second, the religion of the

extreme Anglican rationalists, as Phillip Harth
points out in Swift and Anglican Rationalism,
prized clarity and simplicity and de-emphasized
paradox and mystery, the supernatural aspects of
religion. The religion of the deists, as exemplified in the revealing title of Toland's Christianity Not Mysterious, diminished the sense of the
Marvellous generally associated with the hidden
ways of God as deus absconditus. Third, the secular view of history, discussed in Carl L. Becker's
The Heavenly City of the Eighteenth Century Philosophers, substituted the theory of progress for
the providential view of history; the good life on
earth, the Earthly City, the best of all possible
worlds replaces the beatific vision of God in Paradise, Augustine's City of God, as the end of history. As the shifting meaning of the word prudence[4] in the seventeenth and eighteenth centuries
indicates, human planning, calculation, and foresight supersede God's wisdom, government, and
providence as the important elements in man's history. Both J. B. Bury's The Idea of Progress and
Herbert Butterfield's The Statecraft of Machiavelli illustrate how this "new history" rejected fortune, chance, and accident--the well-known nicknames or handmaidens of Providence--as significant
forces in history. To cite the passage Bury
quotes from Montesquieu's Considerations on the
Greatness and Decadence of the Romans (1734):

> It is not Fortune who governs the world,
> as we see from the history of the Romans.
> There are general causes, moral or physical, which operate in every monarchy,
> raise it, maintain it, or overthrow it;
> all that occurs is subject to these
> causes.[5]

Or, as Machiavelli said in the twenty-fifth chapter of The Prince, "How Much Fortune Can Do in Human Affairs and How It May Be Opposed": "I certainly think that it is better to be impetuous
than cautious, for fortune is a woman, and it is
necessary, if you wish to master her, to conquer
her by force."[6]

This view of Fortune as an ineffectual power in history, as a weak, vulnerable woman, conflicted with Fielding's views on the subject of chance, the influence of Fortune or Providence in history. As discussed in Chapter II, Fielding in <u>The Champion</u> (Dec. 6, 1739) stressed the crucial role that Fortune plays in the histories of men and nations. In agreement with Plato who offered "a religious respect to chance and fortune," with the Romans who honored their goddess Fortuna by building a special temple for her, with the Anglo-Saxons who settled controversies by lots, Fielding accepted the divinity of Fortune, its providential aspect. In this essay he compares life to a game of hazard rather than to a game of chess:

> in which latter [chess], among good players, one false step must infallibly lose the game; whereas in the former [hazard], the worst that can happen is to have the odds against you . . . ; and we often see a blundering fellow who scarce knows on which side the odds are, dribble out his bad chance upon the table, and sweep the whole board; while the wisest players, and those who stick close to the rule, lift their eyes and curse the dice.

Also in this essay Fielding examines the life of Oliver Cromwell, "the child of fortune," as another testimony of Fortuna's divinity; the Puritan hero owed his success in large measure to "the wonderful effects of chance."[7] Scattered throughout Fielding's novels are other statements about his belief in luck. He writes in <u>Joseph Andrews</u>, "Plato and Aristotle, or somebody else, hath said, <u>that when the most exquisite cunning fails, chance often hits the mark, and that by means the least expected</u>" (p. 195, Bk. II, ch. xv). He cites the same quotation from Virgil in both <u>Joseph Andrews</u> (p. 195, Bk. II, ch. xv) and <u>Amelia</u> (p. 307, Bk. XII, ch. viii): <u>Turne, quod optandi divum promittere nemo/Auderet, volvenda dies, en attulit ultro</u> ("What none of all the gods could grant thy vows, that, Turnus, this suspicious day bestows." Of course Fielding alludes to Fortune throughout Tom Jones. Since this topic has been examined in detail in Chapter II, it suffices here to recall two of the more important passages:

> But Fortune, who is a tender parent, and often doth more for her favourite offspring that neither they deserve or wish . . . . (p. 32, Bk. I, ch. xi)

> Notwithstanding the sentiment of the Roman satirist, which denies the divinity of Fortune, and the opinion of Seneca to the same purpose; Cicero, who was, I believe, a wiser man than either of them, expressly holds the contrary; and certain it is, there are some incidents in life so very strange and unaccountable that it seems to require more than human skill and foresight in producing them. (p. 678, Bk. XIV, ch. viii)

In acknowledging chance as a powerful factor in history, in ascribing such a prominent role to Fortune in his novels, in emphasizing the ubiquity of luck in the lives of "histories" of both the major and minor characters in his novels--Fielding presents Fortune and Providence as intelligible mysteries, as wonderful paradoxes that conflict with the scientific laws and mathematical certainties of the age of reason. For example, whereas Newton's God, the deity in the eighteenth century version of the chain of being, plays a static, noninterfering role in the universe except when he acts the part of repairman or deus ex machina, the goddess Fortuna as "tender parent" or Alma Mater takes a special interest in the lives of her children. She blesses Tom Jones when he is born and welcomed into Allworthy's home, when he reaches manhood and falls in love with Sophia, when he travels the road to London and meets Mrs. Waters, and when he is saved from hanging during his adventures in London. Omnipresent and energetic, Fortune favors Tom throughout his entire life, at the beginning, middle, and end of his history.

Also Fielding takes particular care to distinguish Fortune's intervention from the interference of god machinery. His caveat in Tom Jones (p. 333, Bk. VIII, ch. i) enjoins the author to introduce "supernatural agents as seldom as possible." In the novel itself Fielding himself promises "none of that supernatural assistance" to deliver his hero, leaving him to discover "some natural means of fairly extricating himself from all his distresses" (p. 781, Bk. XVII, ch. i). Thus in her active yet subtle role, in her interested yet unofficious conduct, Fortune's motherly love and female modesty differ from the aloof detachment and sudden assertion that tend to characterize the watchmaker-repairman god of Newtonian metaphysics.

The intelligible mystery of fickle Fortune acting as a handmaiden of a reasonable Providence also contradicts the rationalist and fideist tendencies in eighteenth century religion. Whereas the "unorthodox" Anglican rationalists, as Phillip Harth puts it, and the deists separated reason and revelation, exalting man's ability to know God "naturally" without the aid of Biblical revelation or the need of faith to believe in His miracles; whereas the Puritans and the fideists, such as Dryden in Religio Laici ("So pale grows Reason at Religions sight," l. 10), elevated the power of faith over reason, deriving religion exclusively from revelation and belittling nature[8]--Fielding does not separate reason from faith or dichotomize nature and revelation. He not only criticizes pure rationalists like Square or deists like the "Rule-of-Right" men but also satirizes fideists like Trulliber in Joseph Andrews, a clergyman who puts faith above works. "Fellow, dost thou speak against faith in my house? Get out of my doors," Trulliber mutters to Adams as he refuses to lend money or offer hospitality to a fellow clergyman (p. 192, Bk. II, ch. xiv). Fielding ridicules both the abuse of reason, the false prudence of politic characters like Blifil and Jonathan Wild who reduce right reason to Hobbesian "reckoning," and the abuse of faith, "the pernicious principles of Methodism" he attacks in Tom Jones (p. 361, Bk.

VIII, ch. viii). As Parson Adams says in his repudiation of Whitefield's theology, "the detestable doctrine of faith against good works" was coined in hell: it leads to such <u>non sequiturs</u> as, "Lord, it is true I never obeyed one of thy commandments, yet punish me not, for I believe them all" (p. 82, Bk. I, ch. xvii). Fielding's orthodox views on the harmony of reason and faith in theological matters, then, relates to his concept of Fortune as a logical mystique and Providence as an intelligible mystery--a notion that requires both understanding and belief, in the same way that Fielding's heroine, Sophia (<u>sophia</u>), means wisdom or knowledge and exemplifies the sublime or miraculous.

The idea of Providence in Richardson's <u>Pamela</u> and Defoe's <u>Robinson Crusoe</u>, which Fielding satirizes in <u>Joseph Andrews</u> and <u>Jonathan Wild</u> through the naive beliefs of Parson Adams and Mrs. Heartfree respectively, especially relates to fideistic religion. For, in their understanding of God's ways, Pamela, Crusoe, Adams, and Mr. and Mrs. Heartfree either divorce belief from knowledge or separate works from faith. Fielding rejects the oversimplifications of Providence which often result from fideism, such as the virtue-rewarded formula of Richardson or the predestination view in <u>Robinson Crusoe</u>. For example, when Pamela quotes the chain of being notion of Providence in the following lines, it shows how Richardson conceives of God's government as a simplistic idea rather than as a wonderful miracle:

>   Wise Providence
> <u>Does various parts for</u> various mind dispense:
> The <u>meanest slaves</u>, or those who <u>hedge and ditch</u>,
> Are <u>useful</u>, by their sweat, to feed the <u>rich</u>. (p. 272)

Richardson further reduces Providence to a categorical system when, at the end of the novel, he cites Mr. Williams as clear proof that "Providence will at last reward . . . piety" and presents Pamela's parents as undeniable evidence to show that "Providence never fails to reward . . . honesty and integrity" and offers Pamela as a conclusive exemplum to teach "that no danger or distress . . . can be out of the power of Providence to obviate or relieve" (pp. 530-31). In the case of <u>Robinson Crusoe</u> the protagonist depicts his shipwreck and solitude on the island as entirely a matter of God's absolute, arbitrary command, not as the misuse of his own free will or the consequence of his own imprudence. Exaggerating God's powerful hand in his own history, Crusoe diminishes man's actions and choices and resigns himself to the decrees of Fate. He writes in his journal (June 28): " . . . God had appointed all this to befall me; that I was brought to this miserable circumstance by His direction, he having the sole power, not of me only, but of everything that happened in the world" (p. 94, "I Am Very Ill and Frightened"). Fielding satirizes these reductionist ideas of Providence by showing how Parson Adams and the Heartfrees manipulate this concept without understanding it; how their glib use of expressions like "trust in Providence," "the will of God," "God disposes all things for the best" renders them meaningless cliches, not rich commonplaces. Fielding portrays the folly of the naive providential view when Adams exhorts Joseph to submit and resign himself to the will of God yet finds himself unable to accept the disposition of Providence when he hears about the drowning of his young son. Fielding also ridicules this simplistic version of God in <u>Jonathan Wild</u> when Heartfree returns home and is shocked at the sudden disappearance of his wife. Forthwith, instead of acting to learn of her whereabouts, he commences a long soliloquy on the <u>de contemptu mundi</u> topos and rationalizes in Stoic fashion that neither he nor his children have reason for sorrow: "Why, the same Being to whose goodness and power I entrust my own happiness is likewise as able and as willing to procure theirs" (p. 118, Bk. III, ch. ii). Relying solely on faith and trusting naively in Providence, these simple-minded believers ignore prudence or right reason, practical knowledge about the here and the now, and they restrict man's active role in creating his own history by confusing Providence with Fate. Unlike Crusoe, Adams, or Heartfree, Fielding's magnanimous heroes, such as Allworthy, Wilson, and Amelia synthesize reason (prudence) with faith (trust in Providence) and live an active life full of charitable "works," not sola fide.

In addition to clashing with conceptions of science and religion, the nature of Providence in Fielding's novels also opposes the grandiose philosophies of history that abounded in the eighteenth century, such as the theory of progress espoused by the Philosophes, which envisioned utopias and foresaw the future as an upward and onward journey; the Great Man theory of history expressed by Cardinal Richelieu's gesture of striking out the word "unfortunate" from the dictionary, the interpretation of history that Fielding satirizes in Jonathan Wild; and the myth of objectivity and detachment perpetuated by the chronologist and antiquarian who associate Truth with the accumulation of facts and data. Directly or indirectly, Fielding's novels as "histories" attack all of these misconceptions. For example, the nature of the journey in Tom Jones and Joseph Andrews, the circuitous course followed by the protagonists on the road to London, their various peregrinations off the main road, their experiences of going off course, losing direction, or getting lost in the night indicate that the history of Tom Jones or Joseph Andrews is no clear, easy climb from low to high, no smooth, quick ascent from poverty to riches as in the case of Richardson's Pamela. The fact that evil in the form of a cruel squire interrupts the pastoral existence of Wilson's country life, which reminds Parson Adams of the golden age, and the fact that Blifil's machinations occur at "Paradise Hall" both shatter the idea of an earthly utopia, the shallow optimism of the theory of progress.[9] Likewise, Fielding also denies the Great Man view of history which, in its view of life as a game of chess rather than hazard, eliminates both Fortune and Providence and regards success as a matter of shrewd calculation and politic prudence. All the Great Man or Jonathan Wild types in Fielding's novels who cross out the word "unfortunate" from their dictionary, however, experience "the insults of Fortune" or "the interposition of Providence" as a result of their hubris. Fireblood's ironic betrayal of his famous teacher, Jonathan Wild; Joseph's unbelievable punctilio about his male chastity in Lady Booby's bedroom; Sophia's shocking escape to avoid marriage with Blifil; and Robinson's accidental meeting with Amelia and his sudden confession of Murphy's fraud can all be viewed as God's punishment or judgment in history, as wonderful acts of justice that further prove the Interposition of Providence, as Fielding entitles his minor work on the nature of divine intervention in matters of crime. Dr. Harrison's quotation from Homer at the end of Amelia reinforces the idea: "If Jupiter doth not immediately execute his vengeance, he will however execute it at last" (p. 306, Bk. XII, ch. viii).

Finally, Fielding takes to task the chronologist and the antiquarian who measure the truth of history by the amount of verifiable data, facts, and statistics which they amass. Fielding refers to the chronologist in Tom Jones (p. 40, Bk. II, ch. i) as "the painful and voluminous historian, who, to preserve the regularity of his series, thinks himself obliged to fill up as much paper with the detail of months and years in which nothing remarkable happened, as he employs upon those notable eras when the greatest scenes have been transacted upon the human stage." That is, the chronologist who models his work upon a mechanical conception of order, a clock or a calendar, overlooks the Wonderful events of history and confines his narrative to a rigid system. Like the scientist who discovers all the missing links in the great chain of being and eliminates all chasms or empty spaces, the chronologist, in the "regularity of his series," leaves no blank pages or open dates--a practice that Fielding ridicules in Jonathan Wild when the historian delivers a pompous apology for "a blank in this history," the hiatus of an unduly short chapter dealing with Wild's early travels (p. 43, Bk. I, ch. vii). Just as the chain of being in the eighteenth century eliminates mystery or surprise, the chronologist omits the sense of the Marvellous in history, never distinguishing the "remarkable" or "extraordinary" actions from the insignificant episodes. In defiance of the chronological method of narrative, Fielding claims that the history of Tom Jones will sometimes stand still and sometimes fly and will emphasize "what really happened" instead of what time or date it is. Imitating Homer's epic style throughout his work, with the in medias res beginnings, the flashbacks into the past, the projections into the future--as seen, for example, when Odysseus recites his adventures to King Alcinous and when Wilson narrates his history to Parson Adams--Fielding avoids the pseudo-scientific, documentary style of Defoe and Richardson who carefully record dates and observe an exact chronological sequence. As a narrator Fielding shuns Richardson's guise of editor-novelist and Defoe's pose as the factual historian.

It is clear, then, why Fielding in Tom Jones vows to write a "history," not a "system." In rejecting these different scientific, religious, and historical schemes, which either exclude, delimit, or oversimplify the sense of the Wonderful, Fielding emancipates himself from the univocal view of an idee fixe or grandiose generalization, the "one certain method" or "unerring rule or right" that he exposes in his novels. The mathematical methodology and scientific technique that view all matters as problems to be solved with a definitive answer fail to distinguish between the puzzle that is to be solved once and for all and the mystery or miracle that constantly creates wonder. Whereas these various systems of thought in science, religion, and history all try to provide final, conclusive answers, as reflected in the well-known catch phrases--virtue-rewarded, rape Fortune, trust in Providence, sola fide, Whatever is, is right, return to nature--or attempt an exhaustive, comprehensive treatment, such as the plenitude of the chain of being and the corresponding fullness of the chronological history, Fielding's novels do not provide ultimate solutions to the riddles of the universe. Rather they present partial glimpses into the mystery of being which is penetrated by the divinity of Fortune and the miracles of Providence--a deeper insight, a more subtle possession, a more intimate familiarity with a reality that is limitless, inexhaustible, and teeming in its fullness, as plenteous as the "feast" of Nature that Fielding describes in the beginning of Tom Jones. In keeping with this idea of the inexplicable, the boundless or immeasurable aspect of the Marvellous, Fielding ends his novels on a strong note of wonder, not in a tone of certainty --wonder in the traditional sense of being in suspense as to the cause, being unable to explain completely the surprising, coincidental events. In Aristotle's words, "And a man who is puzzled and wonders thinks himself ignorant . . . " (Metaphysics, 982b). Although the conclusions of Fielding's novels depict the revelation of the "full secret" of Joseph's parentage, Tom's birth, and Amelia's legacy, these discoveries are not intended as the last phase or final solution of a detective mystery but as the experience of a miracle which brings on wonder, the first step toward knowledge, the beginning of all philosophy as Plato says in the "Theaetetus." That is, the ignorance of the man who wonders whets his intellectual appetite and excites inquiry; it is only partial knowledge of a great subject or profound mystery, not the skeptical doubt expressed in Montaigne's "Que sais-je?" According to St. Albert the Great's explication of Aristotle's idea of wonder: "Hence wonder is the movement of the man who does not know on his way to finding out, to get at the bottom of that at which he wonders and to determine its cause" (Commentary on the Metaphysics of Aristotle, II, 6).[10]

This type of movement and inquiry characterizes the conclusions of Fielding's novels. Thus at the end of <u>Tom Jones</u>, when Tom's true history is disclosed and Blifil's villainy is uncovered, Allworthy finds himself rapt in amazement in his meeting with Mrs. Waters: "'I need not, madame,' said Allworthy, 'express my astonishment at what you have told me; and yet surely you would not, and could not, have put together so many circumstances to evidence an untruth.'" He continues to show this astonishment when he senses the handiwork of Providence; he remarks, "Good heaven! by what wonderful means is the blackest and deepest villainy sometimes discovered" (p. 846, p. 847, Bk. XVIII, ch. vii). Similarly, Fielding describes Wilson's state of mind at the end of <u>Joseph Andrews</u> as in a condition of awe. When he hears the mention of a stolen child and a strawberry birthmark, he is so thunderstruck that he both cries and rejoices at the same time: " . . . abandoning himself to the most extravagant rapture of passion, he embraced Joseph with inexpressible ecstasy, and cried out in tears of joy, 'I have discovered my son, I have him again in my arms'" (p. 415, Bk. IV, ch. xv). Likewise, in the final chapters of <u>Amelia</u>, when Dr. Harrison learns the strange truth that Booth and Amelia are the heirs of Mrs. Harris's estate, he waits before he tells Amelia, "for this wise and good man was fearful of making such a discovery all at once to Amelia, lest it should overpower her . . . " (p. 302, Bk. XII, ch. vii). When Amelia is eventually told about her marvellous good fortune, she grows faint, needs to sit down, and asks for a glass of water. This experience of shock, excitement, or awakening that Allworthy, Wilson, and Amelia undergo when they come in contact with the Marvellous is best described in St. Albert the Great's <u>Commentary on the Metaphysics of Aristotle</u>:

> Now, wonder is defined as a constriction and suspension of the heart caused by the amazement at the sensible appearance of something so portentous, great, and unusual, that the heart suffers a systole. This effect of wonder, then, this constriction and systole of the heart,

springs from an unfulfilled but felt desire to know the cause of that which appears portentous and unusual.[11]

Thus whereas the "systems" of science, religion, and history diminish the importance of miracles, the role of Fortune, or the status of Providence, Fielding's novels reassert the Marvellous. Instead of acknowledging the dearth of the Wonderful, Fielding depicts its plethora. That is, he comments that wonder is not only superabundant at the climax of a plot but also profuse at the beginning and middle of a good story that imitates Nature: " . . . every writer may be permitted to deal <u>as much</u> in the wonderful as he pleases; nay if he <u>thus</u> keeps within the rules of credibility, the <u>more</u> he can surprise the reader the more he will engage him (<u>Tom Jones</u>, p. 338, Bk. VIII, ch. i; italics mine). Wonder is plentiful throughout a man's life, increasing with age rather than ending in childhood., Unlike the Stoic who associated wisdom with the attitude of <u>nil admirari</u> and regarded a forty year old man as above the astonishment of a child, Fielding's heroes, like Allworthy, Wilson, and Amelia--who all embody true wisdom and the cardinal virtue of prudence--continue to be amazed in their old age or maturity. Also the Wonderful, superabounding in nature and history, is ubiquitous in the lives of <u>all</u> men, in the "histories" of the minor characters in each novel, such as the man of the hill and Mrs. Fitzpatrick, as well as in the lives of the heroes. Thus Fielding, who uses the comic-epic mode, is in a sense writing an informal theodicy in his novels--justifying the ways of God to man and "to the hight of this great argument," to borrow Milton's famous phrase, asserting eternal Providence, defending the Judaeo-Christian view of history from the scientific, religious, and historical misconceptions of Providence that prevailed during the eighteenth century.

B. Science

Whereas the new science posited a general providence that ordered the universe, it denied the idea of a particular providence that cared for all individuals. God's activity, relegated to Nature or to the act of creation, did not interfere in history, in the lives of each and every person. Hence the new science challenged the Biblical conception of God as numbering the hairs on the heads of all men, as providing for the lilies of the field and the birds of the air, and caring for the least among men. Fielding, however, shows that God's Providence is both general and particular and thus affirms the Biblical view of Providence. As M. C. D'Arcy states the idea in The Meaning and Matter of History:

> In the Christian dispensation, Providence is looked upon as both universal and particular. As particular it means that every individual is cared for . . . . As universal, it means that though history is made by the co-operation and clash of human wills, God works in and through it, so that His purposes are fulfilled. This is the idea of Providence which has prevailed in the West and wherever Christianity has penetrated, and it lies behind the attempts of various Christian thinkers in the past to sketch a providential view of history.[12]

Fielding's minor work, Interposition of Providence, especially stresses God's government as a particular providence interested in the lives of individual men. Citing numerous examples from various religious works and other pieces of literature, Fielding shows the active intervention and special concern of Providence in the detection and punishment of murder. God's omniscience, which penetrates all places and watches all men and overlooks no detail, exposes the most secretive, cunning acts through secondary causes and natural means. Fielding speaks of the crime of murder as a vice that especially prompts the intervention of Providence: "The divine providence hath been pleased to interpose in a more immediate manner in the detection of this crime than any other." By "the most unaccountable, indeed miraculous means," by "preternatural interpositions," by "a supernatural and miraculous interposition of Providence," wonderful acts of justice are effected.[13] The source of amazement lies in the strange, unexpected, and unsystematic manner that villainy is often detected--the endless variety of ways and means that Providence utilizes as natural agents and secondary causes to effect its purposes. For instance, in example No. 7 two murderers, many years after the crime, have a violent quarrel in a public place where they accuse each other of the crime. In example No. 25 a murderer tries to put others off his scent by pretending great enthusiasm for discovering the villain and by always carrying a picture of the criminal. However, "His noisy assiduity was observed by a sagacious person . . . ." Another story, example No. 13, depicts an avaricious innkeeper who murders a rich jeweler sojourning at his inn. He then lies and claims that the jeweler died of natural causes when the doctor investigates the death. However, a wolf digs up the corpse; men find the body and take it to the physician who recognizes the true cause of death and accuses the innkeeper. Thus the way that God brings justice to individual criminals in <u>Interposition of Providence</u> or to particular villains in Fielding's novels, such as Blifil, Murphy, and Wild, indicates how divine Providence reflects the same ultimate concern for the life of a single man as for the general harmony of the universe.

This is also the tenor of Fielding's novels, where Providence appears not only in the life of the hero but also in the histories of the minor characters. In <u>Tom Jones</u> two seemingly insignificant characters, the man of the hill and Mrs. Waters, are blessed by divine favor in their marvellous luck, a boon of the same order at Tom's good fortune with Sophia. When Tom rescues the man of the hill from thieves who threaten to murder him, the hero offers the following reflection: "Having missed our way this cold night, we took the liberty of warming ourselves at your fire . . . when we heard you call for assistance, which I must say, Providence alone seems to have sent you" (p. 375, Bk. VIII, ch. x). Likewise, after he saves Mrs. Waters from hanging and rescues her from Northerton, Tom again gives a providential interpretation to the event: "He presently lifted her up and told her he was highly pleased with the extraordinary accident which had sent him thither for her relief, where it was improbable she should find any; adding that Heaven seemed to have designed him as the happy instrument of her protection" (p. 419, Bk. IX, ch. ii). Another example of a particular providence that cares for even the most wretched among men is the episode of the robbery that occurs when Tom Jones and Partridge are journeying from St. Albans to London (p. 593, Bk. XII, ch. xiv). A desperate highwayman, who is later discovered to be Anderson, threatens to shoot Tom unless he delivers the £100 bank note. Refusing to part with Sophia's money, Tom knocks the pistol from the robber's hand and wrestles him to the ground. However, when Tom learns that Anderson attempted the robbery because of the distress and hunger of his five children, Tom not only forgives him but also offers him money to support his starving family--a magnanimous act of generosity, "an act of extraordinary humanity" which so amazes the highwayman that he is brought to the verge of tears. Thus when Providence interposes to befriend men with the surprise of luck, God offers his gifts to all men of all ranks, not to just a few favorites, and extends his love everywhere: to the orphan left in Allworthy's bedroom at Sommersetshire; to the helpless Mrs. Waters attacked at night in the woods; to the unmarried, pregnant Nancy Miller in London. Similarly, when Providence intervenes to detect crime or punish folly, it brings wonderful acts of justice to all men in all places: to Square whom Tom finds in Molly's bedroom; to Northerton whom Tom thoroughly thrashes when he rescues Mrs. Waters, thus repaying Northerton for the time the ensign threw a bottle at Tom's head; to Blifil whom Allworthy renounces as an heir when he learns the secret of his villainy. All these examples illustrate the particular providence of God. In the words of Boethius: "For Providence embraces all things equally, however diverse they are, however infinite."[14]

However, as mentioned earlier, the Christian idea of history holds that God's providence is universal as well as particular. It follows a general plan and acts according to an ultimate purpose, a <u>telos</u>. It involves the harmony of the one and the <u>many</u>. As St. Paul expresses the idea, all things co-operate for the good of those who love God. As <u>Paradise Lost</u> shows, Adam is rapt with wonder when he learns of the great plan behind God's general providence, the linear, teleological view of history that the archangel Michael reveals to him: the Incarnation; the crucifixion of Christ, the second Adam, who will redeem Adam's original sin; the defeat of Satan, Sin, and Death; and the return to an even happier Paradise. Because Adam sees meaning in history and hope in the future--in his own <u>individual</u> destiny as in the future of mankind in <u>general</u>, he exclaims, "O goodness infinite, goodness immense!/That all this good of evil shall produce" (XII, 11. 469-470). Or, as Boethius illustrates in <u>The Consolation of Philosophy</u>, the all-at-onceness (<u>tota simul</u>) of God's omniscient, comprehensive glance which views all events <u>sub specie aeternitatis</u> predicates a general providence or wise government of infinite scope.

Fielding's conception of a general providence seems to be a synthesis of the Old and New Testament, St. Paul, Boethius, Milton and eighteenth century providential apologetics found in the sermons of the clergyman Fielding most admired, "our favourite Dr. Barrow."[15] To begin with the Old Testament version of God's general providence: just as the Hebrews in Exodus leave their home in Egypt and wander in the wilderness like exiles, so too Joseph Andrews, dismissed by Lady Booby, and Tom Jones, expelled by Allworthy, leave their native abodes and lead the life of sojourners. In the same way that the exodus of the Jews often fails to make sense to them, as when they travel in the wilderness and murmur about the lack of food and the threat of the enemy, the journeys of Joseph and Tom also often appear to lack purpose and direction. Joseph's experience at Mrs. Tow-Wouse's inn and Tom's adventure at the inn at Upton mark moments of pell-mell confusion in their lives. This topsy-turvy chaos is especially revealed at Upton where blind chance, not God's government, seems to rule: the goal of each character who arrives at the inn is within sight, yet the special purpose of all these journeys goes unrealized. Squire Western, in mad pursuit of Sophia, just barely misses his daughter; Mr. Fitzpatrick, who is actually in the same house with the wife he has chased all over Ireland and England, fails to discover her; the object of Tom's life, Sophia, is also present at the inn, but Tom is too late in recognizing that fact. It seems as if Whirl, not Providence, is king. Finally just as the Hebrews are led to the Promised Land by a long roundabout course and not by the more direct King's Highway, so too Joseph discovers his father and Tom finds Sophia by following devious paths and byways. Diverted by the sound of robbers from the main thoroughfare that leads back to Booby Parish, Adams and Joseph descend a hill that directs them to Wilson's home and makes possible the reunion of father and son. Distracted from the road to Bristol by a poor guide who loses the way, Tom is delayed in following his desire to go to sea. Then, thrown off course by Mrs. Waters' cry for help, Tom is retarded in his second goal, fighting for the Protestant cause in the North. Then, going out of his way to accompany Mrs. Waters to a safe lodging, Tom arrives at Upton, where Sophia's journey crosses his path and leads him toward his true destiny. The _telos_ of history is often accomplished, not by systematic advances, but by strange peregrinations full of wonderful providential surprises that afford revelations of the general plan and hidden purpose. As Lady Philosophy explains in The Consolation of Philosophy (p. 90), " . . . what may seem unjust confusion in the affairs of men is directed by Providence toward the good." Indeed the journeys of Tom Jones and Joseph Andrews are as winding and as purposive as the course of the water that flows through Allworthy's estate and as the pilgrimage of the Hebrews in Exodus.

Although the journey often appears aimless or retrogressive, it has both a definite end for the sojourner and an ultimate purpose that involves the lives of many others besides the history of the traveler. For example, according to the Christian philosophy of history, the story of the Jews, the chosen people, goes beyond that race of people to embrace all men. According to the divine promise given Abraham, "And your descendants shall possess the gate of their enemies, and by your descendants shall all the nations of the earth blass themselves" (Genesis 22:17-18). That is, the history of the Jews indicates that God's Providence is a particular one with regard to the Hebrews and a general one with regard to mankind. As Saint Augustine puts the matter in the City of God (Bk. X, ch. xxxii): "This way does not belong, then, to one but to all nations; and the Law and the Word of the Lord did not remain in Sion and Jerusalem, but went forth that it might spread throughout the world."[16] Likewise, the history of Tom Jones brings happiness not only to the hero but also to a host of major and minor characters: to Sophia, to Allworthy, to Squire Western, to Mrs. Miller, to Nightingale, to Mrs. Waters, to Partridge, to Anderson, etc. By the same token the history of Joseph Andrews transcends the marital bliss of Joseph and Fanny and diffuses joy into the lives of Mr. and Mrs. Wilson, Gammer and Gaffer Andrews, Parson Adams, and the pedlar. Just as everyone eventually arrives at a commonplace, London, in Tom Jones and just as everyone gathers at another general meeting place, Booby Parish, at the end of Joseph Andrews, so too one history affects many lives. As Fielding's last sentence in Tom Jones reads, " . . . there is not a neighbor, a tenant, or a servant, who doth not most gratefully bless the day when Mr. Jones was married to his Sophia." In this way Providence creates a kind of universal history and appears at the end of Fielding's novels as general in its care for all men as well as particular in its concern for the hero. Thus Fielding's view of Providence contradicts the Newtonian or deistic version that eliminates God from history and confines Him to Nature.

C. Religion

Just as Fielding attempts to rescue the Christian idea of history from the scientific notion of Providence--God as an unmysterious being, a clear and distinct general idea, a self-evident "unerring rule of right"--so too he tries to free it of the superstition and irrationality connected with the fideistic conception of Providence, that is, God as an inscrutable, cryptic deity; God as absolute, arbitrary Will rather than true right Reason--the doctrine of voluntarism held by such thinkers as William of Ockham, Duns Scotus, Luther, and Calvin.[17] As stated throughout Chapter II, Fielding represents Fortune, the handmaiden of Providence as "intelligibly mysterious," not as darkly unfathomable. To put it another way, as Etienne Gilson suggests in The Unity of Philosophical Experience, " . . . if we do not know God, the reason is not that God is obscure, but rather that He is a blinding light."[18] Or, as Lady Philosophy remarks in The Consolation of Philosophy, distinguishing between the divine and human mode of knowledge, "Therefore whoever seeks the truth knows something: he is neither completely informed nor completely ignorant" (p. 108). It is this half-revealed, half-concealed open secret that creates the experience of bedazzlement at the end of Fielding's novels where the Wonderful is not irrational but beyond reason, where the effect is clear but the cause remains hidden. Ending on a note of revelation, the clarity of Fielding's novels toward their conclusions resembles the illumination of the sun that exceeds the limits of human vision, not the lucidity of a geometrical proof that is commensurate with human reason. Thus it is important to distinguish between the darkness of the truly Marvellous, which is always commingled with light, and the darkness of superstition, which is pure unrelieved obscurity. Likewise, the ignorance of one who wonders as the first step toward philosophy needs to be differentiated from the ignorance of the credulous person who believes in ghosts.

In the characters of Partridge, Parson Adams, and Heartfree Fielding portrays the irrationality of the naive providential view that portrays God as Fate, a Will without Reason. Just as all three characters lack right reason or true prudence and hence are dominated by will or passion--the psychology of voluntarism where, to use Shakespeare's phrase, "reason panders will"--so likewise their conception of Providence portrays God as governed by His will rather than by His reason; a deity Who does what he pleases or likes rather than what is just or in accordance with natural law and right reason. In Partridge's case the passion of fear constantly overrules his rationality. Relying on his own "inner light," so to speak, and disregarding Tom Jones' common sense observations, Partridge emerges as a kind of mad enthusiast who imagines ghosts, witches, and demons. When he and Tom arrive at the man of the hill's cottage at a time of total darkness, Partridge regards the old woman housekeeper as a witch. When they approach the Gypsies, again in the dead of night, Partridge remarks, "They can be nothing but ghosts or witches, or some evil spirits or other, that's certain," and adds, "for, sure, such darkness was never seen upon earth, and I question whether it can be darker in the other world" (p. 580, Bk. XII, ch. xii). Partridge's fear or awe is of course a species of Gothic terror, the pseudo wonder of sensationalism divorced from knowledge or "light." Hence Partridge's superstition is usually aroused at night when total darkness or Partridge's ignorance prevails. Confusing the Monstrous with the Marvellous, Partridge sees an irrational, freakish Supernature that is as arbitrary and foolish as Partridge himself. Just as Partridge's whim decides to call the Gypsies demons or to interpret a dream of riding on a white mare as a sign of good fortune, so too in his story Providence acts in the same preposterous, willful way. The tale that Partridge narrates to Tom and the man of the hill tells about Frank, a young man who apprehended a thief. After the thief is hanged, poor Frank is haunted by spectres until one night, "in a long, narrow, dark lane," the thief's ghost waylays and beats him. Thus, associating Supernature with tangible forms like ghosts, witches, and demons and with certain definite times of the day, such as nighttime, and prophesying future events through dreams, Partridge reduces the Marvellous to a formula, a pseudo science like alchemy of astrology. While Partridge's inscrutable Supernature differs radically from Square's clear ideas, both occultism and the new science seek a final, univocal answer to the mystery of being and presume that their all-encompassing theories represent infallible truth. When Tom laughs at the ridiculous ghost story, Partridge defends it as an absolute certainty: "Besides, Frank told me he knew it to be a spirit, and could swear to him in any court in Christendom" (p. 387, Bk. VIII, ch. xi).

In his encounter with thieves at night Parson Adams in Joseph Andrews also lets reason pander will and allows his irrational fear of the robbers to conjure up ghosts in his imagination: "And did you not mark how it vanished?" cries he: "though I am not afraid of ghosts, I do not absolutely disbelieve them" (p. 387, Bk. III, ch. ii). As a victim of superstition and Gothic terror Adams contradicts all of his sound Boethian statements about the rationality of Providence. There is a reason or purpose for everything that happens, Adams explains to Joseph after Fanny has been kidnapped. To quote from Adams' simplified version of The Consolation of Philosophy:

> Joseph, if you are wise, and truly know
> your own interest, you will peaceably and
> quietly submit to all dispensations of
> Providence, being thoroughly assured,
> that all the misfortunes, how great so-
> ever, which happen to the righteous, hap-
> pen to them for their own good.

Adams insists that there is a divine rationale for the vicissitudes of Fortune, despite man's inability to see God's plan:

> for as we know not future events so
> neither can we tell to what purpose any
> accident tends; . . .
>
> . . . for as we know not to what purpose
> any event is ultimately directed; so
> neither can we affirm from what cause it
> originally sprung. (pp. 314-315, Bk. III,
> ch. xi)

However, in emphasizing the supreme intelligibility and divine wisdom of God's Providence, Adams oversimplifies the problem of evil and comforts Joseph like one of Job's friends: "You are a man, and consequently a sinner; and this may be a punishment to you for your sins." Thus Adams eliminates the mystery of God's justice, what Garrigou-Lagrange in his book Providence calls "the Divine Incomprehensibility," a phrase that aptly describes Job's encounter with God: "so much that is transparently clear to us and at the same time so much that is profoundly obscure."[19] In his counsel to Joseph, Adams admits man's ignorance and Providence's incomprehensibility ("we know not to what purpose any event is ultimately directed"), yet he contradicts his own words. For Adams acts omniscient and denies the mystery of suffering when he tries to connect Joseph's misfortune to his sin. Like righteous Job, good-natured Joseph, who has just fought like a great-souled hero in an epic battle to defend Fanny from kidnappers, exclaims: "Oh! you have not spoken one word of comfort to me yet!" (p. 315, Bk. III, ch. xi).

Remembering from The Consolation of Philosophy the tenet of Lady Philosophy that all fortune is good, Adams forgets that only from the divine point of view, sub specie aeternitatis, does this truth make complete sense. From the limited human perspective, as Joseph explains in the lines he quotes from Shakespeare:

> Yes, I will bear my sorrows like a man
> But I must also feel them as a man
> I cannot but remember such things were
> And were most dear to me. (p. 316, Bk. III, ch. xi)

The view of Providence, then, shared by Job's friends, Adams, and naive providentialists like Robinson Crusoe is simply a version of the virtue-rewarded, vice-punished formula of Richardson. It detracts from the divine incomprehensibility, the conception of Providence as both rational and unknowable, as both intelligible and mysterious. As Boethius comments on the paradox:

> "This is an old difficulty about Providence," Philosophy answered . . . . "The cause of the obscurity which still surrounds the problem is that the process of human reason cannot comprehend the simplicity of divine foreknowledge." (p. 108)

Or, as Saint Augustine illuminates the problem in the City of God:

> God often shows His intervention more clearly by the way He apportions the sweet and the bitter. For if He visited every sin here below with manifest penalty, it might be thought that no score remained to be settled at the Last Judgment. On the other hand, if God did not plainly enough punish sins on earth, people might conclude that there is no such thing as Divine Providence. So, too, in regard to the good things of life. If God did not bestow them with

patent liberality on some who ask Him, we could possibly argue that such things did not depend on His power. On the other hand, if He lavished them on all who asked, we might have the impression that God is to be served only for the gifts He bestows. (p. 46, Bk. I, ch. viii)

It is significant that Fielding criticizes the doctrine that "virtue is the certain road to happiness and vice to misery, in this world" as an unchristian idea because it "is indeed destructive of one of the noblest arguments that reason alone can furnish for the belief of immortality" (<u>Tom Jones</u>, p. 691, Bk. XV, ch. i). In other words, the wonderful interpositions of Providence and the miracles of Fortune in human life do not complete the work of justice.

Like Partridge and Parson Adams, Mr. and Mrs. Heartfree in <u>Jonathan Wild</u> also manipulate the concept of Supernature. When Heartfree discovers the sudden disappearances of his wife, he does not grieve over the fact or view it as an evil, tragic event--in the way that Joseph bemoans the loss of his Fanny. Instead Heartfree rationalizes the evil into good: the death or elopement of his wife does not strike him as a loss of human life but as a lesson in the vanity of human wishes. Comparing a man's delight in his wife to a child's pleasure with a toy, to a "bubble in the water" and "a picture in the clouds," Heartfree regards his sorrow with Stoic apathy and decides to wonder at nothing: "The delights of most men are as childish and as superficial as that of my little girl; a feather or a fiddle are their pursuits and their pleasures through life, ever to their ripest years, if such men may be said to attain any ripeness at all" (p. 116, Bk. III, ch. ii). After showing a contempt of the world where Fate reigns ("How mean a tenure is that at the will of Fortune, which chance, fraud, and rapine are every day so likely to deprive us of"). Heartfree than meditates on the glories of heaven, "those beautiful mansions" where Providence presides. That is, he confines Providence to the afterlife and thus divorces God from history. Instead of viewing Fortune as the handmaiden of Providence, he esteems her as the supreme ruler in human affairs--a goddess whose whimsical antics require Stoic indifference. When Heartfree examines the lot of his children without a mother, he rationalizes partial evil into universal good: "The hind may be more happy than the lord, for his desires are fewer, and those such as are attended with more hope and less fear" (p. 118, Bk. III, ch. ii). Experimenting with different theories to explain the problem of evil and suffering, Heartfree, in this long soliloquy, shifts from Stoic to mystic to deist. Thus Heartfree either equates Providence with a Fate that he cannot resist except by Stoic apathy, or he relegates God to a supernatural realm that awaits him after death, or he systematizes Providence in accordance with deism where this life is the best of all possible worlds. Mrs. Heartfree, on the other hand, portrays Providence as a <u>deus ex machina</u> that will always intervene to befriend the helpless. Saved from rape by hairbreadth escapes time and again in an episodic series of improbable adventures on the sea, Mrs. Heartfree "providentially" eludes the lust of Jonathan Wild, the French Count, an English captain, a hermit, and a chief magistrate. The moral of her story, as she explains in her <u>non sequitur</u>, is that "PROVIDENCE WILL SOONER OR LATER PROCURE THE FELICITY OF THE VIRTUOUS AND INNOCENT" (p. 201, Bk. IV, ch. xi).

In all of these simplified accounts of Providence, human free will is denied or minimized. Man is not regarded as a being who co-operates with Providence and shapes his history through intelligent choices and active, charitable works. The Boethian notion that "divine Providence does not preclude freedom of the will"--an important point also in <u>Paradise Lost</u> ("Our voluntary service he requires,/Not our necessitated," V, 11. 539-540)--is contradicted. For all these characters show either imprudence in their decisions or apathy in their actions. Partridge, fearing ghosts, wants to run in the opposite direction when he hears cries for help; Parson Adams counsels resignation and submission when Joseph wants to pursue Fanny; Heartfree imitates the self-sufficiency and wise indifference of the Stoic; and Mrs. Heartfree is completely passive as she is buffeted here and there on the ocean. In one form or another these naive providentialists separate reason from faith or intellect from will or works from faith. Partridge and Adams' belief in ghosts, Heartfree's faith in an afterlife, Mrs. Heartfree's trust in Providence can all be classified as forms of "fideism" or mysticism devoid of reason. By their blind faith in the power of witches (Partridge), Fate (Heartfree), or Providence (Adams and Mrs. Heartfree) as the sole forces in the universe or history, they depreciate the role of human responsibility and hence the value of moral works. When they do act, as when Mrs. Heartfree trusts Jonathan Wild and goes to Holland with jewels to rescue her husband or as when Parson Adams rushes out of bed without any clothes on to answer a woman's cry of "rape!"--the naive providentialists act with good will and noble intentions but not with the prudence associated with intellect or right reason. As good-natured but imprudent fools, they depict characters of sensibility, not sense, who embody Shaftesbury's idea of benevolence: virtue as an instinct of natural affections seated in the will rather than a principle of conscience that resides in the mind; the sentimental notion of "the mighty good heart" rather than the classical-Christian concept that "virtue is knowledge."

As briefly discussed in Chapter II, Fielding's novels show that man's history involves the riddle of chance and choice, the co-operation of Providence and free will, the exercise of right reason as well as a hope in the future and a trust in Providence. The ideal of magnanimity treated in Chapter III reveals that Fielding's heroes and heroines embody both the natural cardinal virtues of prudence, justice, fortitude, and temperance and the supernatural theological virtues of faith, hope, and charity--that is, a synthesis of nature (reason) and revelation (faith). Since these ideas have been explored in the chapters on <u>Tom Jones</u> and <u>Amelia</u>, it suffices here to contrast the naive providential view of Fielding's good-natured, imprudent characters with the more orthodox Christian philosophy of history reflected by Fielding's heroes, the characters who combine classical right reason with Christian <u>agape</u>, that is, the view of Providence found in the Bible, <u>The Consolation of Philosophy</u>, and <u>Paradise Lost</u>-- Fielding's chief sources.

When Adams, Joseph, and Fanny suddenly arrive at the home of the Wilsons during the course of the night, it is a random occurrence. To avoid the robbers whom they have overheard or the apparitions that Adams imagines, they proceed off the main course until, by chance, Adams' foot slips and causes him to roll down a steep hill that brings them within sight of Wilson's cottage. However, out of this accidental misfortune or "fall" from high to low from the top of the hill to the bottom arises providential good luck; out of evil arises the good--the idea of the fortunate fall (<u>felix culpa</u>). As a result of Parson Adams' fall (evil) an even greater happiness (good) than a stranger's hospitality ensues. For as an indirect result and as an ultimate consequence of Adams' fall, the miraculous revelations at the end of the novel occur: Wilson finds his lost son, Joseph discovers his true father, and Fanny uncovers the real identity of her parents. Parson <u>Adams</u>' fall of course recalls Adam's Fall, the source of the <u>felix culpa</u> topos that Milton treats in <u>Paradise Lost</u>. When Adam recognizes his fortunate fall, he exclaims:

> O goodness infinite, goodness immense!
> That all this good of evil shall produce,
> And evil turn to good; more wonderful
> Then that which by creation first brought
>   forth
> Light out of darkness! (XII, ll. 469-478)

Fielding clearly incorporates the notion of the fortunate fall in Tom Jones as well as Joseph Andrews. For when Tom is expelled from Somersetshire or banished from "Paradise" hall, Fielding explicitly compares him to Milton's Adam: "The world, as Milton phrases it, lay all before him; and Jones, no more than Adam, had any man to whom he might resort for comfort or assistance" (p. 270, Bk. VII, ch. ii). However, just as Adam in the passage above views his redemption as "more wonderful" than his creation, so too Tom's deliverance from prison in his London adventures or "salvation," so to speak, at the end of the novel is even more miraculous than his strange birth in the opening scene of the novel.

The Biblical narrative of Joseph and his brethren, one of the sources of the history of Joseph Andrews, provides a Biblical analogue of the fortunate fall and reinforces this mystery of good coming from evil and Providence creating greater wonder in the future than in the past. Like the Biblical Joseph, the favorite son of his father, who was unexpectedly thrown into a pit by his brothers and then sold into slavery and finally condemned as a prisoner by Pharoah and Potiphar--Joseph Andrews, the especial servant of Lady Booby, also experiences the tragedy of the sudden fall from high to low. Stripped of his livery because he will not comply with Lady Booby's amorous advances and more than his namesake would lie with Potiphar's wife, Andrews is brusquely dismissed. Just as Joseph is thrown into a pit, sold as a slave, and reduced to a prisoner--falling from high to low to lowest--Andrews is discharged from his position, then robbed and beaten by thieves, and afterwards abused by Mrs. Tow-wouse, the innkeeper, as a naked vagabond. These experiences of Fielding's character and the Biblical Joseph represent categorical tragedies, the injustice of life. Like Job's suffering or Adam's Fall, like Joseph's loss of Fanny or Tom's exile from Somersetshire, they signify evils that cause despair--a temporary disbelief in Providence and a hopelessness about the future. That is, no one who actually suffers the tragedy of a fall quickly assents to the idea of a "fortunate" fall or "happy" sin, not even Parson Adams, for he experiences uncontrollable grief when he hears the report of his drowned son. When Joseph tries to comfort Adams by reiterating the parson's own famous words of consolation, "Yes, surely," says Joseph, "and in a better place, you will meet again never to part more," Adams pays no attention and continues crying. A fall strikes all men in the same way it affects Adams in this episode as he resembles Adam or Man in the way he suffers the universal human dilemma, responding in a natural way to tragedy-- acknowledging evil as evil and not calling it a disguised form of good or trying to be above pleasure and pain. Here, in his own personal loss, Adams responds like Job rather than Job's comforters, expressing the universal suffering of man that the cries of Milton's Adam and Tom Jones in their experiences of a fall also epitomize as well as Job:

> Thus <u>Adam</u> to himself lamented loud . . .
> . . . .
>   On the ground
> Outstrecht he lay, on the cold ground,
>   and oft
> Curs'd his Creation, Death as oft accus'd
> Of tardy execution, since denounc't
> The day of his offense. (<u>Paradise Lost</u>, X, 1. 845 ff.)

> Here he [Tom Jones] presently fell into the most violent agonies, tearing his hair from his head, and using most other actions which generally accompany fits of madness, rage, and despair. (p. 255, Bk. VI, ch. xii)

Thus, as the story of Joseph in Genesis and the history of Joseph Andrews and Tom Jones illustrate, Providence does not eliminate tragedy or prevent evil. Rather it undoes or amends the misfortunes precipitated by the folly and wickedness of men, "working wonderfully in and through history," to quote from William G. Pollard's Chance and Providence, "to transform and redeem the damage and hurt wrought in the world by the evil acts of sinful men and in the end accomplishing far more than could ever have been expected or hoped for."[20] In the Biblical story Joseph, after he saves his brothers and father from famine, says to his brothers after the death of Jacob, "As for you, you meant evil against me; but God meant it for good, to bring it about that many people should be kept alive, as they are today" (Genesis 50:19). In short, the paradox of the fortunate fall differs from the deistic tenet, the clear and distinct idea of "all partial evil, universal good" and the oversimplification of Boethius's statement that "All Fortune is good." Only from a providential point of view, from the "eternal now" of divine omniscience is the world a Divine Comedy. From the human experience of Adam and Job, of Joseph Andrews, Tom Jones, and Parson Adams, the sudden fall from high to low is always a tragedy that causes wonder at the mystery of suffering and the injustice of life. Thus when Parson Adams comforts Joseph with paraphrases from The Consolation of Philosophy and Heartfree rationalizes the disappearance of his wife as a disguised form of good, they both in essence eliminate the problem of evil and the incomprehensibility of Providence. This is the basic error of both the deists and the naive providentialists. As Boethius observes, "Only to divine power are evil things good, when it uses them so as to draw good effects from them" (p. 96; italics mine).

To say that good arises out of evil presupposes a prior tragedy that, from the human perspective, represents a categorical evil, not happiness in disguise. Because Providence has foreseen this fall, it can "provide" only because it has prescience. Thus Providence does not contradict free will as the naive providentialists imply. As Lady Philosophy remarks in The Consolation of Philosophy, "foreknowledge does not impose necessity on future events" (p. 109). This is also Augustine's point in his discussion of the *felix culpa* in the City of God:

> Here, too, God foresaw the fall, the disregard of His law, the desertion from Good, yet He left man's free choice unchecked, because He also foresaw to what good He would turn man's evil. (p. 509, Bk. XXII, ch. i)

In order for the miracle of the *felix culpa* to occur, the reality of evil must be acknowledged as an undeniable fact. It is only *after* a fall or tragedy, not as a direct result *of it* or a necessary consequence of the event, that good arises out of evil. That is, although God does not cause or create tragedy or equate evil with good, He permits the possibility of tragedy since He grants man free will--fallible freedom--man being, in Milton's phrase, sufficient to have stood or free to fall. Through the abuse of free will and right reason Joseph's brothers sell him into slavery, Lady Booby expels Joseph Andrews, and Blifil maligns Tom Jones. They all, in Joseph's phrase, "meant evil" to an innocent person. At the actual moment of the sudden fall there is of course no sense of any *felix culpa* as all the cries of grief cited earlier indicate. It is only in retrospect at the end of the story and in the fullness of time or history that Joseph can say "God meant it for good" or Milton's Adam can utter "That all this good of evil shall produce" or the dismissal of Joseph Andrews and the banishment of Tom Jones emerge as "fortunate" falls.

None of these wonderful events could be foreseen or predicted through human prescience. The hidden intentions of God, the subtle workings of Providence, the real meaning of history are not as simple or self-evident as Parson Adams and the Heartfrees believe or as clear and distinct as the deists suggest. "You are asking about the greatest of all mysteries," one of Lady Philosophy's answers to Boethius's questions about Providence, "one which can hardly be fully explained" (p. 90), is an attitude which the naive providentialists overlook. Assuming a kind of omniscience about divine matters, they reduce the <u>art</u> of God's government to a perfect science--as if they had unlocked the secrets of God's incomprehensibility in the same way that Newton uncovered the hidden laws of Nature. However, in Fielding's novels "the glory of God," to borrow Bacon's phrase, "is to conceal a thing," not to appear with the sensationalism of a <u>deus ex machina</u>: to camouflage Himself in the motley diversity of Fortune, the handmaiden of Providence in <u>The Consolation of Philosophy</u>, with all her ups and downs; to hide His deepest intentions by acting through human agents, natural means, and commonplace happenings; to make use of a boundless variety of ways and means--the ill-nature of Lady Booby who banishes Joseph as an outcast as well as the good-nature of Wilson who provides hospitality and welcomes Joseph into his home; the lowliness of a poor Merry Andrew who helps Tom find Sophia as well as the greatness of the magnanimous Allworthy who adopts Tom and his son; the comedy at the inn at Upton that inspires Tom to change his goal from joining the soldiers to finding Sophia as well as the tragedy of Tom's duel with Fitzpatrick that leads to Jenny Jones' revelation about his birth. This is the whole gist of Fielding's <u>Interposition of Providence</u>, where he shows the countless, inexhaustible natural ways and human instruments that Providence uses as secondary causes to reveal the crime of murder: the dog (example 1), the crane (example 12), the wolf (example 13); the stings of conscience (examples 2, 3, and 4); the mutual accusation of two murderers (example 7); a dream (example 22). This is also a central point in <u>The Consolation of Philosophy</u>, the multitude of instruments and agents that serve Providence:

> Therefore, whether Fate is carried out by divine spirits in the service of Providence, or by a soul, or by the whole activity of Nature, by the heavenly motion of the stars, by angelic virtue or diabolical cleverness, or by some or

all of these agents, one thing is certain: Providence is the immovable and simple form of all things which come into being . . . . It follows then, that everything which is subject to Fate is also subject to Providence, and that Fate itself is also subject to Providence. (p. 92)

In the example of Parson Adams' fortunate fall down the hill that leads him to Wilson's home, Fielding also shows how Fate or Fortune is subject to Providence and how Providence orders events through an amazing variety of means. The wonder accrues because a <u>small</u> incident (Adams' accidental slipping down a hill) eventually leads to a <u>great</u> revelation, because <u>confusion</u> (getting lost in the night) leads to a total <u>clarification</u>, because <u>evil</u> (the threat of robbers in the night) leads to <u>good</u>, and because the <u>playful</u> antics of Fortune help to accomplish the <u>serious</u> purposes of Providence. Along with these paradoxes the incident also illustrates what Boethius calls "the problem of Providence and free will" (p. 115). Lady Philosophy's point that "divine Providence does not preclude free will" (p. 108). Although Providence, through the agency of Fortune, directs events toward a happy ending, Wilson, by his hospitality and charity toward strangers, chooses to co-operate with the divine plan. God proposes; man disposes. Exercising right reason by ascertaining that Parson Adams is a true clergyman, not a robber disguised in a cassock, and that Joseph is the fiancé of Fanny, not her ravisher, Wilson couples prudence with good-nature and thus illustrates the difference between the true Fielding hero and the good-natured but imprudent providentialist. Trusting entirely in Providence and neglecting the role of right reason and human actions, the naive providentialists deny the paradox of freedom and Providence. For example, Wilson, as he explains to Adams in his history, conducted "the most diligent search" after the Gypsies stole his infant son whereas Parson Adams counseled Joseph to "peaceably and quietly submit to all the dispensations of Providence" (p. 315, Bk. III, ch. xi) after the squire's henchmen capture Fanny. Easily assuming that all falls are fortunate by their very nature and failing to perceive that tragedy or evil is but one of the agents of Providence and only sometimes a means of good, they deny the marvellous, wonderful art of Providence, which acts in the surprising and paradoxical and hidden ways spoken of in the Bible, Paradise Lost, and The Consolation of Philosophy, to name only the most primary sources of Fielding's Christian philosophy of history.

D. History

Fielding's novels also try to rescue the traditional Christian idea of Providence from the distortions of historians as well as from the misconceptions of science and religion. In Narrative Form in History and Fiction Leo Braudy observes how the period between 1700 and 1754 in England witnessed a dearth of significant historical writing. Partisan historians viewed events from their Tory or Whig bias, and of the hundred or so histories published during the first half of the century "most of these were either specialized studies of biblical and ecclesiastical history or bare chronologies."[21] Sensationalistic rogue's lives and criminal biographies were passed off as "histories," as W. R. Irwin's The Making of Jonathan Wild clearly shows. And in The Art of Biography in Eighteenth Century England Donald Stauffer notes the odd mixture of "sensationalism and research," "scandal and scholarship," "antiquarian zeal and pure vulgar curiosity" that characterized many eighteenth century histories and biographies.[22] It is in this context that Jonathan Wild satirizes contemporary practices of historians, for the novel is full of both the sensationalism of romance and the pedantry of scholarship, the improbable sea adventure of Mrs. Heartfree and the esoteric footnotes of the narrator-historian, such as his gloss on "hats."

To recall Fielding's major criticisms of histories, he blamed bare chronologies written by "the painful and voluminous historian"; the accumulation of data as Truth compiled by the pedantic scholar; the "systems," like the Great Man theory, imposed by partial historians; and the rejection of the Marvellous in history, the elements of Providence and Fortune, in the names of scientific objectivity. Through the character or persona of the biographer in <u>Jonathan Wild</u> Fielding attacks all of these errors of historians. First, Fielding mocks the bare chronology type of narration. In chapter II of the novel the historian provides a lengthy, tedious, matter-of-fact account of Jonathan Wild's genealogy, tracing his ancestry from the time of the Anglo-Saxons to the recent history of the Wild family. Written in the style of "Mathematical Plainness" that follows the ideal of clarity proposed by the Royal Society--"the primitive purity, and shortness, when men deliver'd so many <u>things</u>, almost in an equal number of <u>words</u>"-- the whole passage adheres to the criteria of the famous Royal Society statute on language (1728): " . . . the Matter of Fact shall be barely stated, without any Prefaces, Apologies, or Rhetorical Flourishes . . . ." Thus, piling fact upon fact in the most prosaic style, the historian relates the lineage of the Wild family tree and encompasses a period of several hundred years in a matter of a few pages. Then, proceeding in exact chronological sequence, the historian in chapter III gives an account of Wild's birth and parents, which in turn is followed by a chapter on Master Wild's boyhood. In fact, this biographer is so preoccupied with preserving "the regularity of his series," to recall Fielding's comment on the painful, voluminous historian in <u>Tom Jones</u> (p. 40, Bk. II, ch. i), that he apologizes for the lacuna in one of the chapters, the unduly brief description of Master Wild's travels, the lack of verifiable data to account for this period of the hero's life: "To confess a truth, we are so ashamed of the shortness of this chapter . . . " (p. 43, Bk. I, ch. vii). Although the biographer acknowledges that no extraordinary events transpired during this time, "not one adventure worthy the reader's notice," he still feels embarrassed about his lack of detail, the "blank in this history," as he is bound by the chronologist's obligation, as Fielding puts it in <u>Tom Jones</u> (p. 40, Bk. II, ch. i), "to fill up as much paper with the detail of months and years in which nothing happened" as with the great, epic moments of history.

Second, in <u>Jonathan Wild</u> Fielding also ridicules the accumulation of facts, details, statistics, and documents as the equivalent of Truth, the kind of illusion that Defoe perpetrates in his novels when he poses as the "editor of this account" in the preface to <u>Robinson Crusoe</u>--that is, the historian's adaptation of the scientist's inductive method. To create the aura of detachment and objectivity, the historian of <u>Jonathan Wild</u> presents himself as a reporter of facts who produces documentary evidence and cites authoritative sources. For example, he adduces five different letters to a creditor that all offer essentially the same excuses for the delay of payment (pp. 93-94, Bk. II, ch. vii). The letters are not only repetitious, a useless multiplication of examples, but also irrelevant to the subject, a curious digression. As another small item of information, the historian includes one of Wild's love letters to Laetitia, his "MOST DEIVINE and ADWHORABLE CREETURE," an epistle "which we here insert . . . as we take it to be extremely curious . . . " (p. 130, Bk. III, ch. vi). To the historian this letter is striking only because of its oddity, the irregular, eccentric spelling habits of his hero:

> I doubt not but those IIs, briter than the son, which have kindled such a flam in my hart, have likewise the faculty of seeing it. It would be the hiest preassumption to imagin you eggnorant of my loav. (pp. 130-131, Bk. III, ch. vi)

In other words, in these two examples the type of information that the historian uses as evidence actually reveals the petty quality of his own mind more than it illuminates the subject of his biography. He reflects a quality of the worst travel writers, what Fielding condemned in his preface to The Journal of a Voyage to Lisbon as a perversion of knowledge, "that lowest degree of it which is the object of curiosity," a trait that is "the leading principle in weak minds only." Further claims of authenticity on the historian's part include the dialogue between Jonathan and Laetitia (p. 135, Bk. III, ch. viii), a conversation "overheard and taken down verbatim" by "a friend of mine"; "the only copy" extant of Jonathan Wild's eloquent speech on the liberties of Newgate prison (pp. 166-170, Bk. IV, ch. iii); and a list of his famous maxims on the attainment of greatness, aphorisms "which were after his decease found in his study" (pp. 215-216, Bk. IV, ch. xv). For these reasons the historian's vainglory boasts about "that strict attachment to truth and impartiality which we have professed in recording the annals of this great man" (p. 171, Bk. IV, ch. iv). Like the travel writer who is, to quote again from the Voyage to Lisbon, "inflamed with the glory of having seen what no man ever did or will see but himself," the narrator of Jonathan Wild, like the traveler, displays that "vanity of knowing more than other men," of recording facts that serve no purpose other than to flaunt the pedant's vain learning, his pride in the possession of esoteric, curious information inaccessible to others. Thus when the historian records Wild's last words with the ordinary of Newgate, a dialogue on eschatology "taken down in shorthand by one who overheard it," the biographer brags that this manuscript represents "one of the most curious pieces which either ancient or modern history hath recorded" (p. 204, Bk. IV, ch. xii). As if this pomposity were not enough, he offers as final, irrefutable evidence, not of Wild's sublime greatness, but of his own trivial mind, the following bit of arcana, as useless as it is rare:

    JONATHAN   * * * * * If once convinced * * * * *
    * no man * * lives of * * *

> * * * * * whereas sure the
> clergy * * opportunity * * better
> informed * * * * * all manner
> of vice * * * (p. 205, Bk. IV, ch. xiii)

It is this type of mind, then, that Stauffer refers to when he speaks of the "wedding of curiosity and methodical antiquarianism" in eighteenth century biographers and historians.[24]

Third, Fielding satirizes the historian's love of system in <u>Jonathan Wild</u>, his inveterate bias toward his hero, his prepossession with the Great Man theory of history, his mania about "uniformity of character." In the first chapter of the biography the narrator states his thesis: " . . . as we are to record the actions of a GREAT MAN, so we have nowhere mentioned any spark of goodness which had discovered itself either faintly in him . . . ." In the last chapter of the biography the historian restates his thesis: "Now, in Wild everything was truly GREAT, almost without alloy . . . . But surely his whole behaviour to his friend Heartfree is a convincing proof that the true iron or steel GREATNESS of his heart was not debased by any softer metal." That is, he begs the question. Assuming as self-evident what he has in no way proved, the historian ends as he begins, that is, offering his thesis as his conclusion. Hence he contends in the first chapter that Jonathan Wild's pure greatness remains untainted, bearing no trace of the impurities that lowered the esteem of other famous men, such as the clemency of Alexander the Great and the largesse of Julius Caesar. Then in the final chapter the narrator again rides this hobbyhorse:

> Nor had he any of those flaws in his
> character which . . . have (as I hinted
> in the beginning of this history) by the
> judicious reader been censured and despised.
> Such was the clemency of Alexander and Caesar . . . . (p. 218, Bk.
> IV, ch. xv)

In short, in contrast to the sense of the Marvellous that superabounds in the endings of Fielding's other novels, the finale of Jonathan Wild is a foregone conclusion presented in a nil admirari tone. Unlike Fielding's other novels or histories where the narrator (of course Fielding himself) portrays the unsystematic epic view of things--the immense variety of human nature, the constant mutability of Fortune, the idea of the one and the many, and the motley sense of comedy--the historian in Jonathan Wild prizes his work for its perfect consistency and lack of all contradiction, for its preservation of "the great perfection called the uniformity of character," its idea of the One at the expense of the many.

While the historian offers his opening thesis as his final conclusion in a tour de force of circular reasoning, the middle portions of the biography, the argument in support of the proposition about Jonathan Wild's greatness, also reveal shaky logic. For the narrator adjusts, distorts, manipulates, and slants the facts and evidence to conform to his preconception, his premise that greatness is incompatible with goodness. Hence when Master Wild utters his first sound and happens to pronounce the difficult "th" syllable, his biographer interprets it as an omen of future glory, a sign that "he was certainly born to be a GREAT MAN" (p. 28, Bk. I, ch. iii). When the young prodigy cheats Count La Ruse at cards and steals from his pockets, the gamester admires the precocity of the boy genius--another presentiment of greatness as "men of great genius as easily discover one another as freemasons can" (p. 32, Bk. I, ch. iv). The biographer not only regards evil as good and cheating as genius but also refers to lust as love and rape as honor. Wild's lust for Laetitia, which the biographer tries to justify as "an honourable sort of passion," provokes him to ravish her. However, prior to resorting to violence and attempting rape, Wild tried to seduce Laetitia with the more gentle method of a lie, a promise of marriage--an act of tenderness and honor which, according to the biographer, exonerates the hero from all guilt: "but he was so remarkably attached to decency, that he never offered any violence to a young lady without the most earnest promises of that kind, these being, he said, a ceremonial due to female modesty . . ." (p. 49, Bk. I, ch. ix). Wild again displays the sincerity of a lover and a sense of male honor when he meets Molly Straddle. To rationalize the hero's affair with this prostitute and to eliminate the contradiction between Wild's avowed love for Laetitia and his recent amour with Molly, the biographer offers two reasons to defend the perfect uniformity of Wild's pure greatness. First, the hero does not belong to that effeminate race of men who "tie themselves to a woman's apronstrings" and who indulge in "that mean, base, low vice, or virtue as it is called, of constancy" (p. 77, Bk. II, ch. iii). Second, after Wild's sensual appetite is satiated with the pleasures of Molly, he quickly turns all his thoughts to his beloved Laetitia and rushes to her apartment. The biographer goes on in the same vein throughout the rest of the novel, referring to Wild's tyranny over his gang in terms of his heroic "transcendant qualities." Thus when Wild tries to exploit Bagshot by demanding more than his fair share of the booty, he outshouts him in a ranting speech--a form of despotism which the biographer interprets as evidence of "a bold heart, a thundering voice, and a steady countenance" (p. 73, Bk. II, ch. ii). When Wild bribes his henchmen to perjure Thomas Fierce and thus have him executed, the biographer commends his "policy, or politics, or rather pollitrics" (p. 89, Bk. II, ch. v). When Blueskin and other members of the gang threaten to revolt against their leader, Wild immediately quells the rebellion by informing the law about the crimes of the head of the conspiracy and thereby intimidates his other dupes--an act of treachery that earns him the epithets of "resolute," "timely," and "expeditious" from his biographer. Thus like Procrustes, who refused to adjust his bed and hence either cut off the legs of his victims or stretched their bodies to fit it, the historian in Jonathan Wild--rather than modify his theory to fit the facts--twists, exaggerates, and bends his evidence to make it conform to his system.

Fourth, Fielding criticizes the historian's treatment of the Marvellous or "the Prodigious," the term used in Jonathan Wild. On the one hand, the biographer purports to expel all supernatural elements and incredible fictions from his factual, documented narrative. On the other hand, despite the illusion of scientific objectivity and impartial detachment on the part of the narrator, the life of Jonathan Wild is filled with absurd improbabilities, what Fielding generally calls the Monstrous. The biographer guarantees us that no mythical sea monsters or animals will suddenly appear to rescue his hero when he is abandoned on the ocean. He assures the reader,

> The truth is, we do not choose to have any recourse to miracles, from the strict observance we pay to the rule of Horace:
>
> Nec deus intersit, nisi dignus vindice nodus--
>
> the meaning of which is, "Do not bring in a superagent when you can do without him." (p. 107, Bk. II, ch. xii)

When a reprieve arrives at the last minute to save Heartfree from the gallows, the biographer reminds the reader of a historian's integrity: he would prefer to see one half of humanity hanged rather "than have saved one contrary to the strictest rules of writing and probability" (p. 177, Bk. IV, ch. vi). Finally, he contrasts his own excellent work, based on "the truths of history," with mediocre books, "the extravagances of romance" (p. 171, Bk. IV, ch. iv).

However, the life of Jonathan Wild is replete with the extravagances of romance, the god machinery of mythology, and the Prodigious. Supernatural agents are introduced during Wild's birth, as Mercury and Priapus visit his mother in her dreams--an event that the scientific historian, forgetting his caveat about miracles, alludes to as "wonderful" and "preternatural." The other "remarkable incident" that attended Mrs. Wild's pregnancy was the "most marvellous glutinous quality" in her fingers, an omen that clearly presaged the dexterous hands of her most adroit son, the greatest thief of his time. Although no sea monster appears from the bottom of the deep to succor Wild when he is adrift on the ocean, Alma Mater performs the same function: "She, therefore, no sooner spied him in the water than she softly whispered in his ear to attempt the recovery of his boat, which call he immediately obeyed, and, being a good swimmer, and it being a perfect calm, with great facility accomplished it" (p. 108, Bk. II, ch. xii). By substituting Nature or Alma Mater for the mythological deus ex machina, the biographer feels he has avoided the Prodigious. Finally, as mentioned earlier in this chapter, the adventures of Mrs. Heartfree on the sea are as imaginary and preposterous as any of the "extravagences of romance." Nearly raped by a host of admirers, perfunctorily delivered each time by the mechanical intervention of Providence, Mrs. Heartfree narrates this portion of the story which appears as unauthentic as the spurious adventures of Robinson Crusoe, which Defoe called "a just history of fact." Indeed Fielding intends this portion of Jonathan Wild as a parody of Robinson Crusoe and other such travel books. For one of Mrs. Heartfree's deliverers and later one of her would-be ravishers is a hermit dressed in outlandish garb; a castaway on an island who has dwelled in a cave for over thirty years; a religious penitent who has devoted himself to a holy life of prayer; a prudent, industrious man who can offer Mrs. Heartfree the products of his labor--venison, brandy, and fruits; a cautious man who lives in fear of wild beasts and arms himself with gun and powder. These are of course all the well-known features of Defoe's famous character. Thus, despite all of his intentions to write a true matter-of-fact history, the biographer of Jonathan Wild produces an imaginary romance. Going to all lengths to follow the criterion of consistency or uniformity of character, he contradicts himself and commits non sequiturs. Intending to purge his history of the Marvellous, he introduces elements of the Monstrous.

Fielding's point, then, is clear: Poetry (literature), as Aristotle stated in the Poetics, is often a higher form of truth than either History or Philosophy. Historians in love with useless facts or minute particularities, such as the biographer's preoccupation with curiosities in Jonathan Wild, or philosophers in love with theories or systems, such as the biographer's generalization about GREATNESS, both divorce the union of the individual and the universal, the harmony of the many and the one which is the basis of Fielding's art and the principle behind the divine art of God's Providence. Just as Shakespeare's Prospero in The Tempest, who personified Providence in the play, performs his magic in a playful, spontaneous, creative, masterful way--making use of both good agents like Ariel and evil instruments like Caliban; working through diverse natural means such as the four elements of earth, air, fire, and water (e.g., Ariel says, "I come/ . . . to fly,/To swim, to dive into the fire, to ride/On the curl'd clouds," I, ii, ll. 189-192); reflecting the wonderful variety of God's Being, His power, omniscience, justice, mercy, wisdom, and beauty; creating order out of chaos, transforming an uninhabitable desert into a humane society, making a great thing, a true civilization, from a small thing, a mere island--so too divine Providence in Fielding's novels proceeds in the same unsystematic, sportive, various, and astonishing ways: accomplishing great things through small means, blending the Supernatural into Nature and History, concealing the rationality of Providence amid the fickleness of Fortune, in short, camouflaging the wisdom of God as the play of a child in the spirit of the book of Proverbs (8:27-31):

> When he established the heavens, I was
>   there, . . .

>when he marked out the foundations of the earth,
>then I was beside him, like a little child;
>and I was daily his delight,
>rejoicing before him always,
>rejoicing in his inhabited world
>and delighting in the sons of men.[25]

Just as Prospero the artist or magician unites his sense of work and his sense of play, causing both delight and instruction, so too God the artist also combines a sense of vocation and avocation, a sense of purpose--a general and particular providence--and a sense of play, the antics of Fortune, the game of hide and seek. In the same way that Miranda, meaning Wonderful, is the natural child of Prospero the player and magician, a work of art whose beauty and virtue surpass all the excellences of other women ("But you, oh, you," says Ferdinand, "So perfect and so peerless, are created/Of every creature's best," III, i, ll. 46-48); the wonder in Fielding's novels, an effect of miracles, a result of the handiwork of Providence, transcends the rigid systems of science, religion, and history in the eighteenth century that tend to deny the childlike spontaneity, creative freedom, and skillfull virtuosity of God as Player and Artist. Instead of acknowledging God's copious amplitude and inexhaustible variety, these systems delimit the infinite Being of God summarized in His name of "I am that I am"; they reduce Providence to an uncreative repairman, a perfunctory deus ex machina, an inexorable Fate, or a mere superstition. Thus it is the essence of Providence to beget miracles, the begotten of God, as naturally as Prospero fathers Miranda; to mix with the givenness of things and be immanent in Nature, History, and Fortune to accomplish divine intentions, in the same way that Prospero works his magic through such natural agents as a tempest, the love between man and woman, and the four elements in order to fulfill his higher purposes; to govern the whole universe as well as to number the hairs on a man's head as a matter of play just as

Prospero's power and wisdom penetrate all parts of the island and influence the lives of all men through his magic.

NOTES TO CHAPTER IV

[1] Herbert Butterfield, *The Origins of Modern Science* (New York: The Free Press, 1968), p. 229.

[2] J. B. Bury, *The Idea of Progress* (New York: Dover Publications, 1955), p. 73.

[3] E. A. Burtt, *The Metaphysical Foundations of Modern Physical Science* (New York: Doubleday Anchor Books, 1954), pp. 295-298.

[4] Prudence, as practiced by Defoe's Robinson Crusoe, Richardson's Pamela, and Fielding's politic characters in no way adheres to the traditional meaning of the word. Johnson's *Dictionary*, for example, defines *prudence* in terms of the cardinal virtue, as his definition and quotation illustrate: "Wisdom applied to practice."

[5] Bury, p. 145.

[6] Niccolo Machiavelli, *The Prince* (New York: New American Library, 1952), p. 123.

[7] *Works*, ed. Henley, XV, 87-91.

[8] Phillip Harth, *Swift and Anglican Rationalism* (Chicago and London: Univ. of Chicago Press, 1969), pp. 21-22.

[9] J. B. Bury clearly explains all the implications of the eighteenth century idea of progress: "It is based on an interpretation of history which regards men as slowly advancing--*pedetentim progredientes*--in a definite and desirable direction, and infers that this progress will continue indefinitely. And it implies that . . . a condition of general happiness will ultimately be enjoyed, which will justify the whole process of civilization; . . . There is also a further implication. The process must be the necessary outcome of the physical and social nature of man; it must not be at the mercy of any external will; otherwise there would be no guarantee of its continuance and its

issue, and the idea of Progress would lapse into the idea of Providence." (Ibid, p. 5)

[10] Quoted by J. V. Cunningham, Woe or Wonder (Denver: Swallow Paperbooks Edition, 1964), p. 78.

[11] Quoted by Cunningham, p. 77.

[12] M. C. D'Arcy, The Meaning and Matter of History (New York: Meridian Books, 1961), p. 133.

[13] Works, XVI, 116-119.

[14] Boethius, The Consolation of Philosophy (New York: Bobbs-Merrill, 1962), p. 91. All further references are taken from this edition; page numbers will be included in the body of the text.

[15] Martin Battestin's The Moral Basis of Fielding's Art (Middletown, Conn.: Wesleyan Univ. Press, 1964) and Aubrey Williams' article, "Interpositions of Providence and the Design of Fielding's Novels," South Atlantic Quarterly, 70 (1971), both indicate the extent of Fielding's knowledge of eighteenth century sermons. Some of the best known divines that Fielding read and respected include--along with Barrow--Tillotson, Hoadley, Clarke, and Sherlock. The secondary sources Fielding uses in his compilation of God's judgments in Interposition of Providence also include a number of theological works, for example, Wanley's The Wonders of the Little World: Or a General History of Man (London, 1678).

[16] Augustine, City of God (Garden City, N.Y.: Image Books, 1958), p. 201. All further references come from this edition; page number, book and chapter citation will hereafter be incorporated in the text.

[17] R. H. Hoopes, Right Reason in the English Renaissance (Cambridge, Mass., 1962), p. 107. This study offers an illuminating exposition of the relationship between the virtue of right rea-

son and the rationality of God's Providence; man, being created in the divine image, imitates the rationality or foresight of God inasmuch as he practices right reason. In surveying the history of the idea, Hoopes shows how the psychology of voluntarism and the notion of God as Will rather than Reason challenged the natural law tradition of classical antiquity and medieval Christendom-- the tradition found in thinkers like Plato, Aristotle, Cicero, the Stoics, Aquinas, Hooker, and the Cambridge Platonists.

[18] Etienne Gilson, *The Unity of Philosophical Experience* (New York: Scribner, 1965), p. 109.

[19] Reginald Garrigou-Lagrange, *Providence* (St. Louis, Mo. and London: Herder, 1946), p. 123.

[20] William G. Pollard, *Chance and Providence* (New York: Scribner, 1958), p. 132.

[21] Leo Braudy, *Narrative Form in History and Fiction* (Princeton, N.J.: Princeton Univ. Press, 1970), pp. 21-22.

[22] Donald A. Stauffer, *The Art of Biography in Eighteenth Century England* (Princeton, N.J.: Princeton Univ. Press, 1941), pp. 233-234.

[23] Quoted by Richard F. Jones, "Science and English Prose Style in the Third Quarter of the Seventeenth Century," in *The Seventeenth Century* (Stanford, Cal.: Stanford Univ. Press, 1951), p. 86.

[24] Quoted by Hugo Rahner, *Man at Play* (New York: Herder and Herder, 1967), p. 19. In his chapter, "The Playing of God," Rahner cites important texts from Greek philosophers and the Church Fathers, Plato, Heraclitus, Philo of Alexandria, Clement of Alexander, Apollonius Rhodius, Origen, Gregory Nazianzen, and Maximus Confessor, to show how the idea of the Divine Wisdom's playing and dancing, the creation of the world as a kind of ball play, is an integral aspect of the classical-

Christian tradition, the *philosophia perennis*.

CHAPTER V

CONCLUSION: FIELDING'S MARVELLOUS AND THE EIGHTEENTH CENTURY SUBLIME

The classical-Christian idea of the Wonderful underwent a transformation during the eighteenth century. The theories of the sublime that prevailed during the period, as expounded by representative critics like Boileau, Dennis, Addison, Akenside, and of course Burke, all conflicted with the traditional view of the Marvellous. Essentially, the Sublime as an eighteenth century version of the Wonderful was an attempt to reinstate and dignify the Marvellous during a time when the idea suffered a loss of repute as a result of the new science. Having purged Nature of all superstition and supernatural explanations of phenomena, the new science, as seen in Thomas Sprat's observation that the "cours of all things goes quietly along, in its own true channel of Natural Causes and Effects,"[1] associated the Marvellous with ignorance, the state of unenlightenment. The neo-classical view stated by Pope that "fools admire" whereas "men of sense approve"[2] also implies a view of wonder as a nonintellectual state of mind that conflicts with the norm of clear ideas and ratiocinative logic. This is also the import of Burke's statement: "It is our ignorance of things that causes all our admiration and chiefly excites our passions."[3] In these quotations wonder or admiration is not a condition of partial knowledge or the beginning of philosophy, as it is for Aristotle, but a state of total darkness or sheer ignorance.

To reconcile the Marvellous, the unexpected and improbable, with the Natural--the predictable laws of nature, the chain of cause and effect, explanations through physical causes rather than hidden agents--the concept of the Sublime became a solution. As David B. Morris's <u>The Religious Sublime</u> discusses this problem: "Many eighteenth-century poets answered this question with the sublime in nature; floods, mountains, whirlwinds, blizzards, and volcanos possessed the literary advantage of being simultaneously natural and marvellous."[4] In his article, "Donne and the Wane of Wonder," Dennis Quinn also comments on the same phenomenon: "Having banished wonder from nature, men began to cast about for something to wonder at."[5] The Sublime offered such an outlet, and it lent itself to a mechanical explanation of the Wonderful in terms of an empirical psychology, as eighteenth century views of the rainbow illustrate. The rainbow is traditionally regarded as the image of the Wonderful, for in the Greek myth Iris, the goddess of the rainbow, is the child of Thaumas, which means "wonder." However, eighteenth century scientists and philosophers, basing their theories of light and color on Newton's <u>Opticks</u>, analyzed the rainbow as a problem of motion and denied Iris her divine origin. Alfred North Whitehead summarizes this eighteenth-century physics of light in the following way:

> Whatever theory you choose, there is no light or color as a fact in external nature. There is merely motion of material. Again, when the light enters your eyes and falls on the retina, there is merely motion of material. Then your nerves are affected and your brain is affected, and again there is merely motion of material . . . . Nature is a dull affair, soundless, scentless, colorless.[6]

Critics were to perform a similar task for the sublime, explaining the dynamics of the mind in terms of a materialistic psychology, the physical and emotional effects of the sublime in terms of secondary causes and the association of ideas, so that the sublime experience becomes scientifically verifiable--an effect whose cause is clear, not hidden as in the classical-Christian idea of wonder.

Although it tried in many ways to accommodate the Natural and the Marvellous, the eighteenth century idea of the Sublime did not affirm the Classical-Christian theory of the Wonderful but rather marked a new departure. Using Longinus's *Peri Hupsous* as an ancient text to justify the notion of the sublime, the various commentators of *On the Sublime* offer divergent interpretations of Longinus's precise meaning. As Morris explains the situation: "Longinus actually provided no clear definition of the sublime--creating a vacuum which a multitude of eighteenth century critics rushed to fill."[7] For example, whereas Boileau's conception of the sublime in *Traite du Sublime ou de Merveilleux dans le Discours Traduit du Grec de Longin* (1674) defines the emotion as "that extraordinary and marvellous quality (*cet extraordinaire et ce merveilleux*) which strikes in a discourse, and which enables a work to elevate, ravish, and transport (*qui fait qu'un ouvrage enleve, ravit, transport*)"--thus limiting wonder to a mere sensation or ecstatic feeling and disregarding it as the first step toward knowledge--Fielding's description of Sophia in *Tom Jones* (p. 109, Bk. IV, ch. ii), "A Short Hint of What We Can Do in the Sublime . . . ," praises the heroine for both her physical beauty and mental acumen: "Her mind was every way equal to her person." Since Sophia possesses prudence, charity, and beauty, Fielding understands the sublime as a synthesis of the true, the good, and the beautiful, as an experience that does not merely ravish or transport but pleases and teaches as well as moves--*docere*, *conciliare*, *movere*, to cite Cicero's terms from *De Oratore* and *Orator*--in the way that Sophia delights everyone with her goodness and instructs Tom in the sense that as he pursues her on the journey, he acquires *sophia* or wisdom; of course she also moves or ravishes Tom with her beauty. Thus Fielding does not isolate the sublime as the aesthetic quality par excellence; he does not separate the sublime from the beautiful or the good as many of the aestheticians of the day preferred to do, namely, Thomson, Akenside, and Burke, to name but a few. When Thomson in the summer portion of The Seasons cites the ravenous wolves and voracious sharks as examples of the sublime, he connects sublimity with evil. When Burke in the Philosophical Enquiry relates sublimity to violence, dread, and pain, he too approaches the identification of sublimity with evil. Fielding, on the other hand, associates virtue and beauty as two integrated aspects of the sublime: "It is truly said of Virtue, that, could men behold her naked, they would all fall in love with her."[9] Whereas Fielding always distinguishes between the Marvellous and the Monstrous, the critics of the sublime tend to blur this distinction as darkness, ugliness, and evil-- what Fielding generally calls the false sublime of "the deformity of vice" as opposed to the "true beauty of virtue"--come to be honored as elements of the real sublime. Burke, for example, cites Milton's description of Death in the second book of Paradise Lost as a locus classicus of true sublimity:

> The other shape
> If shape it might be called that shape
>   had none
> Distinguishable, in member, joint, or
>   limb;
> Or substance might be called that shadow
>   seemed;
> For each seemed either; black he stood
>   as night;
> Fierce as ten furies; terrible as hell;
> And shook a deadly dart. What seemed
>   his head
> The likeness of a kingly crown had on.

Burke comments, "In this description all is dark, uncertain, confused, terrible, and sublime to the last degree,"[10] thus relating sublimity more to the ugliness of evil than to the beauty of virtue.

Fielding's Longinus, whom he praises as one of the "noble critics" in the rank of Aristotle and Horace among the ancients and Dacier and Bossu among the moderns, is not the same Longinus whom John Dennis champions in The Advancement and Reformation of Modern Poetry and in The Grounds of Criticism in Poetry (1701 and 1704 respectively). Following the cues of Boileau, Dennis, although he does not reject the moral or didactic aspect of literature, nevertheless stresses the emotional impact of the sublime, which, he explains, is evoked by religious ideas that convey "Enthusiastick Passions": admiration, terror, horror, joy, sadness, and desire." According to Dennis's reading of Longinus, poetry is "an Art, by which a Poet excites Passion," and "A Poet . . . is oblig'd always to speak to the heart."[12] On the other hand, Fielding interpreted Longinus, not as an apologist for passionate enthusiasm in literature, as the chief authority of a preromantic school of literature that challenged the rigid rules of neoclassical theory--a common view of Longinus during the period. Rather, Fielding admired Longinus as a classical critic, a learned man of "taste," a quality that Fielding defined in the Covent-Garden Journal as "a nice harmony between the imagination and the judgment,"[13] that is, as a rational faculty, not an aesthetic je ne sais quoi. In praise of Longinus, Fielding quotes the lines of Pope from An Essay on Criticism, where Pope places Longinus in a great tradition and treats him as a successor rather than as an innovator--a line of succession that includes Aristotle, Horace, Dionysius, Petronius, Quintilian. In short, Fielding esteemed Longinus as a classical thinker, a member of the triumvirate to which Aristotle and Horace belonged, not as a pre-romantic forerunner or founder of the School for Taste that cultivated sensibility and praised Longinus for the emotional and subjective basis of his criticism. Although Fielding does not cite his favorite passages from Longinus, the following excerpts from On the Sublime reflect principles consonant with Fielding's own classicism:

> For that is really great which bears a repeated examination, and which it is difficult or rather impossible to withstand, and the memory of which is strong and hard to efface. In general, consider those examples of sublimity to be fine and genuine which please all and always.
>
> For art is perfect when it seems to be nature, and nature hits the mark when she contains art hidden within her.[14]

The first passage refers to the criterion of universality, the <u>quod ubique, quod semper</u> touchstone, as the measure of great art. The second passage is a paraphrase of Aristotle's "Art imitates Nature" and Horace's "Art is the ability to conceal art." All three ideas are of course commonplaces of the classical tradition.

Fielding's discussion of the true sublime in his "Preface to the Miscellanies and Poems," where he examines <u>admiration</u> in its generic sense of wonder, an effect of heroic virtue or magnanimity, an aspect of praise evoked by moral greatness, differs from the treatment afforded the sublime by Addison who relates the idea in his <u>Spectator</u> papers to "the pleasures of the imagination." In <u>Spectator</u> No. 412 Addison explains the sublime pleasures of the imagination as powerful sensations originating in "the Sight of what is <u>Great, Uncommon</u>, or <u>Beautiful</u>." As examples of greatness he mentions "the Prospects of an open Champian Country, a vast uncultivated Desart, of hugh Heaps of Mountains, high Rocks and Precipices, or a wide Expanse of Waters"[15]--the familiar list of convenient sublime objects and ideas that can be found in many writers of the sublime during the period; for example, Dennis, Baillie, and Burke all provide a handy list of ready-made topics for sublimity. Fielding, however, did not confine the idea of the Wonderful to any prescribed formula or associate it with only a set number of topics, such as ". . . Thunder, Tempests, raging Seas, Inundations, Torrents, Earthquakes, Volcanos, Monsters, Serpents, Lions, Tygers . . . ,"[16] to cite Dennis's list. While many eighteenth century writers and critics connected the sublime, in Morris's phrase, "with a set of conventional subjects, forms, and techniques,"[17] such as the Bible, the epic, Milton, the grandeur of Nature, the attributes of God (especially his power and wrath), and the last things of eschatology, Fielding does not equate the greatness of sublimity with the power of size, the awesomeness of Nature, or the gravity of religion. In <u>Joseph Andrews</u> and <u>Tom Jones</u> Fielding mingles the seriousness of epic with the lightness of comedy--the motley affair of the "comic epic poem in prose" where the sublime appears in the guise of the ridiculous, not the solemn. In <u>Amelia</u> greatness appears, not in the form of a strong military hero like Captain Booth or a fierce dueller like Colonel James, but in the cloak of a meek woman like Amelia and an unworldly clergyman like Dr. Harrison. Sublimity is a matter of moral quality, a <u>magna anima</u>, not physical size or measurable quantity, the "GREAT GREATNESS" of a Jonathan Wild. As Fielding remarked in the "Preface to the Miscellanies and Poems," greatness without goodness is a contradiction: ". . . it seems to me in nature to resemble the false sublime in poetry," where bombast poses as eloquence. Throughout his novels the miracles of Providence, the handiwork of God and the evidence of His power, do not manifest themselves as overt expressions of might. Instead the greatness of God's providence works through simple, little things, such as Sophia's muff or a strawberry birthmark; insignificant, low characters, such as Mrs. Waters in <u>Tom Jones</u>, the pedlar in <u>Joseph Andrews</u>, and Robinson, the prisoner in <u>Amelia</u>; commonplace, ordinary occurrences, like the journey to London or Tom Jones' hunting with Squire Western. The miracles of Providence, in Fielding's eyes, testify to God's playfulness and lightheartedness as much as to his earnestness and strength--the idea of the divine wisdom "always at play, playing through the whole world"[19] (Proverbs 8:30)--for Providence often camouflages itself in the antics of frolicsome Fortune.

Whereas the poets and critics of the sublime regarded the infinity of God and the grandeur of Nature as the epitomes of sublimity--Burke commenting that "The ideas of eternity and infinity are among the most affecting we have"[20] and Addison alluding to "that rude kind of Magnificence which appears in many of these stupendous Works of Nature" (Spectator No. 412)--Fielding's portrait of the sublime Sophia invokes placid deities like "sweet Zephyrus" and "lovely Flora" and exorcises the ruder deities, "noisy Boreas" and "bitter-biting Eurus." That is, he summons the more gentle, serene, calming aspects of Nature rather than the violent, awesome, or shocking parts. In describing Sophia's sublimity in terms of soft breezes (the soothing qualities that Zephyrus symbolizes as he rises from his "fragrant" bed and whispers "delicious" gales) and in terms of delicate flowers (the pied beauty and variegated colors of Flora, as the goddess "gently" moves along the "verdant mead" until "the whole field becomes enamelled")--Fielding parts company from the theorists of the sublime who based their notion of greatness upon terror, obscurity, and vagueness rather than upon stillness, clarity, and color-- the idea of sublimity that receives its fullest expression in Burke's Philosophical Enquiry into the Origin of our Ideas of the Sublime and Beautiful (1757). In the Philosophical Enquiry Burke cites as sources of the sublime certain categories that are all exclusive of either calm, light, or color. To quote from Samuel Monk's commentary on Burke's list of sublime topics:

> They are obscurity, where darkness and uncertainty arouse dread and terror (II, 3); power, where the mind is impelled to fear because of superior force (II, 5); privations, such as darkness, vacuity, and silence, which are great because they are terrible (II, 6); vast-

ness, whether in length, height, or depth, the last being the most powerful source of the sublime (II, 7); infinity, or any object that because of its size seems infinite (II, 8).[21]

With his emphasis on privations like darkness, vacuity, and silence, Burke divorces greatness from light, color, and familiarity--the locus of the sublime for Fielding. It is only brilliant, blinding light--such as the scorching sun of summer, a thunderbolt, or an eclipse--that constitutes the sublime in the aesthetics of Burke and Thomson. Making this point in the second part of the Philosophical Enquiry, Burke provides another example from Paradise Lost, the description of the fallen Satan, who still retains some of his original lustre:

> as when the sun new risen
> Looks through the horizontal misty air
> Shorn of his beams; or from behind the moon
> In dim eclipse disastrous twilight sheds
> On half the nations; and with the fear of change
> Perplexes monarchs.[22]

The power of this passage depends, Burke remarks, on the images of "the sun rising through mists," and the eclipse, that is, sudden displays of light or dark. In Thomson's The Seasons it is the glorious effulgence of the summer sun which makes that season profoundly sublime; the sun burns "with ardent blaze" and "looks gaily fierce o'er all the dazzling air" (ll. 637-638). Notwithstanding the greatness and majesty of the glorious sun, darkness is still more evocative of sublimity than light, for Burke prefers "sad and fuscous colors, as black and brown, or deep purple"[23] as more emblematic of sublimity than bright colors. In short, by emphasizing the extremes of light and dark, the theorists of the sublime separate the sublime from the common light of day and the familiar colors of Nature, where Fielding locates the Marvellous.

In addition to Flora's painting the earth with her most iridescent colors to prepare the ground for the sublime Sophia, whom Fielding also describes in terms of bright hues, as having black hair, red lips, a white neck, and a complexion "more of the lily than the rose," Allworthy's magnificent estate in Somersetshire too conflicts with conventional eighteenth century attitudes toward the sublime. Here Fielding situated the sublime in another scene of tranquillity that also reflects the gentleness of Zephyrus and Flora: "It was now the middle of May, and the morning was remarkably serene . . . ." He paints the picture with bright, natural colors where everything is visible to the naked eye, not with blinding light or dreadful darkness: it is the month of May when Nature traditionally beautifies herself with a wonderful panoply of hues and tones, the iridescence of the rainbow. Further, Fielding indicates the clarity of the view from the top of the hill, the open vistas, "a most charming prospect," the lake "which was seen from every room in the front," and the light of dawn. There is nothing in the picture that is "dark, uncertain, confused, terrible," to recall Burke's epithets for the sublime. Hence whereas sublimity to Fielding means the clear, the visible, the colored--the enamelling of Flora, the painting of Nature in the spring--to Burke greatness represents the vague, the imagined, and the obscure. "A clear idea," he remarks, "is therefore another name for a little idea," and "dark, confused, uncertain images have a greater power on the fancy to form the grander passions."[24] To put it another way, Fielding conceives of literature in the tradition of Horace's <u>ut pictura poesis</u>, painting as the sister art of poetry, while Burke, in the preromantic school, views the highest literature as suggestive, connotative, and indefinite, as an imitation of music rather than painting.

In contrast to the sublime sensation that Boileau speaks of as a ravishing, transporting force, that Dennis discusses as an "Enthusiastick Passion," that Burke treats as the perturbation of terror, the experience of the sublime or Marvellous in Fielding's novels, although it animates or inspires, does not discompose the emotions but quiets them. Wonder to Fielding signifies contemplation, the rest or recollection that is prerequisite to philosophizing, the absence of busyness and distraction. Leisure, as the Greek skole and the Latin scola indicate, is the basis for knowledge, the sine qua non of a school, for the classical words mean "leisure." The Greek a-scolia and the Latin neg-otim (literally, "unrest") refer to a state of being unleisurely, that is, unreceptive to knowledge or inspiration, overpreoccupied with business or neg-otiation. Or, as Josef Pieper shows in Leisure: The Basis of Culture, the verb "be still" in the well-known verse from the Psalms, "Be still and know that I am God" (65: 11), is translated from the Greek skulasate in the Septuagint version, a word that means "have leisure," "wonder," or "go to school" as easily as "be still."[25] In Covent-Garden Journal No. 24 Fielding, discussing the vice of sloth in terms of busyness and restlessness, shows how the sin relates to the state of unleisureliness, the obsession with idle, frivolous activity which is a form of malaise. He cites the phrase from St. Paul's letter to the Thessalonians: "Doing no work, but busying themselves in impertinence." He quotes from an unnamed Roman writer and translates the Latin thus: "Puffing and sweating to no purpose; employed about many things, and doing nothing." Fielding glosses the Greek πολυπραγμοσυνη as "a vain curiosity and diligence in trifles," and he alludes to Dr. Barrow's phrase, "to be impertinently busy, doing that which conduceth to no good purpose."[26] Fielding offers a similar point in the "Preface" to The Journal of a Voyage to Lisbon, where he castigates the vain curiosity, the trivial mind, and the restless activity of the mediocre travel writer whose frenetic pursuits allow no leisure for the contemplation of significant truths.

Also the characters in Fielding's novels receive good luck and experience the miracles of Providence only when they are in a state of leisure or rest, when they are "standing still" rather than "flying." For example, in Joseph Andrews Mr. Wilson, although he conducted a diligent investigation to recover his lost son when Joseph was stolen in his infancy and although he has not despaired of sometime discovering him in the future, is not frantically busy or constantly moving to realize his goal. In fact, Mr. Wilson, although industrious in tending his garden and raising his family, finds ample leisure during the day to take exercise, to play with his children, and to enjoy the conversation of his wife. He remarks to Parson Adams, "For I have experienced that calm serene happiness, which is seated in content, is inconsistent with the hurry and bustle of the world" (pp. 266-267, Bk. III, ch. iv). Likewise, Tom Jones, in his journey to London, is not possessed like a monomaniac who concentrates on only one thing, his dream of finding Sophia. As his many excursions off the main road indicate, Tom takes an interest in the variety of life, the many as well as the one--what Fielding calls "conversation" or "Experience," the knowledge of "every kind of character, from the minister at his levee, to the bailiff in his sponging-house; from the duchess at her drum, to the landlady behind her bar" (Tom Jones, p. 599, Bk. XIII, ch. i). Both Wilson and Jones approach life in the spirit of the "ingenious traveller" who slows his pace to relish the beautiful sights of Devon and Dorset and to appreciate the prodigious variety of Nature, unlike the "money-meditating tradesman" who never delays his progress and marches straight ahead with only one object in mind (Tom Jones, p. 531, Bk. XI, ch. ix). In Fielding's novels, then, providential good fortune is received as an unexpected gift in a state of leisure or contemplation rather than earned as a calculated reward in the pursuit of business. As Fielding implies in the conclusion of Jonathan Wild, heaven is given whereas hell is bought: "A man may go to heaven with half the pains which it costs him to purchase hell." The same sentiment appears in the "Preface to the Miscellanies and Poems": " . . . that while it is so easy and safe, and truly honourable, to be good, men . . . wade through difficulty and danger, and real infamy, to be great, or, to use a synonomous word, villains."[27] Thus the gift of luck blesses those who are open, receptive, and still; those who wait for Fortune and cooperate with it when it comes, not with those rapists of Fortune who try to force their destiny with the ceaseless activity of scheming and calculating. Fortune befalls the truly patient, such as Amelia, not the indolent like Heartfree or the restless like Jonathan Wild for whom "the truest mark of GREATNESS IS insatiability." Commenting on the verse from Job, "God giveth songs in the night" (35:10), Josef Pieper's remark is especially apropos to Fielding's idea of rest as creative and dynamic: "Moreover, it has always been a pious belief that God sends his good gifts and his blessings in sleep. And in the same way his great, imperishable intuitions visit a man in his moments of leisure."[28] For it is when Tom is resting at an inn rather than travelling on the road that he receives an illumination. At the ale house where Tom and Partridge see a performance of a puppet show, Tom learns tidings of his Sophia from the Merry-Andrew and marvels at "the extraordinary manner in which he <u>received</u> his intelligence" (italics added)--a <u>surprise</u> that compels Tom to ponder or contemplate the words of Partridge: "'two such accidents could never have happened to direct him after his mistress if Providence had not designed to bring them together at last'" (p. 566, Bk. XII, ch. viii).

On the other hand, neither Burke nor the other critics of the sublime relate wonder to being leisurely, still, or contemplative. Instead they equate wonder or sublimity with terror and fright rather than with quiet or calm. Tracing the root meaning of the words for wonder in various languages, Burke concludes that wonder and its synonyms like astonishment and admiration are all equivalents of fear:

Several languages bear a testimony to the affinity of these ideas. They frequently use the same word to signify indifferently the modes of astonishment or admiration and those of terror. Θάμβος is in Greek either fear or wonder; δεινός is terrible or respectable; αἰδέω to reverence or to fear. <u>Vereor</u> in Latin is what αἰδέω is in Greek. The Romans used the verb <u>stupeo</u>, a term which strongly marks the state of an astonished mind, to express the effect either of simple fear or of astonishment; the word <u>attonitus</u> (thunderstruck) is equally expressive of the alliance of these ideas; and do not the French <u>etonnement</u> and the English <u>astonishment</u> and <u>amazement</u> point out as clearly the kindred emotions which attend fear and wonder?

Since terror is the chief aspect of wonder, "the ruling principle of the sublime," its essential purpose is to excite the emotions rather than to order or purge them, to affect the imagination and thus arouse "the grander passions," which Burke associates with "strength, violence, pain, and terror" rather than to produce what Sir Joshua Reynolds in the eighth discourse of <u>Discourses on Art</u> called <u>repose</u>, "a relief of the mind from that state of hurry and anxiety which it suffers . . ." (p. 121). Instead of bringing on repose, the sublime, according to Burke, "hurries us on by an irresistible force."[29] The sublime, then, is an "idea," not in the Platonic or Aristotelian sense, but as defined by Locke, Hartley, and the British empiricists: an idea as a bundle of impressions, a cluster of simple sensations that cumulate to form complex sensations or "ideas." That is, the sublime process whereby the awesomeness of Nature, a thunderstorm or tempest, stirs "the grander passions" (Burke's phrase), thus causing the state of transport or ravishment that Boileau speaks of, which in turn leads to such operations of the mind as the association of ideas and the pleasures of the imagination, is an essentially mechanical

Butterfield, Herbert, 148, 149

Caesar, Julius, 107, 108, 114, 186

Calvin, John, 167

the cardinal virtues, 33, 80, 102, 114, 129, 174, 215

Cervantes, Miguel de, 31, 34

chain of being, 57, 58, 59, 74, 151, 153, 156, 157

The Champion, 11, 12, 13, 29, 74, 105, 106, 112, 129, 132, 140, 150

charity, 80, 81, 84, 85, 87, 129, 132, 134, 138, 175

Christ, 106, 107, 108, 110, 113, 141

Christianity Not Mysterious, 149

Cibber, Colley, 9, 13, 20, 23, 24, 29, 31, 49

Cicero, 9, 123, 151, 201

City of God, 149, 166, 171

The Civilization of the Renaissance in Italy, 9

Classical and Christian Ideas of World Harmony, 66

Considerations on the Greatness and Decadence of the Romans, 149

The Consolation of Philosophy, 166, 167, 169, 171, 175, 178, 180, 182

contemplation, 213

Coomaraswamy, Ananda, 1, 2

The Covent-Garden Journal, 12, 108, 109, 203, 209

Crane, R. S., 75

Cromwell, Oliver, 74, 75, 105, 150

Dante, 10

D'Arcy, M. C., 161

de contemptu mundi, 154, 172

Defoe, Daniel, 20, 21, 22, 25, 29, 34, 38, 153, 157, 184, 190

deism, 43, 147, 149, 152, 167, 173, 178, 179

Descartes, 55, 68, 75, 148

deus ex machina, 16, 17, 18, 151, 173, 180, 190, 192

"A Dialogue between Alexander the Great and Diogenes the Cynic," 110, 114

The Discarded Image, 3

Discourses on Art, 2, 212

Dennis, John, 203, 204, 205, 209, 215

Dodington, George, 12, 116

Don Quixote, 31, 49, 214

Don Quixote in England, 140

"Donne and The Wane of Wonder," 68, 200

Dryden, John, 135, 152

duelling, 117, 118, 119, 129

Empiricism, 200, 212, 213

The Enduring Monument, 9

Epistle to the Satires, 109

"Essay on Conversation," 109

Essay on Criticism, 5, 203

"Essay on the Knowledge of the Characters of Men," 11, 22, 38, 41, 48, 64, 121, 122, 123, 125, 126, 137, 140, 141

Essay on Man, 56, 58

Exodux, 164

faith, 152, 153, 154, 155, 157, 174, 175

Familiar Letters, 14

fate, 155, 168, 172, 173, 181, 191

The Fathers or The Good-Natured Man, 116

fideist, 152, 153, 167, 174

form, 71, 72, 73, 79, 97, 98, 101, 213

fortunate fall, 175, 176, 177, 178, 179

Fortune, 74-86, 89, 92-97, 105, 149-153, 156-159, 167, 170-173, 180, 181, 183, 187, 191, 192, 211

gambling, 128

Garrigou-Lagrange, 170

Gilson, Etienne, 86, 95, 96, 167

glory, 9, 12, 13, 19, 49, 111, 114, 115

good-nature, 41, 66, 81, 103, 114, 116, 118, 129-134, 138, 181

Gothic terror, 168, 169, 199-216

great and good, 113, 114, 115, 116, 117, 122, 132, 135, 138, 142

Great Man theory of history, 155, 183, 186, 205

greatness, 105-143, 191, 204, 205; see magnanimity

The Grounds of Criticism in Poetry, 203

Gulliver, 19, 20, 34, 42, 48, 68, 141

Gulliver's Travels, 19, 43, 141

Hagstrum, Jean, 14

Hardison, O. B., 9, 10

Harth, Phillip, 152

Hartley, David, 212

The Heavenly City of the Eighteenth Century Philosophers, 149

Hebrews, 164

heuresis, 4, 18, 35, 37

history, 74, 160, 164, 174-182, 182-194

Hobbes, Thomas, 33, 123, 152

Homer, 24, 25, 31, 32, 33, 34, 35, 70, 114, 134, 135, 156, 157, 213, 214

Honor, 108, 111, 112, 118, 119, 121, 122, 123, 128, 129, 130-136

Hooker, Richard, 80

Hope, 174, 175

Horace, 9, 12, 17, 69, 203, 204, 208

Human Nature, 5, 48, 67, 68, 80, 124, 134

Hume, David, 213

humility, 106, 108, 109, 129, 138, 142, 143

hypocrisy, 122

The Idea of Progress, 67, 148, 149

230

The Iliad, 24, 31, 34, 114, 135, 214

Inquiry into the Cause of the Late Increase of Robbers, 108, 112, 114-116, 126

Interposition of Providence, 156, 161, 162, 180

inventio, 2, 3, 16, 18, 20, 31, 32, 34, 45, 67

Irwin, W. R., 182

Job, 170, 171, 176, 177

Johnson, Samuel, 19, 20, 43, 70, 71, 73

Jonathan Wild, 11, 18, 21, 107, 110, 112, 114, 131, 153, 154, 155, 156, 172, 182-193, 210

Joseph, 176, 177, 214

Joseph Andrews, 7, 10, 11, 17, 18, 20-50, 112, 150, 153, 155, 159, 166, 176, 178, 205, 210, 214

A Journey from this World to the Next, 40

Journal of a Voyage to Lisbon, 6, 16, 41, 185, 209

Judaeo-Christian view of history, 160, 164, 166

judgment, 32, 35, 46, 47

Julian, 40, 67

The Laws of Ecclesiastical Polity, 80

Leisure: The Basis of Culture, 209

Lewis, C. S., 3

Lobo, Father, 43, 44

Locke, John, 59, 212

Longinus, 69, 141, 201, 203

Lovejoy, A. O., 58

Luther, Martin, 167

Lynch, W. F., 67

Lyttleton, George, 96, 109

Machiavelli, Niccolo, 75, 123, 149

magnanimity, 105-144, 204

The Making of Jonathan Wild, 182

Mandeville, Bernard, 124

Maritain, Jacques, 4, 36, 50

the Marvellous, 17, 19, 41, 42, 45, 49, 60, 62, 65, 68, 72, 74, 76, 77, 85, 88, 89, 96, 98, 99, 100, 109, 110, 113, 125, 140, 141, 147, 149, 156, 158, 159, 160, 162, 168, 169, 182, 187, 189, 199-216

The Meaning and Matter of History, 161

Metaphysics, 158

The Metaphysical Foundations of Modern Physical Science, 148

Methodism, 152

mimesis, 6, 70

Milton, John, 7, 81, 134, 139, 160, 164, 176, 179, 202, 205, 213

The Mirror and the Lamp, 3

"A Modern Glossary," 108, 130, 135, 136

Monk, Samuel, 206, 213

the Monstrous, 7, 17-22, 41, 43, 45, 48, 68, 69, 110, 111, 121, 125, 141, 169, 189, 191

Montaigne, Michel, 158

Montesquieu, 149

Morris, David B., 200, 201, 204

Narrative Form in History and Fiction, 182

natural law, 80, 168

nature, 5-8, 60, 61, 63, 65-67, 69, 71, 73, 74, 80, 89, 94, 97, 148, 152, 158, 161, 175, 190, 191, 200, 201, 205, 206, 207, 208, 213, 214

neo-classicism, 70, 71, 73, 89, 199, 203

new science, 147, 161, 169, 199

Newton, Isaac, 147, 148, 151, 152, 167, 180, 200

nil admirari, 160, 172, 187

noble savage, 43, 44

"of Good-Nature," 117, 129, 130, 132

Of Tragedy, 213

"of True Greatness," 12, 116, 121, 132,

epistemology. It involves, as Monk puts it, "the vibration of the nerves":[30] "merely the hurrying of material, endlessly, meaninglessly,"[31] according to Alfred North Whitehead. David Hume, who applied his empirical philosophy to literary criticism in Of Tragedy (1757), clearly exemplifies how a sublime critic destroys the classical-Christian notion of contemplation. Confusing the quiet of contemplation with the boredom of sloth, Hume regards the human mind as constantly hungering for external stimuli and diverting novelties, craving for sensations of any kind that will distract it from its native apathy:

> No matter what the passion is: let it be disagreeable, afflicting, melancholy, disordered; it is still better than that insipid langour which arises from perfect tranquility and repose.[32]

Hence this eighteenth century empiricist understanding of idea as an accumulation of sense impressions provided by external stimuli, as a series of sensations that result in the transport of the sublime feeling, or as an excitation that arouses the lethargy of the mind conflicts with the Aristotelian notion, where idea is a synonym for form or essence--a perennial truth or eternal principle of intelligibility, the concrete universal which the mind contemplates or wonders at in a state of repose, not agitation.

Finally, Fielding associates sublimity with the harmony and proportion of variety, not with the disorder and confusion unleashed by Nature's destructive forces or symbolized by Milton's descriptions of Death and Satan, Virgil's personification of Fame, and Homer's portrait of Discord-- favorite literary passages of Burke which he cites as illustrations of his notion of greatness. Variety to Fielding means more than novelty, change, or picturesqueness, what Addison calls the new or uncommon that diverts the mind and prevents satiety: "It is this that recommends Variety, where the Mind is every Instant called off to something new, and the Attention not suffered to dwell too long, and waste it self on any particular Object" (<u>Spectator</u> No. 412). Rather, variety to Fielding signifies a principle of order or cosmos, the philosophical idea of the one and the many, the life force itself as manifested in Nature's prodigality, God's goodness, the copiousness of a great work of art, and the generosity of man. From the abundant garden of Mr. Wilson ("here was variety of fruit and every thing useful for the kitchen") to the "prodigious variety" of Nature's feast, the bill of fare offered in the first chapter of <u>Tom Jones</u>, to the "amazing variety of meadows and woods" that adorn Allworthy's estate to Nature's profusion at Eshur, Stowe, and Wilton ("Here Nature indeed pours forth the choicest treasures which she hath lavished on this world.") to the "immense variety" of fish "in such abundance . . . such inexhaustible stores" that Fielding marveled at in the voyage to Lisbon prior to his death--he stresses Nature's bounty and love of individuation. In showing how divine Providence works in diverse, irregular ways, operating through the fickleness of Fortune in all her different moods, using every species of man from the great Allworthy to the lowly Merry-Andrew as heavenly agents, and exerting both a particular providence in the lives of individuals and a general providence that cares for the whole as well as the part, that acts as the God of Nature as well as the God of History--Fielding acknowledges the principle of the one and the many in the Christian idea of history. By mixing comedy and epic in <u>Joseph Andrews</u> and <u>Tom Jones</u>; by mingling an imitation of <u>Don Quixote</u>, a satire of <u>Pamela</u>, the classical idea of biography, the form of Homer's <u>Iliad</u>, and the story of Joseph and his brothers in <u>Joseph Andrews</u>; by harmonizing the histories of the man of the hill, Mrs. Fitzpatrick, and Nightingale with the History of Tom Jones and by integrating the histories of Leonora and of Leonard and Paul with the History of Joseph Andrews as variations on the theme of Prudence--Fielding shows how the principle of variety or "art of contrast" operates in his own work. Likewise, the wise man's art of living practiced by Fielding's heroes and heroines involves a blend of the natural cardinal virtues and the supernatural theological virtues, a union of the wisdom of the serpent and the gentleness of the dove; the enjoyment of many pleasures, not one satisfaction ("The wise man gratifies every appetite and every passion while the fool sacrifices all the rest to pall and satiate one," (<u>Tom Jones</u>, p. 226, Bk. VI, ch. iii); the "conversation" or first-hand experience "with all ranks and degrees of men," the knowledge of men and manners cited by Fielding in the epigraph to Tom Jones, "Mores hominum multorum vidit"; and the different rhythms of "the ingenious traveller . . . who always proportions his stay at any place to the beauties, elegancies, and curiosities which it affords" (<u>Tom Jones</u>, p. 531, Bk. XI, ch. ix). Thus sublimity, in Fielding's notion of the Marvellous, is an effect of order or cosmos, not of chaos or whirl--the common association in the eighteenth century when, to quote from Dennis's list again, " . . . Tempests, raging Seas, Inundations, Torrents, Earthquakes . . . " create the sublime sensation. It is the harmony of the one and the many that comprises the art of Nature, the art of God, the art of literature, and the art of living--art which is sublime, not because it terrifies the human imagination through the astonishment of fear or distracts the human mind from the tedium of daily life through the novelty of change, but because it gratifies the intellect's love of order, what Aristotle in the <u>Poetics</u> calls "the instinct for harmony," which Aristotle regards as inherent to the nature of man as his instinct for imitation, "implanted in man from childhood."[33] In fact, Fielding, even as a magistrate interpreting the English constitution, viewed it in light of this universal principle of order, man's inborn love of a harmony based on eternal first principles capable of infinite variation. Comparing the English Constitution to climate, which is "changing and variable," in contrast to soil, which is "uniform and permanent," Fielding once again affirms that the sublimity of variety rests upon the harmony of the one and the many, even as the greatness of the English Constitution ensues from the music between the parts and the whole:

> The Greek philosophy will, perhaps, help us to a better idea; for neither will the several constituent parts, nor the contexture of the whole, give an adequate notion of the word. By the Constitution is, indeed, rather meant something which results from the order and disposition of the whole; something resembling that harmony for which the Theban in Plato's Phaedo contends; which he calls ἀόρατόν τι καὶ ἀσώματον something invisible and incorporeal. For many of the Greeks imagined the soul to result from κρᾶσις or composition of the parts of the body, when these were properly tempered together; as harmony doth from the proper composition of the several parts in a well-tuned instrument: In the same manner, from the disposition of the several parts in a state, arises that which we call the Constitution.[34]

NOTES TO CHAPTER V

[1] *The History of the Royal-Society of London* (London, 1667); quoted by David B. Morris, *The Religious Sublime* (Lexington, Ky.: Univ. Press of Kentucky, 1972), pp. 40-41.

[2] Quoted by Samuel H. Monk, *The Sublime* (Ann Arbor: Univ. of Michigan Press, 1960), p. 32.

[3] Edmund Burke, "A Philosophical Inquiry into the Origin of Our Ideas of the Sublime and Beautiful" in *Eighteenth Century Poetry and Prose*, eds. Louis I. Bredvold, et al. (New York: Ronald Press, 1956), p. 1167. All further references to Burke's essays are taken from this anthology.

[4] Morris, p. 41.

[5] Dennis Quinn, "Donne and the Wane of Wonder," *A Journal of English Literary History*, 36, No. 4 (Dec., 1969), 642.

[6] Quoted by Marjorie Hope Nicolson, *Newton Demands the Muse* (Hamden, Conn.: Archon Books, 1963), p. 147.

[7] Morris, p. 31.

[8] Quoted by Monk, p. 31.

[9] *Works*, ed. Henley, XIV, 300.

[10] Burke, p. 1166.

[11] John Dennis, "The Grounds of Criticism in Poetry," *The Select Works of John Dennis* (London, 1718); quoted by Monk, p. 51.

[12] *The Critical Works of John Dennis*, ed. Edward Niles Hooker (Baltimore, Md., 1939-1943), 1: 336; 1: 127; quoted by Morris, p. 48; p. 49.

[13] *The Covent-Garden Journal* (Jan. 11, 1752); quoted by F. Homes Dudden, *Henry Fielding* (Oxford:

Clarendon Press, 1952), II, p. 924.

[14]Longinus, "On the Sublime," Criticism: The Major Texts, ed. Walter Jackson Bate (New York: Harcourt, Brace, & World, 1952), p. 65; p. 70.

[15]Eighteenth Century English Literature, eds. Geoffrey Tillotson, et al. (New York: Harcourt, Brace, & World, 1969), pp. 335-336. All further references to the Spectator are taken from this anthology.

[16]The Critical Works of John Dennis, 1: 361; quoted by Morris, p. 74.

[17]Morris, p. 155.

[18]Works, XII, 246.

[19]Quoted by Josef Pieper, Leisure: The Basis of Culture, tr. Alexander Dru (New York: Random House, 1963), p. 32.

[20]Burke, p. 1167.

[21]Monk, p. 93.

[22]Burke, p. 1167.

[23]Quoted by Monk, p. 95.

[24]Burke, p. 1168; pp. 1167-1168.

[25]Pieper, pp. 20-21; p. 19; p. 65.

[26]Works, XIV, 146-149.

[27]Works, XII, 244.

[28]Pieper, p. 42.

[29]Burke, pp. 1165-1166.

[30]Monk, p. 96.

[31] Alfred North Whitehead, *Science and the Modern World*; quoted by Nicolson, p. 147.

[32] *Criticism: The Major Texts*, ed. Bate, p. 193.

[33] *Criticism: The Major Texts*, ed. Bate, p. 21.

[34] "An Inquiry into the Causes of the Late Increase in Robbers," *Works*, XIII, 9-10.

BIBLIOGRAPHY

Augustine, Saint. *The City of God*. Garden City, N.Y.: Image Books, 1958.

Bate, W. J., ed. *Criticism: The Major Texts*. New York: Harcourt, Brace, & World, 1952.

──────────. *From Classic to Romantic*. New York: Harper Torchbooks, 1961.

Battestin, Martin. *The Moral Basis of Fielding's Art*. Middletown, Conn.: Wesleyan Univ. Press, 1964.

Boethius. *The Consolation of Philosophy*. New York: Bobbs-Merrill, 1962.

Boyd, John D., S. J. *The Function of Mimesis and Its Decline*. Cambridge, Mass.: Harvard Univ. Press, 1968.

Braudy, Leo. *Narrative Form in History and Fiction*. Princeton: Princeton Univ. Press, 1970.

Bredvold, Louis I., et al., eds. *Eighteenth Century Poetry and Prose*. New York: Ronald Press, 1956.

Brown, Lloyd W. "The Person of Quality in the Eighteenth Century." *Dalhousie Review*, 48 (1968), 171-84.

Brown, Norman O. *Love's Body*. New York: Vintage, 1966.

Burckhardt, Jacob. *The Civilization of the Renaissance in Italy*. New York: Modern Library, 1954.

Burtt, E. A. *The Metaphysical Foundations of Modern Physical Science*. New York: Doubleday Anchor Books, 1954.

Bury, J. B. *The Idea of Progress*. New York: Macmillan, 1933.

Butterfield, Herbert. *The Origins of Modern Science*. New York: The Free Press, 1968.

Cibber, Colley. *An Apology for His Life*. London: J. M. Dent and New York: E. P. Dutton, n. d.

Coomaraswamy, Ananda. *Christian and Oriental Philosophy of Art*. New York: Dover Books, 1956.

Crane, R. S. "The Concept of Plot and the Plot of *Tom Jones*" in *Critics and Criticism*, ed. R. S. Crane (abridged edition). Chicago: Univ. of Chicago Press, 1957.

Cunningham, J. V. *Woe or Wonder*. Denver: Swallow Paperbacks, 1964.

D'Arcy, M. C., S. J. *The Meaning and Matter of History*. New York: Meridian Books, 1961.

_____. *The Mind and Heart of Love*. Cleveland and New York: Meridian Books, 1964.

Defoe, Daniel. *Robinson Crusoe*. New York: Signet, 1961.

Dudden, F. Homes. *Henry Fielding*. 2 vols. Oxford: Clarendon Press, 1952.

Fairchild, Hoxie Neale. *Religious Trends in English Poetry*, vol. 1. New York and London: Columbia Univ. Press, 1964.

Fielding, Henry. *Amelia*. 2 vols. New York: E. P. Dutton, 1962.

_____. *Jonathan Wild*. New York: Signet, 1962.

_____. *Joseph Andrews*. New York: Modern Library, 1950.

_____. *Tom Jones*. New York: Modern Library, 1950.

_____. The Complete Works of Henry Fielding, Esq., ed. W. E. Henley. 16 vols. New York: Croscup and Sterling, 1902.

_____. The Works of Henry Fielding. Philadelphia: John D. Morris, 1902.

Garrigou-Lagrange, Reginald, O. S. B. Providence. St. Louis, Mo. and London: Herder, 1946.

Gilson, Etienne. The Unity of Philosophical Experience. New York: Scribner, 1965.

Gunn, J. A. W. "Interest Will Not Lie: 17th-Century Political Maxim." Journal of the History of Ideas, 39 (Oct.-Dec., 1968), 551-64.

Hagstrum, Jean H. Samuel Johnson's Literary Criticism. Chicago: Univ. of Chicago Press, 1967.

Hardison, E. B. The Enduring Monument. Chapel Hill: Univ. of North Carolina Press, 1962.

Harth, Phillip. Swift and Anglican Rationalism. Chicago: Univ. of Chicago Press, 1969.

Hoopes, R. H. Right Reason in the English Renaissance. Cambridge, Mass.: Harvard Univ. Press, 1962.

Irwin, W. R. The Making of Jonathan Wild. New York: Columbia Univ. Press, 1941.

Jones, Richard F. "Science and English Prose Style in the Third Quarter of the Seventeenth Century" in The Seventeenth Century. Stanford: Stanford Univ. Press, 1951.

Lewis, C. S. The Discarded Image. Cambridge, Eng.: Cambridge Univ. Press, 1967.

Lovejoy, A. O. The Great Chain of Being. New York: Harper Torchbooks, 1960.

Lynch, William F., S. J. Christ and Apollo. New York: Mentor-Omega, 1963.

Machiavelli, Niccolo. The Prince. New York: New American Library, 1952.

Maritain, Jacques. Art and Scholasticism and the Frontiers of Poetry. New York: Scribner, 1962.

_____. Creative Intuition in Art and Poetry. Cleveland and New York: Meridian Books, 1966.

_____. A Preface to Metaphysics. New York: Mentor-Omega, 1962.

McNamee, Maurice J., S. J. Honor and the Epic Hero. New York: Holt, Rinehart, and Winston, 1960.

Monk, Samuel H. The Sublime. Ann Arbor: Univ. of Michigan Press, 1960.

Morris, David B. The Religious Sublime. Lexington, Ky.: Univ. Press of Kentucky, 1972.

Nicolson, Marjorie Hope. Newton Demands the Muse. Hamden, Conn.: Archon Books, 1963.

Pieper, Josef. The Four Cardinal Virtues. South Bend: Univ. of Notre Dame Press, 1966.

_____. Leisure: The Basis of Culture, tr. Alexander Dru. New York: Random House, 1963.

Pollard, William G. Chance and Providence. New York: Scribner, 1958.

Price, Martin. To the Palace of Wisdom. Garden City, N.Y.: Doubleday & Company, 1964.

Quinn, Dennis. "Donne and the Wane of Wonder." *A Journal of English Literary History*, 36

(Dec., 1969), 626-47.

Rahner, Hugo, S. J. *Man at Play*. New York: Herder and Herder, 1967.

Reynolds, Joshua Sir. *Discourses on Art*. Indianapolis: Bobbs-Merrill, 1965.

Richardson, Samuel. *Pamela*. New York: Norton, 1958.

Spitzer, Leo. *Classical and Christian Ideas of World Harmony*. Baltimore: The Johns Hopkins Press, 1963.

Stauffer, Donald A. *The Art of Biography in Eighteenth Century England*. Princeton: Princeton Univ. Press, 1941.

Swift, Jonathan. *Gulliver's Travels and Other Writings*. New York: Modern Library, 1958.

Tillich, Paul. *The Eternal Now*. New York: Scribner, 1963.

Tillotson, Geoffrey, et al., eds. *Eighteenth Century English Literature*. New York: Harcourt, Brace, & World, 1969.

Williams, Aubrey. "Interpositions of Providence." *South Atlantic Quarterly*, 70 (1971), 265-86.

Wilson, Mona, ed. *Johnson: Prose and Poetry*. Cambridge, Mass.: Harvard Univ. Press, 1963.

INDEX

Abraham, 166

Abrams, M. H., 3

Adam, 175, 176, 177

Addison, Joseph, 199, 204, 206, 213

adultery, 125, 126, 130

The Advancement and Reformation of Modern Poetry, 203

agape, 129, 138, 175

Akenside, Mark, 199, 202

Alexander the Great, 107, 108, 110, 111, 114, 186

Amelia, 18, 136-141

Amelia, 11, 22, 105-143, 150, 156, 205

Anglican rationalists, 149, 152, 159

An Apology for His Life, 31, 49

Aristotle, 1, 7, 8, 36, 58, 69, 70, 71, 73, 150, 158, 191, 199, 203, 204, 212, 213, 215

The Art of Biography in Eighteenth Century

England, 182

Augustine, St., 149, 166, 171, 179

Austen, Jane, 20

Bacon, Francis, 49

Barrow, Dr., 164, 209

Bate, W. J., 73

The Battle of the Books, 7, 8, 20

Becker, Carl, 149

biography, 23, 182-186

Boethius, 164, 169, 173, 178, 181

Boileau, 199, 201, 203, 208, 212

Bossu, 203

Boyd, John D., 4, 5

Braudy, Leo, 182

Burckhardt, Jacob, 9, 13, 17, 19

Burke, Edmund, 199, 202, 204-208, 211-213

Burtt, E. A., 148

Bury, John B., 67, 148, 149

227

137, 139

On the Sublime, 201, 203, 204

Opticks, 147, 200

originality, 19

The Origins of Modern Science, 148

Pamela, 21, 23, 24, 31, 35, 38, 49, 153, 214

pantomime, 39

Paradise Lost, 7, 58, 140, 164, 173, 175, 177, 182, 202, 207

Pasquin, 9, 15, 20

Paul, St., 102, 106, 132, 143, 164, 209

Peri Bathous, 13, 141

Peri Hupsous, 201

Petronius, 203

Pieper, Josef, 26, 209, 211

philosophia perennis, 2, 4

Philosophes, 147, 148, 155

Philosophical Inquiry into the Origin of Our Ideas of the Sublime and Beautiful, 199-216

Plato, 74, 140, 150, 158, 212

Pliny, 17

Poetics, 1, 36, 58, 70, 191, 215

Pope, Alexander, 5, 9, 13, 20, 56, 58, 96, 109, 135, 137, 141, 199, 203

poverty, 126, 127

predestination, 153

"Preface to the Miscellanies and Poems," 113, 115, 140, 204, 205, 211

Preface to Shakespeare, 70

primitivism, 43, 45

Principia, 147

problem of evil, 170, 173, 178

progress, 147, 148, 149, 155, 194

providence, 21, 58, 80, 147-193

prudence, 26-33, 38-41, 48, 80, 81, 83, 114, 132-134, 149, 152, 155, 160, 168, 174, 181, 194, 214

233

Puritans, 152, 160

Quinn, Dennis, 62, 68, 200

Quintilian, 203

rainbow, 200

Religio Laici, 152

The Religious Sublime, 200

Rasselas, 3, 73

rationalist, 152

reason, 152, 153, 155, 168, 169, 174, 175

revelation, 152

Reynolds, 2, 3, 20, 34, 37, 212

Richelieu, 75, 155

Richardson, Samuel, 20, 21, 22, 23, 29, 31, 34, 35, 38, 86, 153, 155, 157, 171

right reason, 33, 167, 168, 174, 175, 179, 181, 195-196

Robinson Crusoe, 22, 42, 43, 171, 190

Robinson Crusoe, 21, 25, 43, 153, 154, 184, 190

romance, 44, 69, 189, 190

Royal Society, 183

Samuel Johnson's Literary Criticism, 14

Scotus, Duns, 167

The Seasons, 202, 207

Seneca, 151

sensibility, 174, 203

Shaftesbury, 41, 174

Shakespeare, 65, 71, 168, 191

Shamela, 22, 24

Spectator, 204, 214

Spitzer, Leo, 66

Sprat, Thomas, 199

Stoics, 123, 129, 154, 160, 172, 173, 174

The Statecraft of Machiavelli, 149

Stauffer, Donald, 182, 186

Swift, 7, 8, 9, 19, 20, 141

sub specie aeternitatis, 171

sublime, 109, 110, 113, 114, 117, 121, 135,

140, 141, 143, 153, 199-216

The Tempest, 65, 191

Terence, 90

"Theaetetus," 158

the theological virtues, 80, 102, 114, 129, 175, 215

theory of progress: see progress

Thomson, James, 202, 207

Toland, 149

Tom Jones, 4, 5, 6, 8, 11, 17, 18, 21, 23, 36, 39, 42, 46, 55-98, 132, 134, 137, 140, 155, 156, 158, 160, 162, 166, 167, 172, 176, 183, 184, 201, 205, 210, 211, 214, 215

Tom Thumb, 21, 115, 141

travel, 19, 41, 43, 44, 45, 46, 47, 48

The Unity of Philosophical Experience, 167

utopia, 45

variety, 20-50, 213, 214, 215

Vernoniad, 112

Virgil, 150, 213

virtue, 77, 79, 85, 86, 105, 108, 109, 112, 113, 120, 125, 140, 141, 153, 157, 171, 172, 174

voluntarism, 167, 168

Voyage to Abysinnia, 43, 44

Whitefield, George, 153

Whitehead, Alfred North, 200, 213

wisdom, 40, 41

wise fool, 35, 41

wit, 32, 35, 46, 47

William of Ockham, 167

wonder, 19, 68, 69, 115, 117, 140, 143, 158, 159, 168, 178, 181, 191

the wonderful, 58, 62, 69, 74, 85, 88, 97, 109, 132, 141, 147, 150, 151, 153, 156, 157, 160, 165, 167, 172, 176, 179, 182, 190, 192, 199-216

OHIO UNIVERSITY LIBRARY

Please return this book as soon as you have finished with it. In order to avoid a fine it must be returned by the latest date stamped below.

DEC 0 2 1981

NOV 9 1982

OCT 19 1982
QTR. LOAN

NOV 2 1982

JAN 6 1983

Made in the USA
Columbia, SC
23 July 2021

Also from the Lavish Publishing family

much more than legend. And to think, you thought you knew those old tales so well.

Meet Za and find out what really happened...

Invisible
L.A. Remenicky
http://myBook.to/InvisibleLARemenicky

A bodyguard romantic thriller in this second chance romance…

They found each other. Then the killer found them.

Detective Jackson "Jax" McKenna walks into a psychologist's office and finds that the doctor bears a striking resemblance to his first love, Lainie, who disappeared ten years ago after their disastrous first date ended in violence.

Dr. Elizabeth Parker is really Elaine Wilson, Jax's Lainie. She's been in hiding since the night that changed both their lives. Jax discovers the truth when the killer lets Lainie know he's found her. When Jax and Lainie go on the run to keep Lainie safe, old feelings resurface as the killer threatens their lives.
Can Jax save Lainie and help her stay Invisible?

Also from the Lavish Publishing family

Avoiding Jason's advances and navigating an epic clash of wills, the young woman felt relieved to see graduation day finally arrive. Little did she know, it wouldn't end there. Pregnant and alone, she could only keep her secrets for so long.

After one of the boys is found murdered, the police haul her in, but she denies having done anything wrong. Can she convince them of the truth before all three of the young men fall victim to a killer, forcing her to raise her child alone?

Find out in the action packed thriller...TEACH ME TO PREY.... (New Adult)

The Norn Novellas
A. Nicky Hjort
http://myBook.to/NornNovellas

The Norn Novellas are all chapters in the epic saga of the youngest and most fickle of the four Norn Sisters. The same feisty immortal creature who must escape her inherent inner darkness to learn the meaning of life.

Each story takes a classic fairytale and spins it on its head, as we learn that maybe Norse Mythology was so

Also from the Lavish Publishing family

___

Teach Me to Prey
Samantha Jacoby
http://mybook.to/TeachMetoPrey

Taboo love stories give you a special thrill?

Rebecca Stewart had never let things get personal with her students; a mistake that could cost her far more than a broken heart.

Jason and his friends enjoyed tormenting teachers. When they set their sights on Miss Stewart, nothing would prevent them from bringing her down.